OTHER CULTURES

OTHER CULTURES

Aims, Methods, and Achievements
in Social Anthropology

by

JOHN BEATTIE

Lecturer in Social Anthropology.
Oxford University

THE FREE PRESS
A Division of Macmillan Publishing Co., Inc.
NEW YORK

The Free Press
A Division of Macmillan Publishing Co., Inc.
866 Third Avenue, New York, N.Y. 10022

First Free Press Paperback Edition 1968

Library of Congress Catalog Card Number: 64-16952

Printed in the United States of America

printing number

9   10

TO HONOR

Contents

Preface

IN THIS BOOK I consider some of the contributions which the quite young science of social anthropology can make and has made to the understanding of other people's cultures. I assume that this understanding, like all advances in our knowledge of the world around us, is intrinsically worth while. But I believe, also, that it is more important today than it has ever been before in human history for people to have some understanding of cultures other than their own. I try to show that social anthropology, as one among the social sciences, has its own special contribution to make to this understanding.

Social anthropology does not offer any practical recipes for dealing with the major and pressing problems of human relations that face us today, nor can it tell us how we should live with one another in our shrinking world. But by adding a little more to our knowledge of human society and culture, and so to our knowledge of ourselves, it may help us to understand some of these problems better. Social anthropologists have no special qualifications to discuss power relations between modern states, or to investigate the vast complexities of Western-type governmental, economic or industrial organizations. Still less are they equipped to assess the significance of the innumerable scientific, literary and artistic achievements of several millennia of civilization. But they have a contribution to make, even if it is a very much more limited one.

Fundamentally, it is that they have added significantly to our understanding of the basic social and cultural institutions which, everywhere, bind human beings into living communities. This contribution has been mostly, and most distinctively, made in the context of the small-scale, pre-industrial, often not yet (or not fully) literate societies which still occupy a large part of the globe. But even in more technologically developed countries most people are members of relatively small communities, as well as being more or less closely involved in the vast social and cultural milieux of the modern world. This is so especially, though not only, in rural areas. Social anthropologists increasingly study such 'modern' communities in Europe, America, India and elsewhere.

Their central though not their only concern has been with the investigation of the different kinds of social institutions which characterize the societies they study, whether these be 'civilized' or 'primitive'. Certain kinds of social relationships are institutionalized in all human societies. Thus in every culture there are accepted patterns of behaviour between parents and children, husbands and wives, persons in authority and those subject to it, the people who produce goods and the people who consume them, and so on. But the form and the content of the relationships thus broadly characterized may differ vastly from one culture to another. Grave misunderstandings have arisen and continue to arise because people have attempted to understand the institutions of other, unfamiliar societies in terms of the familiar and unquestioned categories of their own cultures. The greater the differences between the societies concerned, and the less complete the contact already established between them, the greater is the danger of serious misunderstanding. An important contribution of social anthropology has been to demonstrate that the social and cultural institutions of societies remote from our own must be understood, if they are to be understood at all, through the ideas and values current in those societies, and not simply in our own terms. And this kind of comprehension is only possible when the investigator moves, usually literally as well as metaphorically, out of his own culture into the unfamiliar one which he wishes to understand, and 'learns' the new culture as he would learn a new language. (Often, indeed, the field anthropologist's first task is to master an unfamiliar tongue.)

Because social anthropologists are chiefly interested in social and cultural institutions, the central chapters in this book are concerned with the institutions of kinship and marriage, with the maintenance of social order, with economic relations, and with magical and religious institutions. For these between them cover the most important dimensions of the social and cultural lives of the members of most small-scale societies. In these chapters I attempt to summarize at least some of the knowledge that social anthropologists have now acquired about other peoples' ways of thinking about and dealing with these matters. But first of all I discuss, in Part I, some of the questions which social anthropologists have been and are mostly concerned to ask about the societies and cultures they study. That is, I consider the present state of theory in social anthropology. This is necessary partly because the human situations with which social anthropologists deal are often new and unfamiliar, so that new and unfamiliar questions sometimes have to be asked about them. Social anthropologists themselves have by no means always been agreed as to just what are the most useful questions to ask. Thus it is necessary to consider some of the hypotheses about human society and culture which they have worked with, and to try to determine which of them are best adapted to achieve the end sought, that is, the fullest possible understanding of the institutions being studied. So in the first six chapters I ask: what is social anthropology, what kinds of things does it study, and how do social anthropologists go about their work?

This book is not and is not intended to be an original contribution to the subject on the theoretical or on any other level. In several years of teaching social anthropology I have found that many people who are approaching it for the first time find it difficult to fit the diffuse concerns of individual social anthropologists into any common framework. Social anthropology appears to them to be (as no doubt to some extent it is) a hodge-podge of distinct and somewhat tenuously connected interests. So my chief aim is to say, as far as I can in simple and non-technical language, what I think the subject is about. The book contains no diagrams and—I hope—the minimum of jargon. It does not pretend to be comprehensive; many important topics receive only the barest mention or are omitted altogether. It is inevitably selective, and since any selection must be made in the light of certain practical and theoretical interests it is bound also to be in some sense personal. The theoretical standpoint which I have adopted emerges, I think, with sufficient clarity from the first part of the book. I do not think that it differs in any very major respects from that currently held by most of my colleagues in social anthropology in Great Britain, though in some contexts I have attempted to make explicit what is sometimes implicit, and no doubt there are some significant differences in emphasis. I should add, too, that as I did fieldwork as a social anthropologist in East Africa, and so am better informed in African and especially East African ethnography than I am in that of other parts of the world, what may appear to be a disproportionate number of my ethnographic examples (though by no means all of them) are taken from that continent.

In the hope that it may be of some use to readers who wish to learn more about any of the topics discussed, I have appended to each chapter a short list of books for further reading. Here again I have had to be selective. I have listed only a few of the works with which I myself happen to be most familiar and which I have found particularly useful. In many cases a book not mentioned in these lists might equally well, or better, be substituted for one that is. The lists are suggestions only, not prescriptions.

My main theoretical obligations are plain from the book itself, but by far the greatest of them are to my teacher, Professor Evans-

Pritchard. He has read this book in manuscript, and I am grateful to him for much helpful criticism and advice. I owe a similar debt to my friend Dr John Middleton. My wife, Honor Beattie, and Miss Alison Smith have commented helpfully on the text. I should like, also, to record indebtedness to the Center for Advanced Study in the Behavioral Sciences, Stanford, California, where a Fellowship held in 1959–60 provided me with an opportunity to consider a little more fully than before some of the questions discussed in this book.

J. B.

Oxford

PART ONE

1

Introduction and Background

IT IS ONLY QUITE RECENTLY in human history that it has come to be fairly widely—though by no means universally—accepted that all human beings are fundamentally alike; that they share the same basic interests, and so have certain common obligations to one another simply as people. This belief is either explicit or implicit in most of the great world religions, but it is by no means acceptable today to many people even in 'advanced' societies, and it would make no sense at all in many of the less developed cultures. Among some of the indigenous tribes of Australia, a stranger who cannot prove that he is kin to the group, far from being welcomed hospitably as a fellow human, is regarded as a dangerous outsider and may be speared without compunction. Members of the Lugbara tribe of north-western Uganda used to think that all foreigners are witches, dangerous and scarcely human creatures who walk about upside-down and kill people by magic. The ancient Greeks believed that all non-Hellenic peoples were barbarians, uncivilized savages whom it would be quite inappropriate to treat as real people. And many of the citizens of highly advanced modern states today think of people of other races, nations or cultures in ways which are not very different from these, especially if their skin is differently pigmented, or if they hold other religious or political faiths.

At earlier periods in human history, and in the conditions of those small-scale, pre-industrial societies which have survived up to the present day in relative isolation from Western influence, the existence of these universally derogatory stereotypes did not matter very much. Even between neighbouring peoples communications were generally restricted, and between those separated by continents or oceans there was virtually no contact at all. So actual social situations in which ideas about foreigners could be translated into behaviour towards them did not arise very often. Today things are obviously very different. Not only has the world's population 'exploded' in the last century or so, but also communications have developed and are still developing at a fantastic pace. There are now few important centres of human population between which messages cannot be conveyed in a few minutes, people and goods in a few hours. Where once foreigners were a rarity they are now so usual as to be taken as a matter of course, and in any large city a man may encounter people from all five continents in the course of a casual stroll. The platitude that all men are members of a single community is valid today in a real and urgent sense, even though this community is evidently neither harmonious nor well-ordered. What is crucial is that in our time the aims, attitudes and activities of millions of people of other cultures and in other countries than our own (whichever our own may be) are practically important for every one of us as never before.

This is an excellent reason for knowing as much as we can about these other peoples and their cultures, for situations can be dealt with more effectively and fairly when they are understood than when they are not, or worse still, when they are misunderstood. And part of the current interest in that branch of human knowledge which for want of a better term is called social anthropology is due to the fact that it does seem to make some contribution to this kind of understanding. For the past half-century or so social anthropologists have been investigating at first hand the social lives and cultural backgrounds of other peoples, especially though by no means only those peoples who still lack, or lacked until very recently, written literatures and histories and advanced technologies. If such peoples are to be studied at all, they must be studied in the living context of their own societies. For their social and cultural institutions are not, like those of Western civilizations, enshrined in mountains of documents, which would enable us to study them at a distance, as an American scholar can study Russia, say, without ever visiting that country.

Such peoples, whose social systems are usually small in scale and whose technologies are simple, have often been referred to as 'primitive'. Though this term is still commonly used, it is not really very appropriate, for in the temporal sense no existing society can be said to be more primitive than any other. Nor, as we shall see later, can we suppose that present-day 'primitive' societies represent, in Sir James Frazer's words, 'the rudimentary phases, the infancy and childhood, of human society', so that, if they were left alone, African bushmen or Australian aborigines would eventually grow up into fully-fledged Europeans or something like them. It is more plausible to speak of such societies as 'simple', and in many valid senses of the term, technologically and economically for example, their organization obviously is simpler than that of modern industrial societies. Of

4

course this is not to say that the members of such societies are in any sense 'simple'; it is certain that they are not. And often their social and cultural institutions are exceedingly complex. In many contexts it is safer to employ such terms as 'pre-literate' or 'pre-industrial', which are likely both to be more accurate and to sound less condescending.

In any event such societies are usually small-scale ones, and it has been for the most part in the laboratory which they provide that social anthropology has grown up as a distinct branch of social science. We shall see, however, that the hypotheses and techniques which social anthropology uses have a very much wider range of application than just to these simple, small-scale communities in the study of which they were developed.

I do not here discuss in any detail the historical development of social anthropology; fuller accounts are available elsewhere. But it will be easier to see why contemporary social anthropology is the kind of subject it is if we have some idea of what has led up to it. As a branch of empirical, observational science it grew up in the context of the world-wide human interaction which, as I have just noted, has vastly increased in the past century or so. What is most familiar often tends to be taken for granted, and the idea that the study of living human communities was a legitimate scientific interest in its own right only really caught on when detailed information began to become available about hitherto remote and unfamiliar human societies. These had been speculated about since time immemorial, but they could not be scientifically investigated until new, easier and quicker ways of getting about the world made it possible for scholars to visit and observe them.

Thus it was the reports of eighteenth- and nineteenth-century missionaries and travellers in Africa, North America, the Pacific and elsewhere that provided the raw material upon which the first great anthropological works, written in the second half of the last century, were based. Before then, of course, there had been plenty of conjecturing about human institutions and their origins; to say nothing of earlier times, in the eighteenth century Hume, Adam Smith and Ferguson in Britain, and Montesquieu, Condorcet and others on the Continent, had written about primitive institutions. But although their speculations were often brilliant, these thinkers were not empirical scientists; their conclusions were not based on any kind of evidence which could be tested; rather, they were deductively argued from principles which were for the most part implicit in their own cultures. They were really philosophers and historians of Europe, not anthropologists. But they did regard human societies as legitimate

5

objects for study, and some of them thought that universal and necessary laws of society might be discovered, analogous to those which were at that time being so successfully formulated in the natural sciences. So in an important sense they were the forerunners of modern social anthropologists.

These earlier thinkers about human culture and institutions were characteristically concerned with social evolution and progress. To them it seemed plain that some societies were more 'advanced' than others, and there was historical evidence that many of them, in particular the countries of Western Europe, had in recent times developed from a relatively backward condition to a more advanced or civilized one, however 'civilization' might be defined. So it seemed to them to be plausible to suppose that all human societies everywhere had to develop, if they developed at all, through the same or similar series of developmental stages. This way of thinking reflected the evolutionary spirit of the age. In France Boucher de Perthes, on the basis of flint tools discovered at Abbéville, had in the first half of the nineteenth century established a time scale which gave man a vastly greater antiquity than had hitherto been dreamed of. And in Britain the dramatic advance of evolutionary theory in zoology, associated particularly with Charles Darwin, lent support to the idea that the same evolutionary approach could be applied to the history of human society.

These evolutionary hypotheses fitted well with the increased emphasis, also characteristic of the times, on the idea of progress, the notion that on the whole the world was becoming better and better. A number of Victorian scholars, impressed by the striking success of evolutionary theory in the biological sciences where the fossil record was providing increasingly full and convincing evidence, attempted to reconstruct on the same pattern the earlier and by definition the 'lower' stages of human society. Writers like Bachofen in Europe, Maine and McLennan in Britain, and Morgan in America, exercised considerable ingenuity in reconstructing in ample detail what they supposed to have been the earliest stages in social evolution. Thus, for example, Lewis Morgan discussed the three main stages through which 'the lines of human progress' must pass, called savagery, barbarism and civilization. Man had moved from savagery to barbarism when he invented pottery, and to civilization with the invention of writing. And, in Britain, McLennan tried to show that the institutions of marriage and the family as we know them in Western society must have developed from a condition of 'primitive promiscuity' through a number of distinct stages, which included matriliny, when descent was traced through women only, polyandry, when several husbands shared one wife, and finally patriliny, when descent was traced through men only.[1]

Some people still think that all human societies do move through such stages, and that these can be identified. Thus orthodox Marxists support their particular brand of evolutionary theory by reference to Morgan's ideas, which were taken over by Engels. But most modern social anthropologists regard such conjectural reconstructions as at best crude over-simplifications of events which can never be known in detail, at worst fanciful and sometimes absurd inventions. But they seemed a good deal less absurd when they were written than they do now. We must remember that for these writers anthropology was essentially a historical enquiry. Its aim was to discover the origins of human society and of social institutions. So it was natural that as ethnographic information about 'primitive' peoples became increasingly available, anthropologists should use it to illustrate historical, or pseudo-historical, hypotheses which they had already formulated on other grounds. It had not yet occurred to most of them that the unfamiliar, 'primitive' cultures from which they drew their illustrations might be worth investigating in their own right. The common view was that civilized men could have nothing profitable to learn from studying the way of life of a lot of savages. It is reported that even at the end of the nineteenth century the celebrated Sir James Frazer, when asked if he had ever seen one of the primitive people about whose customs he had written so many volumes, tersely replied, 'God forbid!'

Since the conjectures of these writers were about the remote past and not about the present, in the nature of the case their hypotheses could not be either proved or disproved by evidence about contemporary societies, however 'primitive'. In fact, as later became obvious, there is no evidence at all upon which detailed cultural sequences can be established for the earliest stages of human society, nor is it likely that there ever will be any. The argument from 'survivals', which assumed that many existing customs and beliefs are, as it were, fossilized relics of earlier stages in social history, so that the prior existence of earlier stages associated with them might legitimately be inferred, was shown itself to imply unwarranted historical conjecture. Also, and most important, it began to become plain that few societies, if any, have developed in total isolation; always there have been *some* contacts with other human cultures. So far as we know, no society has ever developed anywhere quite free from outside influence.

So, towards the end of the nineteenth century, the naïve evolution-

---

[1] Morgan, Lewis H., *Ancient Society*, London, 1877; McLennan, J. F., *Primitive Marriage*, London, 1865.

7

ary approach to the understanding of the origins of human institutions gradually became discredited, and the rival school of the diffusionists began to become influential. Their approach was no less historical and often hardly less conjectural than the evolutionists'. Correctly observing that it was extremely unlikely that all societies everywhere had evolved or were in process of evolving independently through the same or similar series of stages, they said that cultural change and progress were mainly due to borrowing. They based their reconstructions on the undoubted fact that items of culture could be and very often were transmitted from one society to another. But as far as the remote past was concerned there was hardly more evidence for their conjectures than there had been for those of the evolutionists. So when, early in the present century, Elliot Smith and Perry, who believed with the evolutionists that humanity was progressing from savagery to civilization, claimed that all civilizations everywhere had diffused from an original source in ancient Egypt, their school too became discredited among professional anthropologists.[1]

The trouble with both of these approaches was, of course, that their advocates went far beyond the evidence, as they were bound to do so long as their interest was directed to the remote past, and to the very first beginnings of human institutions and beliefs. For such prehistoric times the only possible evidence must be archaeological, and where such evidence exists the information which it can give us, though highly important, is strictly limited. Thus archaeology can tells us what early men looked like, what they made, and, within very narrow limits, what they did. But it cannot tell us what they thought or believed, or (except in the most general way) the kind of social world they inhabited. Arguments from man's present to his past condition which are unsupported by good historical or archaeological evidence can never be other than merely speculative.

But modern social anthropology owes much to these nineteenth-century scholars, in spite of their errors. Although they were mainly preoccupied with the reconstruction of a past which was lost for ever, they were, like their successors, interested in social institutions and the interrelations between them. Like all social scientists, they were concerned with discovering and recording regularities in human behaviour. Their approach was comparative; they were interested in pointing out similarities between the cultural and social institutions of different societies. And considering the limited ethnographic knowledge then available, it would be unreasonable to expect them to have understood the real social significance of the institutions and

[1] Smith, G. Elliot, *In the Beginning: the Origin of Civilization*, London, 1932; Perry, W. J., *The Growth of Civilization*, London, 1924.

customs they compared. In later chapters we shall see that although, for the most part, we no longer ask the same kind of questions as they did (many of them were in fact unanswerable), none the less some of their ideas and insights have importance for social anthropology today.

By the end of the nineteenth century a considerable amount of miscellaneous ethnographic information had been assembled from all over the world. The most celebrated collection is Sir James Frazer's great compilation of religious beliefs and practices, published in several editions around the turn of the century as *The Golden Bough*. In this great work Frazer, starting with the idea, found in ancient Roman myth, that the priest-ruler, as representative of a god, should be slain and replaced by another before his powers waned, collected a vast body of information about 'primitive' religious and magical practices throughout the world. Like his predecessors, Frazer was mainly interested in origins, but he did claim that social anthropology (he was one of the first to apply the adjective 'social' to the discipline) should seek regularities or general laws. The laws he had in mind, however, were those exemplified in the earlier stages of human society, which were represented, so he believed with the evolutionists, in existing 'primitive' societies. Also, like most of his contemporaries, he was still concerned with isolated 'customs', reported from various parts of the world mostly by people with little or no scientific training, and so inevitably considered apart from the living social contexts which alone could give them real meaning. Frazer's approach is very different from that of modern social anthropologists, but even so the literary skill and imaginative sweep of his work caught the imagination of both scholars and the general reader, and although he is not much read today, the magic is still there.

As the quantity of ethnographic information increased, and its quality gradually improved, it began to dawn on some scholars that this material was too important to be used merely to illustrate preconceived ideas about primitive peoples or about presumed earlier stages of human society. More and more this extensive ethnography was seen to demand some sort of comparative analysis in its own right. And practical concerns stimulated this interest. Colonial administrators and missionaries began increasingly to see that their work would benefit by an understanding of the social and cultural institutions of the populations they dealt with. Some of the best of the earlier monographs on the simpler societies were written by serving missionaries and administrative officers.

So at the beginning of the present century there began to develop a scientific concern with the systematic undertaking of first-hand field studies of human communities which had hitherto been known to scholars only through the piecemeal observations of non-professional observers. Individual field studies, a few of them of very high quality, had been made earlier. Franz Boas's research among the Eskimos in the 1880's was a notable example, and so was Morgan's work among the Iroquois Indians, undertaken more than a generation before.[1] But it was really only in the early 1900's that the systematic collection of information in the field, covering a wide segment of the social and cultural life of particular peoples, came to be generally regarded as an essential part of the social anthropologist's task. An important stimulus in British anthropology was the Torres Straits expedition in 1898, in which a team of anthropologists led by A. C. Haddon undertook a comprehensive field survey of a part of Melanesia. Later, Radcliffe-Brown's study of the Andaman Islanders, undertaken before the first World War, and especially Malinowski's work in the Trobriand Islands of the Western Pacific, undertaken during it, became particularly important influences in modern social anthropology.[2]

It was really with this change of interest from the reconstruction of past societies to the investigation of contemporary ones that modern social anthropology began. From this time onwards social anthropologists could no longer be satisfied with the collection of isolated pieces of information about particular customs or institutions, however skilfully these might be woven into *a priori* theoretical schemes, or however wide-ranging the comparisons based on them. It no longer seemed so worth while as it had to Frazer to collect huge numbers of examples of, say, totemic practices or first-fruit ceremonies from all periods of history and from all corners of the world. There is indeed a case for comparison, and we shall see in Chapter 3 that social anthropology could not get far without it. But first of all it is necessary to be sure that the things that are being compared are really sufficiently like one another to be comparable. In social anthropology this can only be established when the social institutions and customs which it studies have been understood in context, as part of the whole way of life of the people who have them. And the development of fieldwork during the first quarter of the present century has made possible the intensive study of these contexts themselves.

This new concern with people's whole social and cultural backgrounds, studied in the field as going concerns, raised problems of

---

[1] Boas, F., *The Central Eskimo*, Washington, 1888; Morgan, L. H., *League of the Iroquois* (reprinted), New Haven, 1954.

[2] These writers are fully discussed in later chapters.

interpretation and analysis which had not existed for the earlier, 'armchair' anthropologists. The communities now being studied in the field, unlike the complex industrial societies from which most of the investigators came, were usually small in scale, limited in population, and, often, physically more or less separated from neighbouring peoples. For these reasons it was easy to think of them as being in some sense separate and distinct units or totalities, as it were real 'things'. 'Primitive' societies had at last come into their own; they were no longer collectively merely a vast storehouse from which all kinds of exotic materials could be drawn by the diligent researcher. It was now recognized that however different they were from the familiar states of Western Europe, they were none the less systematically organized and viable communities. So, for the first time, the question arose: how are these unfamiliar social and cultural systems to be understood?

French sociological thought, with its analytical, intellectualist tradition, provided the answer. Eighteenth- and nineteenth-century French writers about human society were much concerned with the 'nature' of society and of human social institutions. Their interest lay rather in what human society essentially is than in the history of its development, either generally or in particular cases. Thus Comte, like his predecessor and teacher Saint-Simon, was much concerned to stress that societies are systems, not just aggregates of individuals. Neither an African tribe nor a university town is just a collection of people, any more than a house is just a collection of bricks, or an organism just an aggregate of cells. What makes these entities something more than merely the totality of their component parts is the fact that these parts are related to one another in certain specific and recognizable ways. In the case of human communities, the more or less enduring relationships between different kinds of people are what we refer to when we speak of them as societies.

These French thinkers saw that if societies were systems, they must be made up of interrelated parts. And they thought that these parts must be related to one another, and to the whole society of which they were parts, in accordance with laws analogous to the laws of nature, which, in principle at least, it should be possible to discover. So the understanding of societies, and so of Society with a capital 'S', like the understanding of the physical organisms with which they were either explicitly or implicitly being compared, was to be achieved by discovering the laws of social organization which operated to maintain the whole structure. We shall see in Chapter 4 that this 'organismic' approach to the study of human societies has some grave limitations and can be dangerously misleading. But it did point to the important truth that the customs and social institutions of human communities are somehow interconnected, so that changes in one part of the system may lead to changes in other parts. When this was understood it became possible to ask, and sometimes even to answer, questions about real human societies which arose less readily so long as the 'piecemeal' view of human cultures, which had hitherto been dominant, prevailed. Thus an anthropologist faced with such a custom as, say, mother-in-law avoidance, which is found in many societies far remote from one another, was no longer content merely to record it for purposes of comparison with other apparently similar customs elsewhere; he now asked what the implications of the institutions were for other aspects of the social life of the people in question, for husband–wife relations, for example, or for the pattern of residence.

This 'organic' approach reached its most sophisticated expression in the writings of the French sociologist Émile Durkheim, who is still one of the most important influences in social anthropology. I shall have a good deal more to say about him later, and about some of the topics barely touched upon here. For the moment my concern is to stress that the two most important strains from which the fabric of modern social anthropology is woven are, on the one hand, the fact-finding, empirical, ethnographic tradition represented by British and by much German and American anthropology, and on the other hand, the 'holistic', analytical intellectualism of French social philosophy.

Can we then, at this point, give a preliminary statement of what modern social anthropology is about? Anthropology is by definition the study of man. But obviously no one discipline can possibly study man in all his aspects, though some anthropologists have written as though it could. On the whole, social anthropologists have concentrated on the study of man in his social aspect, that is, in his relationships with other people in living communities. And in fact, as we noted earlier, they have dealt mainly, though not exclusively, with small-scale, pre-industrial, often pre-literate societies. The multifarious dimensions of the social and cultural life of more complex, literate societies have for the most part been left to historians, economists, political scientists, sociologists, and a host of other specialist scholars.

I discuss the relationship between sociology and social anthropology in the next chapter, but we may note here that social anthropologists are sociologists, in so far as they are interested in the different kinds of social relationships they find in the societies they study. And, as sociologists, they consider these relationships more or less independently of the particular individuals who participate in them. Thus a social anthropologist who is studying, say, the political system of an African tribe is interested in the chief-subject relationship in that system, and in the beliefs and expectations which are associated with this relationship, rather than in the particular individuals who occupy the roles of chief and subjects at a given moment. Of course he is interested in people; they are the raw material he works with. But as a social anthropologist his main concern is with what these people share with other people, the institutionalized aspects of their culture. For this reason social anthropologists are not interested in every social relationship in the societies they study; they concentrate mainly on those which are habitual, relatively enduring features of the societies in which they occur. This is so notwithstanding that deviations from social norms may be significant too, especially, as we shall see in Chapter 14, in the context of social change.

In general, however, the social relationships which social anthropologists study are those which are standardized, institutionalized, and so characteristic of the society being investigated. And here one further point may be mentioned; it will be more fully developed later. It is that social anthropologists, in studying the institutionalized social relationships which are their primary concern, have found it essential to take account of the ideas and values which are associated with them, that is, of their cultural content. No account of a social relationship in human terms can be complete unless it includes reference to what it means to the people who have it. The functioning of an ant-hill community, or the sociology of a bee-hive, can be intelligibly described without reference to the mental states of the actors (unless the term 'instinct' be held to simply such reference), about which we have little or no information. But the working of a human community cannot be adequately described without such reference. For human beings have cultures, systems of beliefs and values which are themselves powerful determinants of action, while so far as we know ants and bees do not. Unlike other animals, men live in a symbolic universe, and it is a main theme of this book that this is one of the most important things about them. This is why social anthropologists have been largely concerned with what is commonly called culture, which includes such data as people's religious and cosmological ideas, and have not restricted themselves to a behaviourist description of social relationships considered simply as such.

Some of these points are more fully developed in the chapters that follow. But it is important to realize at the outset that while modern social anthropologists are centrally interested in the various kinds of

13

social relationships which bind people together in communities (and which sometimes set them off from members of other communities), they are interested, too, in people's ideas, their values and beliefs. They are interested in the ways in which the institutions they study are related to one another in living, functioning social systems. And they study these societies at first hand. These are the most important differences between what modern social anthropologists do and the kinds of interests pursued by earlier scholars. Essential to the subject at the present day is the conviction that no social institution can be adequately understood unless it has been empirically investigated, and unless it can be comprehensibly related to its living social and cultural context.

But this does not preclude the investigation of historical communities by the methods of sociology or social anthropology. Some work has been done in this field, notably Homans' study of the English village in the thirteenth century.[1] It is a question of the adequacy of the historical evidence, and of the availability and appropriateness of comparative ethnographic material.

The emphasis today, however, is essentially empirical and functional. This is why contemporary social anthropology is centrally a study of relationships; fundamentally of relationships between different kinds of people, but, at a higher level of abstraction, of relationships between relationships. Let me make this clearer. The point is that the social anthropologist is not *just* interested in the relationship between, say, a particular chief and a particular subject. He is, as we have just noted, interested in the kinds of relationships between chiefs and subjects that are characteristic of the society being studied, and of which the particular case is an example. And further, at the next remove he is interested in the kinds of implications that the institutionalized chief–subject relationship has for other institutionalized relationships in the society; for example, the relationships between different kinds of kin, or the system of land-holding.

We shall find that in modern social anthropology the emphasis is contextual and relational: this will be very plain when we come to consider, in the second part of this book, something of what social anthropologists have actually learned about other cultures. But this does not mean—and this point too will be developed later—that comparison of social and cultural institutions from one society to another is impossible or undesirable. Such comparisons are indeed implicit in the very words we use to describe what we observe. What it does mean is that the social and cultural phenomena which we set

[1] Homans, G., *English Villagers of the Thirteenth Century*, Harvard, 1942.

14

out to compare must first of all be understood in their own proper contexts. Recent social anthropology may claim to have contributed most significantly to this kind of contextual understanding.

SHORT READING LIST

BRYSON, GLADYS, *Man and Society*, Princeton, 1945.
EVANS-PRITCHARD, E. E., *Social Anthropology*, London, 1951.
  (editor) *The Institutions of Primitive Society*, Oxford, 1954.
FIRTH, RAYMOND, *Human Types* (revised edition), London, 1956.
FRAZER, SIR JAMES, *The Golden Bough* (abridged edition), London, 1922.
FRIED, M. (editor), *Readings in Anthropology*, Vol. I, New York, 1959.
LOWIE, R. H., *The History of Ethnological Theory*, London, 1937.
SHAPIRO, M. (editor), *Man, Culture and Society*, New York, 1956.
TYLOR, SIR EDWARD, *Anthropology*, London, 1881.

2

Social Anthropology and Some Other Sciences of Man

(1)

SOCIAL ANTHROPOLOGISTS study people's customs, social institutions and values, and the ways in which these are interrelated. They carry out their investigations mainly in the context of living communities (usually relatively small-scale ones), and their central though not their only interest is in systems of social relations. In later chapters I consider in more detail what social anthropologists mean when they speak of systems of social relations, and of social institutions and values, and I discuss some of the ways in which they may be related to one another, and how they may best be understood. But first it will be useful to say something about social anthropology's relationship to other branches of anthropology, and also to certain other social sciences.

In Britain the term 'anthropology' loosely designates a number of different branches of study which are more or less closely associated, although sometimes the association derives rather from the historical fact that they developed together as 'evolutionary' studies of man, and so were originally taught together, than from any intrinsic relationship. Thus physical anthropology, prehistoric archaeology, primitive technology, ethnology and ethnography are usually subsumed with social anthropology under the rubric of anthropology, while sociology is not, even though its problems and methods overlap with those of social anthropology to a considerable degree. So it is not a bit surprising that the word 'anthropology' means different things to different people. Even when it is qualified by the adjective 'social' it still suggests to some people an interest in bones and head measurements, to others a concern with prehistoric man and his works, to yet others an obsessive interest in exotic, preferably sexual, customs. Because of the confusion which the ambiguity of the word

16

'anthropology' has caused, perhaps it would be a good thing if another name could be found for the subject we are concerned with in this book. But unfortunately no one has yet been able to suggest a better one.

I now discuss briefly the current relationship between social anthropology, as the subject is understood in Britain and the Commonwealth, and some other kinds of anthropology, namely physical anthropology, prehistoric archaeology or pre-history, ethnography and ethnology, and cultural anthropology. I then consider its relationship with history, psychology and sociology. Of course social anthropology has some concern with other branches of knowledge too; political science, economics, human geography, agronomy, even philosophy and theology, to name only a few. This is not surprising, since social anthropologists claim to take at least some account of the whole social and cultural lives of the peoples they study, and all of these disciplines are concerned with aspects of human culture. But although social anthropology often borrows from and sometimes lends to these other studies, the borderline between them and anthropology is not a matter of ambiguity or disagreement. In the case of the subjects discussed in this chapter, however, the link with social anthropology is not only close, but it is also often confused and sometimes disputed.

On the European continent anthropology means physical anthropology. This discipline is concerned with man as a physical organism, and with his place in the scheme of biological evolution. It deals with such topics as the classification of early forms of man, the physical difference between the races of the species *Homo sapiens*, human genetics, and the modes of physiological adaptation and reaction to different physical environments. This study is important and interesting, but it has little to do with the analysis of people's social institutions and beliefs, for differences between these do not seem to correspond to differences in men's biological constitution. Of course the fact that men are physical organisms is (so far as we know) an indispensable condition of their having societies or cultures at all, but it does not tell us why a particular people has the kind of society or culture it has. The studies of physical anthropologists may, however, be very relevant for ethnologists, who are interested in tracing the origins and movements of human populations. For such physical characters as blood types, to say nothing of more obvious features like head shape and skin colour, may help to establish hypotheses about the historical connections between different peoples. It was because the Victorian anthropologists were chiefly interested in the origins of the peoples they studied that physical anthropology went

17

hand in hand with ethnographic enquiry. The earlier field workers thought it just as important to bring back a record of the cranial and nasal indices of their subjects as to report on their customs and traditions. But although physical anthropology has contributed most significantly to the understanding of man and his history as a physical organism, and has helped to clear away some dangerous misconceptions about the nature and significance of race differences (I return briefly to this topic in Chapter 15), it has little to do with the analysis of social institutions and of the beliefs and values associated with them. So no more need be said of it here. A developing field of study which does have some implications for social anthropology, however, even if only analogically, is the investigation of the social behaviour of animals, especially their group behaviour.

Prehistoric archaeology or prehistory investigates and analyses the various remains of early human activity. Since these remains consist either of people's bones or of material objects shaped or made by people (they left no writings to tell us about themselves), prehistoric archaeology's main task is to dig up, identify and classify these relics, to compare them with material from other areas, and to determine the chronological sequences in which they occurred. This branch of knowledge has made great strides in recent years, and has evolved a number of new techniques, such as dendrochronology, carbon dating and aerial photography, which make it possible to classify early human cultures, and to trace developmental sequences, with a great deal of precision. From it we can learn much about what these very early people looked like, and what they made and how they lived. But it can tell us little about their ideas, values and social institutions. And much of what it does tell us, for example about the significance of the magnificent paleolithic cave paintings of France, Spain and the Sahara, is based on analogies with the behaviour recorded of present-day 'primitives' such as the Australian aborigines. So prehistoric archaeology cannot cast any new light on the contemporary patterns of behaviour and belief which modern social anthropologists study. Important and fascinating as it is in its own right, like physical anthropology it has little if any relevance to present-day social anthropology. Their association in many university teaching departments dates from the period when anthropology was essentially a study of origins, and social anthropology had not yet emerged as a distinct subject.

It is now usual, at least in Britain, to distinguish ethnography from ethnology. The term 'ethnography' refers simply to descriptive accounts of human societies, usually of those simpler, smaller-scale societies which anthropologists have mostly studied. In this sense ethnography may be said to be the raw material of social anthropology. But even descriptive studies imply some generalization and comparison, either explicit or implicit. And since today most ethnography is written by social anthropologists, whose theoretical interests determine the kinds of information they wish to record, much modern ethnography inevitably contains or implies a good deal of theory. We shall see in the next chapter that the distinction between description and analysis is by no means a precise one, especially in social anthropology; for even the simplest account of human relationships and values involves interpretation and analysis. We do not *see* social institutions; we infer them from people's behaviour. And the grounds upon which we make such inferences, as well as the kinds of behaviour that we take account of, are determined by our theoretical interests and equipment. Nothing is easier than to misinterpret unfamiliar institutions; plenty of examples are given later. Here I wish only to stress that there is really no such thing as 'pure' ethnography. 'Purely' descriptive studies differ from more theoretically oriented ones rather in the degree and level of abstraction which they involve than in kind. All the same, social anthropology is an empirical study; real people living their daily lives 'on the ground' are its basic subject-matter. First-hand accounts of the culture and social life of human communities, from whatever point of view they are regarded, are what we call ethnography.

The term 'ethnology' is less exact. It was formerly used as a kind of blanket term to designate almost all of the anthropological studies, including physical anthropology and pre-history. It is still sometimes so used in America and on the Continent. But British social anthropologists have found it useful to restrict it to those studies of mostly pre-literate peoples and their cultures which attempt to explain their present in terms of their remote past. In this sense ethnology is the science which classifies peoples in terms of their racial and cultural characteristics, and attempts to explain these by reference to their history or to their pre-history. To take a concrete case, investigations into the origin of a particular type of canoe are ethnological investigations, while enquiries about its contemporary use and its practical and symbolic significance for the people who have it fall within the scope of social anthropology.

I remarked above that the findings of physical anthropologists and pre-historians are for the most part irrelevant to the researches of social anthropologists. But they may be very important for ethnologists, who are interested in reconstructing the past rather than in interpreting the present. Ethnology is really the direct heir to Victorian anthropology; like it, it is a kind of history, though it

19

differs from history in that ethnologists ordinarily lack written records upon which to base their theories. Also, ethnologists have mostly been interested in separate items of culture, whether in the actual objects used or made by people (material culture) or in such topics as myth and folklore. They have inevitably been less concerned with social institutions and values, whose history is usually a good deal more difficult to trace. Social anthropologists may sometimes be ethnologists as well, where information is available about the origins of items of culture in which they are interested, and where this information throws light on their present use or significance. But on the whole present-day social anthropology and ethnology are best regarded as distinct disciplines. With the development in the last half century or so of social anthropology as a distinct subject, both their subject-matter and the kinds of questions they ask have diverged widely, and only confusion can result (and indeed has resulted) from regarding them as the same.

Nowadays a distinction is often drawn between social anthropology and cultural anthropology. Culture has been variously defined since Sir Edward Tylor described it nearly a century ago as 'that complex whole which includes knowledge, belief, art, morals, law, custom and any other capabilities and habits acquired by man as a member of society'.[1] In its broadest sense, 'culture' refers to the whole range of human activities which are learned and not instinctive, and which are transmitted from generation to generation through various learning processes. Often the physical products of human activity are included under the term as 'material culture'. Thus understood, cultural anthropology obviously covers an exceedingly broad field, including practically all the non-biological aspects of human life. Men's social institutions and values, social anthropology's central concerns, occupy only a small part of this range.

To study all this would obviously be a pretty tall order, and most British social anthropologists consider 'culture' too extended a concept usefully to designate a specific field for systematic study. A century ago one scholar might have been able to deal, in some fashion, with the whole life of man, at least of 'primitive' man, on this massive scale; advances in anthropological knowledge and techniques have made it impossible now. In fact, cultural anthropology has to a considerable extent broken down into such separate specialist fields as linguistics, acculturation and personality studies, ethnomusicology, and the study of primitive art. On the whole, American scholars have laid more stress on cultural than on social anthropology, which some of them have regarded as a more restricted

[1] Tylor, E. B., *Primitive Culture*, London, 1891.

20

interest concerned mainly with 'social structure'. This broader view of the content of the subject has led to a wide dispersal of interest over a variety of fields, such as acculturation studies and learning theory, many of which have been but little developed in British anthropology. It has also involved, at least in some degree, a concern with particular aspects or items of culture; with what have been called 'culture traits', rather than with the analysis of cultures or societies as, in some sense, systematic wholes. In this sense, much American anthropology is nearer to ethnology, as I defined it above, than it is to social anthropology as it is understood in Britain.

Historically, the American concern with items of culture rather than with social systems may be partly due to the nature of the ethnographic material most readily available to scholars in that country. Most British social anthropology is based on field studies of peoples whose societies are still 'going concerns', such as island populations in the Pacific and elsewhere, and tribal societies in Africa. But until recently American researchers have had much less ready access to such live material. Most (though by no means all) of the North American Indian groups among which American anthropologists mainly worked had long ago ceased to exist as viable societies, although their members often preserved extensive if piecemeal knowledge of their traditional cultures. So problems of social and political organization could not present themselves with the same urgency as they did in the study of the still viable societies of Africa and the Pacific. Thus rather less work has been done in America than in Britain and the Commonwealth in the analysis of actual communities as working social systems, the field in which recent British social anthropology has made its main contribution. There are important exceptions to this generalization, but it is significant that some modern British social anthropologists would claim that they have been more influenced by the writings of American sociologists (I refer to some of them in later chapters) than by those of American anthropologists.

But however significant these differences in approach—and their importance can be exaggerated—it must be remembered that for the most part they imply only a difference in emphasis: they do not, or at least they should not, imply that social anthropologists and cultural anthropologists study two different kinds of things. Whether the observer's main interest is in society or in culture, the reality which he observes, people in relation to one another, is one and not two. Cultural and social anthropologists sometimes ask different kinds of questions, but however we distinguish these there is a good deal of overlap. I noted earlier that social anthropologists cannot study the social relationships which are their central concern without regard to the beliefs and values associated with them. And in fact most modern social anthropologists regard people's ideas and symbols as an important part of their study, whether these can be shown to be relevant to the understanding of social relationships or not. I return to some of these points later.

There is also a more practical reason why social anthropologists have concerned themselves with the cultures of the people they have studied, including their material cultures and technologies. Very often they have been the only people with any scientific training who have the opportunity of first-hand contact with remote and hitherto unknown communities. So if they do not describe the whole way of life of these peoples, as far as they can, no one else will. And to do so may be a matter of urgency, for many of these cultures are in process of rapid social change, so that if we do not study them quickly it will be too late to study them at all.

(2)

So much for the relationship between social anthropology and other kinds of anthropology. I turn now to its relationship with some other social sciences, first of all with history. Historians are chiefly interested in the past, whether remote or recent; their business is to find out what happened, and why it happened. On the whole, they are more interested in particular sequences of past events and their conditions, than they are in the general patterns, principles or 'laws' which these events may exhibit. In both of these respects their concern is a little different from that of social anthropologists. For social anthropologists are centrally (though not exclusively) interested in understanding the present condition of the culture or community which they are studying. *Qua* historians they ask not 'what happened in history?' but rather 'how did things come to be as they are?' Their point of reference is the particular state of affairs which they are trying to understand. Also, their interest is as a rule explicitly general and comparative, as well as specific to the situation they are studying. Thus, for example, an anthropologist who is investigating a particular kinship system is interested not only in that particular kinship system but also in advancing his understanding of the working of all kinship systems, or at least of all kinship systems of that particular type.

But although the two disciplines are different, social anthropology has a very close relationship with history in two important ways. First, an anthropologist who aims to achieve as complete an understanding as possible of the present condition of the society he is studying can hardly fail to ask how it came to be as it is. This is so notwithstanding that his central interest is in the present, not in the past for its own sake; but often the past may be directly relevant in explaining the present. Thus when I was carrying out a field study in the kingdom of Bunyoro, in western Uganda, I was interested, *inter alia*, in contemporary Nyoro-European relations, and without some knowledge of the history of Western contacts with Bunyoro these would have been quite inexplicable.

A difficulty has been that many of the societies which social anthropologists have studied have no histories, in the sense of documented and verifiable accounts of the past, or at least they had none before the often very recent impact of Western culture. In such societies, the past sometimes is thought of as differing from the present only in respect of the individuals who occupy the different statuses which are institutionalized in the society, for example the statuses of chief, peasant, parent, neighbour. The statuses themselves may be thought of as having continued relatively unchanged since the very beginning of things. Obviously when a people has no history in the sense in which historians use the term, it cannot be studied. But in the twenties and thirties some social anthropologists, reacting against the pseudo-historical hypotheses of the preceding generation, went so far as to imply that history could never be relevant for social anthropologists, whose proper concern is with structural relations, not with historical ones. Some of Radcliffe-Brown's earlier writings express this view, though he later repudiated it. Few social anthropologists nowadays adopt so extreme an approach. Many of them have worked in relatively advanced communities which have documented histories. Also, European contact and the changes which have followed from it have provided histories, not always happy ones, for societies which formerly had none. So most modern social anthropologists do take account of the histories of the societies they study, where historical material is available and where it is relevant to the understanding of the present. Dr. Cunnison's work on the Luapula of Northern Rhodesia is an example, so is Professor Evans-Pritchard's account of the religious order of the Sanusi in Cyrenaica.[1] We shall see in Chapter 14 that the study of social change is by definition a historical one, though it makes use of sociological categories as well.

But history may be important to social anthropologists in another sense; that is, not only as an account of past events leading up to and

---

[1] Cunnison, I., *History on the Luapula* (Rhodes-Livingstone Papers No. 21), Oxford, 1951; Evans-Pritchard, E. E., *The Sanusi of Cyrenaica*, Oxford, 1949.

explaining the present, but also as the body of contemporary ideas which people have about these events, what the English philosopher Collingwood aptly called 'incapsulated history'. People's ideas about the past are an intrinsic part of the contemporary situation which is the anthropologist's immediate concern, and often they have important implications for existing social relationships. Also, different groups of people involved in the same social situation may have very different ideas about the 'same' series of historical events. Thus the history of contact between, say, an African people and a colonial power is likely to be very differently conceived by members of the two groups concerned. In Bunyoro, for example, the military subjection of the country in the nineties was, in the official European view, the necessary suppression of an intransigent native tyrant; in the Nyoro view it was an unnecessary campaign against a king who, while defending his country against unprovoked foreign aggression, showed himself quite ready to come to terms with the British had they permitted him to do so. Opposed 'histories' of this kind are common in colonial history, and they may be of great practical importance, for current action, which may determine the course of subsequent history, may be based on them.

In this sense, history merges with myth, which often enshrines a people's beliefs about their remote and sometimes their not so remote past. But although myths and traditional histories may sometimes give us important clues about past events, they are no substitute for history in the sense of 'what actually happened', for often the events which they describe did not and could not have taken place. An Australian tribesman's belief that he is somehow descended from a totemic species of animal, for example, gives us no insight into tribal origins, though it is culturally informative in other ways. The anthropologist is interested in myth, as he is interested in 'incapsulated' history, chiefly because it may express current attitudes and values, perhaps in symbolic form. Myths nearly always imply some sort of evaluation, some statement of the way in which the people who have the myth think about themselves and about the world, and what they consider to be important. Often myths tend to sustain some system of authority, such as a kingship or a priesthood, with its implicit distinctions of power and status. History and myth, then, are not the same, although there may be an element of history in myth, as there certainly is of myth in history. And social anthropologists are interested in both, for each may throw light on contemporary social and cultural situations.

Even though they are different, the aims and methods of social anthropologists and historians coincide in some degree. Although

24

historians use documentary evidence infrequently available to anthropologists, and anthropologists employ first-hand observation
rarely possible for historians, both are concerned with the description
and understanding of real human situations, and they use whatever
methods are available and appropriate to this purpose. Like
historians (and unlike natural scientists) a social anthropologist can
make the way of life of the creatures he studies intelligible to us only
in so far as he manages to convey to us something of what it would
be like to participate in that way of life oneself. Thus his task is very
largely one of interpretation. An anthropologist who tries to understand, say, why African chiefs in a selected tribe act as they do is not
engaged on an enterprise essentially different from that of a historian
who is trying to understand, say, why Roman emperors of a particular period acted as they did. Both anthropologists and historians
attempt to represent unfamiliar social situations in terms not just of
their own cultural categories, but, as far as possible, in terms of the
categories of the actors themselves. I shall say more in Chapter 6
about this crucial problem of translation; here I am suggesting that
the main difference between anthropology and history lies not so
much in their subject-matter (though generally this does differ), as in
the degree of generality with which they deal with it. Once again, it is
very much a question of emphasis. Historians are interested in the
history of particular institutions in particular places, parliament in
England, for example, or the Hapsburg monarchy. But they are also
concerned, implicitly if not explicitly, with the nature of these institutions themselves. Equally, a social anthropologist who is concerned with, say, the role of chiefs in a particular society must play
the historian to the extent of telling us something about the careers
and activities of individual chiefs. Unless he does this, we shall find
his account empty, formal and unconvincing. So, although in a very
general sense it is true that historians are concerned with what is
individual and unique, social anthropologists, like sociologists, with
what is general and typical, this dichotomy is altogether too simple.
As so often in the social sciences, the difference is largely one of
emphasis.

Social anthropology is not the same kind of study as psychology,
although like all sciences which deal with human affairs, it constantly makes use of psychological terms and concepts. Psychology
is mainly concerned with the nature and functioning of individual
human minds, and although it is generally accepted that human
mentality is a product of social conditioning, the study of that
mentality differs in important ways from the study of the social and
cultural environment which is its context, and each calls for its own

special methods of enquiry. Here again, the differences are very much of level and of emphasis. Both psychologists and social anthropologists (and historians too) deal with the same basic subject-matter, people in relation with other people. But, nowadays, one science cannot do everything, and social anthropology is not so much concerned with the mental experiences of individuals, as with the relationships between people which are institutionalized in particular societies, and with the beliefs and values which they share in virtue of their common culture. Thus while psychology focuses mainly on the individual and also has a physiological interest in human behaviour, social anthropology is concerned rather with the society and the culture which the individual is *in*. Here are some of the different kinds of questions which a psychologist and a social anthropologist might ask, if they were confronted with the same social situation, say (to use an example given by Evans-Pritchard) a criminal court in action. The psychologist might ask: what factors in the life-history of the accused might have led him to commit the offence? what are the mental factors which predispose the jury to bring in one verdict rather than another? why does the judge impose a more (or less) severe sentence than he might have done under the law? In other words, he is chiefly interested in the conditioning factors which lead the individuals concerned in this situation to act as they do. The social anthropologist's questions would be rather different. He might ask: what is the system of legal norms or rules which are applicable in this case? in what kind of social relationships do the actors stand to one another? how, in general, does the community as a whole regard offences of the kinds here being dealt with? That is, he is chiefly interested in the social and cultural implications of the situation.

But although there are evidently two different sorts of interests here, they do not mutually exclude one another; in fact each discipline inevitably uses concepts borrowed from the other. Once again, the important point is that it is not the subject-matter, people in society, that distinguishes the two interests; the difference lies rather in the questions that are asked about them. Just as the organisms biologists deal with are susceptible also of chemical and physical analysis (which does not, however, answer all the questions which the biologist asks), so the situations dealt with by sociologists and social anthropologists may be also analysed by psychologists, but psychology cannot answer the questions which most interest sociologists and social anthropologists.

The interests of these two disciplines are different, then, though their subject-matter is in large measure the same. Sociology (and with it social anthropology) can no more be reduced to psychology than biology can be reduced to chemistry. Following Comte, the French sociologist Durkheim, to whom I have already referred, made a clear and convincing case for the autonomy of sociology as a distinct kind of enquiry from psychology. His point was not that society was a different kind of 'existent' from its component members (though sometimes he incautiously gave that impression); it was rather that since the level of analysis is different, different methods are necessary. He argued that to explain social and cultural phenomena only in terms of individual psychology is to leave out a great deal of sociologically important information. Thus such a phenomenon as a suicide rate cannot be fully understood solely by reference to the individual life histories of the persons who commit suicide in a particular country during a particular period. To begin with, the rate can be predicted with a high degree of accuracy, whereas the future behaviour of particular individuals cannot. Especially, account must be taken, in the society in question, of such social factors as the prevalence of membership in specific groups, such as churches, clubs and even families, and the degree of social integration present in these groups. These factors, like all social data, have psychological aspects, but when the institutions themselves rather than the individuals who participate in them are considered, the questions that arise deal with the interrelationships of social institutions, and with the shared beliefs and values, the 'collective representations', in Durkheim's phrase, that these imply, rather than with individual psychology.

So, broadly, social anthropology differs from psychology in that it studies the cultures and social systems in which men participate, rather than the participants themselves. Like all science it abstracts, but it does so at a different level from psychology. None the less the two subjects are closely interdependent. In recent years there has developed, mainly in America, an important borderline field of study, in which anthropological concepts and methods have been explicitly brought to bear on questions which are essentially psychological, usually in the context of relatively unfamiliar cultures. Margaret Mead's celebrated studies of childhood and adolescence in Pacific communities belong to this kind of anthropology, as also do some of the writings of Ruth Benedict, Clyde Kluckhohn and others.[1] These studies differ from social anthropology as it is understood

[1] Mead, Margaret, *Coming of Age in Samoa*, London, 1929; *Growing up in New Guinea*, London, 1931; *Sex and Temperament in Three Primitive Societies*, London, 1935; Benedict, Ruth, *Patterns of Culture*, Boston and New York, 1934; Kluckhohn, *Mirror for Man*, London, 1950.

in Britain in their primary emphasis on the individual and what his culture does to him, rather than on the society and the culture in themselves. And they differ from 'classical' psychology in the stress they lay on 'acculturation' and processes of learning generally.

Rather as in the case of history, a tendency (itself a reaction against the over-facile psychologizing of the Victorians) to deny that psychology can have any relevance for social anthropology is nowadays being replaced by a recognition of the important contributions it can make to the understanding of people's social behaviour. This recognition is associated with social anthropology's growing concern with what people think, with their systems of beliefs, symbols and values. An important contribution to our understanding of the ways of thought of members of simpler, pre-industrial cultures was made more than a quarter of a century ago by the French philosopher Lévy-Bruhl. His main theme was that 'primitive' thought uses different categories from those of 'civilized' people, and is pre-eminently 'pre-logical' and 'mystical'. Although his views are now out of date, and he seriously over-stated some of his points, his emphasis on the symbolic, non-inferential quality of much human thinking (a quality by no means restricted, as he thought, to 'primitives') has borne fruit in much later work. The impact of Freud, also, on social anthropology, as on human thinking generally, has been considerable, though for the most part indirect. His one incursion into anthropology, his theory of the origin of totemism, is hardly convincing, but his massive demonstration of the primacy of symbolic, non-ratiocinative elements in human thought has had far-reaching influence in the subject.

In fact every field anthropologist must be to a considerable extent a practising psychologist, for a main part of his job is to discover what the people he is studying think, and this is never a simple task. Ideas and values are not given as data; they must be inferred, and there are many difficulties and dangers in such inferences, especially when they are made in the context of an unfamiliar culture. It may well be that there is much to be learned about the less explicit values of other cultures (as well as about those of our own), especially about the kinds of symbolism involved in ritual and ceremonial, through techniques of depth psychology. But a word of warning is necessary. The incautious application in unfamiliar cultures of concepts and assumptions derived from psychological researches in Western society may lead—and indeed has led—to gross distortions. The Oedipus complex, for example, is something to be proved, not assumed, in other cultures. Nevertheless it is likely that as psychologists increasingly work in cultures other than their own (and they are doing this) profitable collaboration between them and social anthropologists will take place.

So far, I have concluded that social anthropology is not history, although social anthropologists are sometimes historians, and that it is not psychology, although it cannot do without psychological categories. But with sociology the case is different. Like sociologists, social anthropologists study social relationships, and if this were a sufficient definition of their subject, it would be difficult to see why they should think of themselves as different from sociologists. In fact not all of them have so thought of themselves. Radcliffe-Brown suggested that social anthropology be re-named 'comparative sociology', thereby at once allying it squarely with sociology as against ethnology and the other historical sciences, and stressing its comparative concern with societies other than the investigator's. But his new name for the subject did not catch on, and this suggests that most social anthropologists do see their subject as at least a little different from sociology. In fact, there are two important differences between what social anthropologists do and what sociologists do. Although these involve no fundamental disjunction between the two disciplines, they do justify the maintenance of the distinction between them, for the present at any rate.

The first important difference is that while sociology is by definition concerned with the investigation and understanding of social relations, and with other data only in so far as they further this understanding, social anthropologists, although as we have seen they share this concern with sociologists, are interested also in other matters, such as people's beliefs and values, even where these cannot be shown to be directly connected with social behaviour. In brief, social anthropologists are cultural anthropologists as well. Although, as sociologists, they are still centrally interested in the manner in which ideas are integrated with systems of social relations (when they are so integrated), it is now plainer than it used to be that it is not always possible to establish such relationships. For example, people's religious and cosmological ideas do not necessarily reflect their social system, though it has sometimes been supposed that they do. And even where such relationships can be established, the anthropologist's interest in people's ideas is by no means exhausted when these connections have been pointed out. He is interested in their ideas and beliefs as well as in their social relationships, and in recent years many social anthropologists have studied other people's belief systems not simply from a sociological point of view, but also as being worthy of investigation in their own right. Recent books by

29

Evans-Pritchard and Lienhardt[1] are examples of such work. In fact, most social anthropologists have always done this to a greater or lesser extent, but they have not always been prepared to admit it. It may be that the study of primitive religions, cosmologies and symbolic systems will one day emerge as a specialized branch of study, separate from the strictly sociological sciences. But this has not happened yet, nor does such a schism seem imminent. Meantime this kind of enquiry remains an integral part of social anthropological research.

The second important difference between social anthropology and sociology is simply that social anthropologists have mostly worked in communities which are both less familiar and technologically less developed, while sociologists have chiefly studied types of social organization characteristic of more complex, Western-type societies. This distinction is by no means a hard-and-fast one; it implies difference in field rather than in fundamental theory, but it has important implications. First, the social systems studied by social anthropologists are usually small in scale, at least in comparison with Western societies, so that a great many of the social relationships which are institutionalized in them are between people who know one another personally. It is in the study of small-scale systems of this kind, where person-to-person relationships are all-important, that the methods of social anthropology have been elaborated, and its main contributions to sociological knowledge have been in this field. It is consistent with this interest that social anthropologists working in Western societies have generally taken as their units rural or village communities, or small sectors of urban ones, rather than whole states or cities, or large-scale governmental or industrial organizations.[2]

It is true that a great deal of sociological research has also been done in small groups, but these have usually been small groups *in* larger societies, and not groups which are more or less coterminous with the whole society. This concern with social systems that are small in scale has led to a particular concern by social anthropologists with the idea of totality, the notion that societies are wholes, or at least can be studied as if they were. The concept derives from French sociological thought, as we noted in the last chapter, but from the point of view of fieldwork it is evidently much more applicable to

[1] Evans-Pritchard, E. E., *Nuer Religion*, Oxford, 1956; Lienhardt, Godfrey, *Divinity and Experience, the Religion of the Dinka*, Oxford, 1961.

[2] Examples of such studies are Arensberg, C., *The Irish Countryman*, London, 1937; Pitt-Rivers, J., *The People of the Sierra*, London, 1954; and Kenny, M., *A Spanish Tapestry*, London, 1961.

a small Oceanic community or an isolated African tribe, than it could be to a large-scale Western society. We shall see in Chapter 4 that although the notion of a 'total social system' has been useful, it has some grave limitations, at least in the sense in which some anthropologists have used it.

Finally, the fact that social anthropologists have mostly worked in unfamiliar cultures has imposed on them a problem of translation which is much less acute for sociologists, though it certainly exists for them too. Sociologists usually speak the same language (more or less) as the people they study, and they share with them at least some of their basic concepts and categories. But for the social anthropologist the most difficult part of his task is usually to understand the language and ways of thought of the people he studies, which may be—and probably are—very different from his own. This is why in anthropological fieldwork a sound knowledge of the language of the community being studied is indispensable, for a people's categories of thought and the forms of their language are inextricably bound together. Thus questions about meanings, and about the interpretation of concepts and symbols, usually demand a larger part of the attention of social anthropologists than of sociologists. None the less, sociology is social anthropology's closest companion discipline, and the two subjects share a great many of their theoretical problems and interests. Social anthropologists are sociologists as well, but they are at once something less, because their actual field of investigation has on the whole been more restricted, and something more, because although they are concerned with social relationships, they are concerned with other aspects of culture as well.

I have now reviewed, inevitably with some over-simplifications and omissions, some of the more important fields of study with which social anthropology has, or had, important links, and with which its boundaries have sometimes been confused. To sum up, its associations with physical anthropology, prehistoric archaeology and prehistory are historical only; today social anthropology has little or no concern with these subjects. It shares its subject-matter with ethnology, and with it possesses a common base in ethnography, but the questions it asks are not ethnological, but relate rather to contemporary society and culture. Its emphasis differs from that of cultural anthropology, but social anthropologists are concerned with culture too. Anthropologists must use history, but for a purpose not itself strictly historical, that is, to understand the present. They must also use psychological concepts, but their chief interest is in the society and culture in which individuals participate, rather than in the individuals considered in themselves. And social anthropology is a kind of

31

sociology, but it does not restrict itself only to strictly sociological problems.

Social anthropologists, more than other social scientists, need to have at least a nodding acquaintance with some of the concepts and methods of a number of other subjects. This is because in the simpler, small-scale societies which they usually study, many of the institutionalized social relationships and values which they are interested in fall in fields which in more complex cultures are studied by specialist disciplines. Thus, for example, social anthropologists should know at least a little of the vocabulary of law and jurisprudence (since they study 'primitive law'), of political science (since they are concerned with relationships of political power and authority), and of elementary economics (since they are interested in production and exchange in the societies they study). But the social anthropologist's claim to treat of these, and other, specialist subjects in the context of his own studies is less arrogant than it may seem. For the relationships which they comprise are, for the most part, small in scale and relatively simple in content. They are effective mostly on a person-to-person level, and since they are for the most part comprehensible to non-specialist members of the cultures concerned, they are also, at least in principle, comprehensible to the anthropologist who has really 'learned' the culture. Nor, in the cultures which social anthropologists mostly study, does the understanding of their social and cultural institutions require, as it would in literate societies, the mastering of a huge quantity of books and documents. This is why social anthropologists, in the restricted context of the small-scale communities in which they work, presume to investigate the several dimensions of social and cultural life; their investigation does not demand the lengthy specialist training which would be necessary for the study of any one of them in a complex, literate society.

Indeed, social anthropology's findings may sometimes be important for the specialist disciplines. For essential features of social structure may sometimes be more plainly manifest in the context of simple social systems than in complex ones. And the analysis of living, though less complex, social systems may illuminate features which are obscured, or implicit, in more complex societies less readily susceptible of first-hand investigation. We shall be better able to assess the kinds of contribution which social anthropology can make to other fields of enquiry when we consider, in the second part of this book, the sort of knowledge about other cultures which it has achieved. Meantime, it may be acknowledged that if the social anthropologist's contributions to the general studies of, say, legal, political or economic systems are to be taken seriously by specialists, he must have at least a working knowledge of elementary theory in these fields. Social anthropology is an eclectic subject, and this is a source of both weakness and strength.

In this chapter I have tried to place social anthropology in the context of some other sciences of man. It should, at least, now be clear what it is not. In the next chapter I discuss in more detail what social anthropologists actually do. This entails consideration of some of the theories about society and culture that underlie their researches.

SHORT READING LIST

BENEDICT, RUTH, *Patterns of Culture*, New York, 1934.
DURKHEIM, É., *Suicide* (English translation), London, 1952.
EVANS-PRITCHARD, E. E., *Essays in Social Anthropology*, London, 1962.
KLUCKHOHN, C., *Mirror for Man*, London, 1950.
KROEBER, A. L., *Anthropology* (new edition), New York, 1948.
LINTON, RALPH, *The Study of Man*, New York, 1936.
RADCLIFFE-BROWN, A. R., *Structure and Function in Primitive Society*, London, 1952.
Method in Social Anthropology, Chicago, 1958.

3

What Social Anthropologists Study: the Need for Theory

(1)

IN THE LAST CHAPTER I said that social anthropologists have made much use of the idea of totality, and I suggested that this was partly because the earlier fieldworkers were chiefly concerned with human communities which were small-scale and relatively easily comprehensible. Some anthropologists, for example, Radcliffe-Brown, have suggested that social anthropologists can and ought to compare whole societies, as though these were some kind of empirical realities. But this is a dangerous and misleading way of thinking, and provides a typical example of Whitehead's 'fallacy of misplaced concreteness', the error of supposing that conceptual entities are 'real' ones, given to the senses like material objects. It derives much of its plausibility from the analogy which is often drawn between societies, which are not 'things', and physical organisms, which are: I examine this analogy more closely in the next chapter.

Since societies are not 'things' in any material sense, they cannot be studied as if they were. The concept of society is a relational not a substantial one; the only concrete entities given in the social situation are people. What we indicate when we use the term 'society' is that these people are related to one another in various institutionalized ways. And the sociologist's and the social anthropologist's job is to find out what these ways are.

Society, then, as a network of relationships, is simply the context in which sociologists and social anthropologists carry out their enquiries. No doubt we shall continue to speak of 'Western society', for example, or of 'Ganda society', as though we were referring to real concrete entities, and not just to particular complexes of relationships. There is no great harm in doing this, so long as it does not lead us to impose substantive models on social, that is relational, systems.

34

It would be rather too cumbersome to use such a term as 'social aggregate' to refer to the empirical reality, the actual sum of people who live in the same territory and who are associated in various ways, as the English philosopher Dorothy Emmet has suggested, reserving the word 'society' for the complex of associations which bind them together. But it would certainly be very much more precise.

But even if societies *were* empirical wholes, like guinea-pigs or frogs, it would still be impossible to study them as wholes. For all analysis, all description even, must be selective. We have to choose certain aspects of anything we wish to study, for we cannot comprehend all its aspects at once. And what social anthropologists do is to abstract from the social behaviour which they observe relatively enduring and institutionalized aspects which seem to hang together and make sense, in reference to some particular interest or question which, consciously or unconsciously, they have in mind. This is how particular social institutions are abstracted and identified. Examples of such institutions are a particular kin relationship, a certain set of rules about who may and may not marry whom, the scope and range of a ruler's authority. It is the institutions which are thus identified and described, not whole societies, that social anthropologists may compare from one society to another. I return later in this chapter to the topic of sociological and cultural comparison; here I wish only to stress that the subject-matter of social anthropology, in so far as it is a kind of sociology, consists in institutionalized social relationships and the systems into which they may be ordered. It does not consist in 'society' or 'societies', somehow given as empirical totalities to the observer.

When I speak of institutionalized social relationships I mean simply to refer to relationships which are familiar and well-established, social usages which are characteristic of the society which has them. Institutionalization is thus very much a matter of degree; some social relationships are more institutionalized than others. But unless a social relationship is institutionalized in *some* degree it is not of direct interest to social anthropologists, though it may concern them indirectly. Thus they may be interested in eccentricity and deviance, but usually only in so far as these divergencies from normal are themselves the objects of institutionalized attitudes (incest is an obvious example), or, in the context of change, where they imply the breakdown of hitherto accepted institutions.

But what is a social relationship? The concept is by no means as straightforward as it may seem. Very simply, when social anthropologists speak of social relationships they are thinking of the ways in which people behave when other people are objects of that

35

behaviour. The social relationship between husband and wife, for example, in a particular society means the ways in which husbands ordinarily behave to their wives, and wives to their husbands, in that society. At this preliminary level, there are always two basic things to be ascertained about any social relationship; whom it is between (e.g. husband and wife, father and son, ruler and subject), and what it is about (e.g. the disposition of property, the exercise of authority, the need to show respect). This dual quality of social relationships is often expressed in the distinction between statuses, what people are; and roles, what as occupants of certain statuses they do. The two aspects have sometimes been combined, as by the American sociologist Talcott Parsons, in the portmanteau concept 'status-role', for each implies the other, and some statuses, for example those of policemen and poets, are wholly or partly defined by reference to the roles which their occupants are expected to perform.

But even though all statuses imply some role or roles, it is not always possible to infer people's statuses from what they do. Some institutionalized statuses are what sociologists call 'ascribed' or 'ascriptive', that is, they are given independently of the role or roles performed by their occupants. Others are based on, and defined by, 'achievement', that is, on what the holders of those particular statuses do. Kinship statuses, for example, are (mostly) ascribed; however a brother behaves he is always a brother: occupational ones (usually) achieved; a farmer is a farmer, for example, because he farms. But very often the same status has both ascribed and achieved aspects; a hereditary king, for example, whose status is so far ascriptive, may be dethroned for incompetence or tyranny, that is, for failure to conform to required standards of achievement.

I said earlier that social anthropologists are necessarily interested in people's ideas and beliefs, as being a no less essential part of their subject-matter than overt behaviour. It should now be growing clearer why this is so. For evidently a social relationship, as I have just defined it, implies something more than just what people are observed to do. To begin with, one cannot observe a status; one must infer it. In human terms, it exists only in being recognized and acknowledged, that is, in people's minds. Essential to all institutionalized social relationships are the kinds of expectations which the parties to it entertain about each other's—and their own—behaviour. This 'reciprocity' or 'complementarity' of expectations, to use Talcott Parsons' phrase, is what makes ordered human social interaction possible; there could be no coherent or meaningful social life, at any rate above the purely instinctual level, if nobody knew what anyone else (or he himself) was going to do next.

So far as human beings in society are concerned, then, social relationships cannot be adequately described without reference to the expectations, intentions and values which they express or imply. It is certainly conceivable that the workings of a human society could be described merely in terms of physical movements in space and time (though the exercise would be a rather pointless one). Or perhaps, like a termite community, it could be described without reference to the ideas or intentions of its members, but with regard only to the consequences of their habitual activities for the preservation of the group. But such an account would be a travesty of sociology. It would leave out all reference to what we most want to know about human societies, what it is that makes them distinctively human, that is, the fact that most human institutions, unlike all insect institutions, are only fully intelligible in terms of the beliefs and values of the people who participate in them. I know of no social anthropologist who has ever attempted to describe any existing human social system in this way. Most of them would agree with the celebrated German sociologist Max Weber that the full sociological understanding of the behaviour of men in society requires that account be taken of what membership in the society means to the people concerned.

So, *qua* sociologists, social anthropologists are concerned both with people's behaviour in regard to one another, so far as this is more or less institutionalized, and with people's ideas about their relationships with one another. These ideas about human relationships may be expectations of certain kinds of behaviour, claims to certain privileges or rights, acknowledgments of certain obligations, recognition of particular statuses, and so on. Here, two different levels of thinking may be broadly distinguished. First, there are people's notions about what they actually do, the manner in which they conceive their own social system and the world they live in. And secondly, there are their beliefs about what they and other people *ought* to do, their legal and moral values or norms. The people themselves may not always clearly distinguish these two levels: thus it may be held in regard to certain kinds of human relationships that they are as they ought to be, and that it is unthinkable that they should be otherwise. The regard in which ritual or 'divine' kings, for example, are held in some societies, provides an example of such a case. But since no mortals (so far as we know) suppose themselves to inhabit the best of all possible worlds, there are always some social relationships in which real and ideal, what is and what ought to be, are distinguished. Not *all* husbands, wives, neighbours, rulers, are perfect.

Social anthropologists who are studying social relationships have, then, to deal with them both on the level of 'what actually happens', and on the level of what people think about what happens. And what they think about what happens is, again, of two kinds; first, what they believe things to be, and second, what they believe they ought to be. Modern social anthropologists writing about communities they have studied almost always give some account of the social relationships they describe on all three of these separate levels, but sometimes they emphasize one level rather than another, and often they do not distinguish them clearly. It is important to do so, however, because they differ significantly, and have to be understood by different methods.

Take, first, the level of 'what actually happens'. The notion is not as simple as it looks. Neither in anthropology nor in any other science are 'facts' given to us fully formed; always construction and interpretation are involved. The facts (for example, the fact that in one society a man may have several wives, in another a woman may have several husbands) are in an important sense 'built up' by the investigator, by inference, based on concepts and presuppositions already in his mind, from what individual people say and do. Of course in a philosophical sense all knowledge, including knowledge of what people say and do, is a construct, compounded of inference as well as observation, and validated by the extent to which it makes sense of already accepted 'facts', that is, of the observer's constructs at the next lowest level of abstraction. The important point to keep in mind is that in studying social relationships we are dealing with different levels of abstraction and interpretation. The level may be that of everyday common sense, or it may be something more precise and consciously formulated, as it must be when quite unfamiliar situations are being dealt with, which do not 'make sense' in terms of our everyday notions.

I return to the difficult problem of sociological interpretation in Chapter 6, where I discuss how anthropologists actually work. Here I want only to make the point that 'what actually happens', however obvious it may seem to be, is at least in some measure the observer's construct or model, usually based on the unanalysed concepts of common sense, that is, of the observer's common sense. And the anthropologist's construct need not coincide with the representation which the people concerned have of the situation being described. This radical opposition has assumed prominence as increasingly intensive fieldwork has shown how very differently different peoples may conceive or 'factor out' their universe, and anthropologists have expressed it in various ways. Thus the American anthropologist Robert Redfield developed the idea of the 'folk' culture, and the French social anthropologist Claude Lévi-Strauss has distinguished the 'statistical model' (the analyst's representation of the system being described) from the 'mechanical model', the same system as its participant members regard it.[1]

Lévi-Strauss's use of the term 'statistical' is significant. For 'what actually happens' is susceptible of quantitative treatment in a way in which, or at least to an extent to which, data of the other two kinds, beliefs and values, are not. Modern social anthropologists are required to do more than merely to describe people's behaviour qualitatively; nowadays they are also expected to support their assertions about what people do (or say they do) with some quantitative evidence. Thus it is one thing to say 'such-and-such a people have the institution of bridewealth, whereby cattle and other goods pass from the bridegroom to the bride's family on marriage'. But it is quite another thing to say that 'in 250 marriages bridewealth was paid in 72 per cent of the sample'. The latter statement, we feel, really gives us 'the facts'.

So statistical treatment is appropriate, sometimes indispensable, at the level of 'what actually happens'. But it is very much less feasible to make quantitative statements of this kind about people's beliefs and values; their ideas about sorcery, for example, or their standards of filial piety. And it should be noted that a statistical assertion, by itself, can tell us nothing, or at least nothing of interest, unless we understand what its terms mean, and such understanding generally requires reference to the folk system of the people concerned. Thus the statistical assertion about marriage and bridewealth which I gave above as an example is sociologically informative only if we understand what 'marriage' and 'bridewealth' mean in the social and cultural context being investigated. For the meanings of even these seemingly simple terms (or rather of the vernacular words which we translate by these terms) may differ in very important ways from one culture to another.

Investigation on the other two levels involved in institutional analysis, beliefs and values, requires not only observation of what people do, but also understanding of what they mean, of their ways of thought. Here the anthropologist's task is not simply the recording of events, it is rather one of interpretation. And this can only be done by attempting, through close personal acquaintance with the people themselves, to understand as far as possible what the basic categories are through which they conceive their social world. In Chapter 6 I discuss some of the ways in which social anthropologists do this, and some of the difficulties of doing it.

[1] Redfield, R., *The Folk Culture of Yucatan,* Chicago, 1941; Lévi-Strauss, C., *Structural Anthropology,* New York, 1963, Chapter 5.

It is, however, worth reverting here to a point already touched on. Although ideal configurations and meanings are essential constituents of social relationships, the social anthropologist is interested in them even where they cannot be shown to be relevant to any particular system of social relationships. Systems of belief can be, and have been, studied by anthropologists as systems in their own right. Indeed it is hard to see how they could be shown to be relevant —or irrelevant—to systems of action until they had first been investigated in themselves. Whether or not a belief is socially relevant cannot be determined until we know what it is. And in fact, as I noted in the last chapter, social anthropologists who have written detailed accounts of primitive religions and cosmologies have not felt themselves at all bound to consider only their social significance. For example Professor Daryll Forde wrote, in his introduction to a collection of essays by social anthropologists about different peoples' ideas of the world they live in, published a few years ago: 'each study seeks to portray and interpret the dominant beliefs and attitudes of one people concerning the place of man *in nature* and in Society' (my italics).[1] The essays, in other words, are about beliefs, not about social relations. It is true that most of the contributors are interested in social relations, and they take note of the implications for them of the ideas they are describing, where such implications can be shown. Again, in the preface to his classic account of the religious ideas of the Nuer of the Southern Sudan, Evans-Pritchard defines his enquiry as a study of 'what they (the Nuer) consider to be the nature of spirit and of man's relations to it'.[2] His book is centrally about religious ideas and practices and not about social relations, and this is so even though the author has in mind the social contexts of the beliefs and rites he describes. So it is plain that, whatever some of them may say about it, social anthropologists are directly interested in systems of beliefs and values, even where these have no direct relevance to systems of social relations.

Nevertheless, even if they are not the social anthropologist's only interest, institutionalized social relationships are certainly his central one. And I have suggested that social relationships are really quite complex abstractions from people's behaviour, implying both a 'factual', behavioural aspect, and an ideal, conceptual one. This can be put another way by saying that social institutions participate at the same time in systems of action and in systems of ideas. As constituents of systems of action they have consequences, and as constituents of systems of ideas they have meanings. Social anthropologists

[1] Forde, D. (editor), *African Worlds*, London, 1954.
[2] Evans-Pritchard, E. E., *Nuer Religion*, Oxford, 1956.

usually take account of both of these dimensions. It is by the systematic interrelating of social relationships on, and between, these two levels that they define and analyse social institutions. For example, such an institution as kingship in a particular society implies a complex of attitudes of respect, authority, obedience, protection, and so on, held by the various categories of persons involved in the institution. And it also implies special patterns of behaviour, appropriate to these various categories of people. These attitudes and their associated behaviour-patterns 'hang together', as it were, in the social field itself, where they form a complex which is meaningful to the people who have them, and which is also causally significant for other institutions in the society. They belong together, too, in the anthropologist's representation of the situation, for they make sense of what he observes, which is in turn determined by his own conceptual interests. I now consider a little more fully how social anthropologists set about understanding the social institutions or complexes of social relationships which they study.

(2)

It may be said that the anthropologist's first task is descriptive: in any empirical enquiry we must know what the facts are before we can analyse them. But it is plain from what I have just said that although the distinction between description and analysis is indispensable it can be misleading, especially in the social sciences. The difference is not simply between studies which imply abstraction and those which do not, for even the most common-sense descriptions are shot through with abstractions, generally unanalysed and implicit ones. This must be so, for a description of anything must be in general terms, and general terms are the names of classes, that is of abstractions, and not the names of things. So description always does more than just describe; to some degree at least it also explains. Theories are involved in even the simplest descriptions; not only do they determine the kinds of facts which are selected for attention, but also they dictate the ways in which these facts shall be ordered and put together. So the important question is not whether an account of a social institution (or of anything else) implies generalization and abstraction, for it is bound to do this. The critical questions are, rather, what is the level of abstraction, and what are the kinds of theories involved? It is especially necessary to be explicit about these matters in social anthropology, for the social situations it deals with are often unfamiliar ones. This means that our common-sense notions about them, implicitly derived from our own culture, are

41

likely to be quite inappropriate and may be gravely misleading. This is why there is a special need for explicit theory in social anthropology, that is, for a systematic consideration of the kinds of questions which are to be asked. For it is not at all obvious *prima facie* what kinds of questions are appropriate to what kinds of data. Owing to deficient theory, anthropologists have often framed their questions in such terms that they are unanswerable.

These considerations also explain why amateurs' accounts of simpler and unfamiliar cultures are rarely as satisfactory by present-day standards as those of professional anthropologists. It is not that they are less careful or conscientious observers; it is simply that the kinds of questions modern social anthropologists ask, and the kinds of interconnections they look for, derive from a body of theoretical ideas which have grown up over the past half-century or so, and which have to be learnt. As in other sciences, though more recently than in most, the amateur's day is over. No scientist can approach his material with, literally, an open mind; he is bound to have some theoretical preconceptions. Since this is so, it is desirable first that these should be as explicit as possible and second, that they should both be appropriate to the kind of material being investigated and be conceived in terms of current theory.

Of course no sensible social anthropologist approaches his study with a set of cast-iron, currently fashionable categories, and then forces his material into them, regardless of its uniqueness and individuality. At the start of a field investigation the appropriateness of any particular body of theory, explanatory framework, or set of questions (all these phrases mean very much the same thing), is bound to be a hit-or-miss affair, subject to continuing revision, modification and reformulation. The difference between the professional and the amateur is not that one has theories about what he is doing and the other has not: nobody in his senses tries to do something without the least idea of what he is trying to do, and his statement of what he is trying to do and how he proposes to do it (if he takes the trouble to make such a statement) is his theory. The difference between them lies rather in the explicitness and appropriateness of their theories, of the questions they are trying to answer. It will become clearer in later chapters that questions which are appropriate in regard to one of the three aspects of social relationships which I distinguished earlier (that is, their aspects as systems of action, systems of beliefs, or systems of values) may be quite inappropriate in regard to another.

Social anthropologists, then, seek to understand the data they study, and what they mostly study are social relationships. Now there are two important ways in which an unfamiliar social relationship can be understood. First, we can learn enough about the culture in which it is found to see the situation as the parties to it see it, and secondly, we can place it in a causal context as both effect and cause. These two kinds of understanding correspond to the two major aspects of human social relationships which I distinguished earlier, their aspect as systems of ideas and beliefs, and their aspect as systems of action. Though analytically distinguishable, these are almost always combined in the actual explanations which social scientists give. But it is worth noting that the first of them, understanding by, as it were, imaginatively putting oneself in the place of the parties to the relationship being examined, is peculiar to the social sciences. It is no part of the chemist's or the physicist's job to identify himself imaginatively with the entities he is studying; to do so would hinder rather than help his researches. But it is an essential part of the social anthropologist's task.

In Chapter 5 I consider further some of the implications of this distinction; first a word must be said on the general notion of explanation in the social sciences, and especially in social anthropology. There are many different ways of explaining things, some appropriate to some kinds of data, others to other kinds, and they are often confused. But what is common to all kinds of explanation is that they relate what is to be explained to something else, or to some order of things or events, so that it no longer appears to hang in the air, as it were detached and isolated. As the social anthropologist Nadel has put it, explanation 'adds meaning to "just so" existence'. What is not fully intelligible when considered in and by itself becomes so as soon as it is seen as a part of a wider whole or process, or as an exemplification of some principle or pattern already understood. So explaining something means putting it in an appropriate context.

Now there are various ways in which things can be related to other things, and so explained: I consider some of them in the next chapter. Here I note only that there is a very broad sense in which it may be said that all explanation, deductively considered, is merely a process of bringing what is to be explained under some general rule or principle. But this is too general for our purpose. Certainly all explanation does involve the assimilation of what is to be explained to some body of existing knowledge, but essentially this process is only classificatory; what we are doing here is referring what is to be explained to some category or class with which we are already familiar. Where we already know something about the class to which our explicandum is referred, then the process of subsuming the particular under the general certainly adds to our understanding of it, and so far it is explanatory. Thus, for example, our understanding of such apparently diverse institutions as the *kula* (in which the natives of some Melanesian islands ceremonially exchange certain ornaments), the *potlatch* (in which members of some North American Indian tribes conspicuously destroy useful goods), and of bridewealth (common in Africa and elsewhere and involving a payment by the groom to the bride's relatives on marriage), is greatly advanced when all these institutions are shown to be special types of the general class of prestations or gift-exchanges. What we are really doing here is bringing what we are attempting to explain within the range of an already existing explanation. So it is not simply the process of generalization that is explanatory—though some have written as though it were—in the last resort what is being invoked is some explanatory synthesis, as yet unspecified, of another kind.

In the next chapter I consider some of the types of explanation which are most used, and most useful, in social anthropology. But first, in order to clear the ground, something must be said about the twin topics of generalization or 'general laws' in social anthropology, and the possibility of sociological comparison.

Anthropologists have differed as to whether general laws exist or not in the social sciences, and, if they do, whether they can ever be discovered. On the whole, those social anthropologists who have thought of the subject as resembling the natural sciences such as biology or chemistry have supposed that such laws can be and eventually will be discovered. But those who have thought of it rather as one of the humanities, closer to such disciplines as philosophy and history, have denied that laws analogous to 'scientific' laws are ever likely to be found in the social sciences. We shall see that the disagreement is very largely a verbal one, depending on what we mean by the term 'law'. It has been further intensified by differences, usually implicit, of moral and religious standpoint. Protagonists of the second view have sometimes written as though they believed that if human behaviour be thought of as governed by necessary and unexceptionable laws, however complex and difficult of discovery these may be, human freedom of choice must be done away with, and with it moral responsibility. The dilemma we are faced with is the familiar problem of freewill; either men's behaviour is determined (and so subject to 'laws'), so that no one can act otherwise than he does, or else it is undetermined, in which case it must be causeless, that is, wholly random and capricious. It is important to note that moral freedom is undermined in either case. In terms of the categories in which we are accustomed to think about our world there is no half-way house.

This is not the place for an exhaustive discussion of this hoary problem. But it may be pointed out that the dilemma, at least as it has presented itself to social scientists, is a false one, resting on a mistaken idea of the nature of knowledge. For, as everybody knows, freewill is a fact of experience: we do make choices, and we know that we could sometimes have chosen to act otherwise than we did. Dr. Johnson very properly observed: 'Sir, we know the will is free, and there's an end on't.' On the other hand, however comprehensive and intellectually compelling 'laws of nature' may be, they are not facts of anybody's experience. They are hypotheses based on inference, justified only by the degree to which they introduce order into our experience and facilitate further advances in our understanding of and control over events. It is reasonable to assume that there must be some order in nature if we are to make any sense of it, as we evidently do. But it does not follow that its order must be identical with that which we hypothetically impute to it for our own purposes, and no reputable scientist would claim that it is.

'Laws of nature', then, are explanatory hypotheses, not statements about the ultimate nature of the universe, and so they have nothing to do with issues of moral choice. Underlying the confusion is Whitehead's 'fallacy of misplaced concreteness', the error of turning concepts into things, epistemology into ontology. Every kind of organized human enquiry either assumes or seeks to establish regularities and coherences in what it deals with, whether it calls these trends, patterns or laws. And the investigator seeks to understand the uniformities he finds, that is, he seeks to explain them. This is no less true in the social sciences than it is in the so-called exact sciences, even though the kinds of understanding appropriate in the social sciences differ in important ways from those appropriate in the 'natural' sciences. In both the investigator is interested in what is general and typical among the phenomena he studies, and in both he seeks to explain the regularities he observes by relating them to wider systems or processes.

In social anthropology at least, the confusion about laws has been further exacerbated by the fact that not all who have been concerned with the question have shown a clear or precise notion of what is meant by a scientific law. Radcliffe-Brown, for example, sometimes wrote as though it were simply a statement of some regularity in nature to which no exception had been observed, of the form 'all A's are B's'. But this is not at all what scientists mean by a scientific law. It is simply a generalized empirical observation, and the regularity which it records, far from explaining anything, is itself just what needs to be explained. A scientific law is not just a statement of a regularity: it is a theoretical synthesis which explains a regularity. It is neither a deduction from already established principles nor an induction from empirical observation, but essentially, as the philosopher Stephen Toulmin puts it, 'the adoption of a new approach'. And although such a synthesis may be expressed in the form of a general proposition, what is explanatory about it is not its generality, nor any kind of regularity in the data it refers to, but essentially the new theoretical synthesis which it proposes.

This is so whatever the range of the new synthesis proposed. An institutionalized relationship of avoidance between a man and his wife's mother, for example, is no less explained when it is shown to be an exemplification of a wider relationship of general respect which subsists between men and their wives' parents in certain societies, than the behaviour of falling bodies is explained when it is shown to exemplify a wider principle about the behaviour of all bodies, though certainly the explanations are on very different levels of generality. Both involve essentially 'the adoption of a new approach' to what is being explained, and it is plain that new approaches, fresh hypotheses, are necessary for advance in any field of human enquiry. This is so even though the range and analytical complexity of any hypothesis must depend both on what is being investigated and on the level of sophistication achieved in the branch of knowledge concerned. And it may be conceded at once that what social anthropologists, like other social scientists, deal with, people acting and thinking in relation with one another, differs in important ways from the 'mindless' data the natural scientists deal with. For example, it is much less susceptible than they are of wide-scale generalization and quantitative treatment.

I develop this point further in the next chapter. Here I wish only to stress that its recognition does not imply that we can never make any significant generalizations about the social behaviour of men in society, or at least of men in particular societies, or that we can never provide satisfactory explanatory bases for these generalizations. Scientific knowledge in any field advances only by seeking the general in the particular, the constant in the flux. But it is now plainer than it used to be that progress in the understanding of the social and cultural institutions of other peoples is to be achieved, at any rate for the present, rather by establishing narrow-range hypotheses (as the American sociologist R. K. Merton puts it) in restricted fields, and by the making of local comparisons on the basis of these hypotheses, than by grand generalizations about all human societies everywhere. It becomes social scientists, perhaps more than other kinds of scientists, to be modest, and no reputable social anthropologist today would offer enlightenment on so grand a scale, or even venture to anticipate being able to do so in the foreseeable future.

As with theory, so with comparison, which implies it. Radcliffe-Brown wanted to call social anthropology 'comparative sociology', but the kinds of comparison which are still most likely to be fruitful are those made between institutions in very similar (and therefore probably contiguous) societies, rather than those drawn between societies of very different types. Thus Professor Schapera has advocated intensive regional studies, embracing all the peoples in particular areas, so that more refined institutional classifications may be arrived at. Such an attempt has recently been made by Professor Mair, in the context of East African ethnography, in her useful paperback *Primitive Government*.[1] Of course in a basic sense social anthropology is essentially comparative, as all science is; comparisons are implicit in the very language which anthropologists use to describe other people's social institutions. When they speak of kings, princes and rulers, of fathers and sons, of priests and laymen, in the societies they investigate, they are implicitly assimilating these kinds of people to categories familiar to them from their own backgrounds. This semantic assimilation is unavoidable; without it there could be no communication. But we shall see later that it is very necessary to keep an eye on these implicit comparisons, for often they lead to misunderstanding. This is one reason why an important part of the social anthropologist's task is to make as explicit and precise as possible the language and categories he uses to describe other people's social and cultural institutions.

On the whole, then, it is more useful to compare institutions which have similar backgrounds or contexts than it is to compare institutions which belong to very different contexts, and which may therefore differ very greatly in social significance and consequence. And evidently the most useful kind of comparison, and so the most useful kind of classification, is that which brings things together not because of extraneous, accidental resemblances (like 'all red-haired men'), but in respect of qualities which are socially important, that is, which are intrinsic to the systematic complexes which are being compared. Much could be learned, for example, by comparing the kingships of the neighbouring and related states of Bunyoro and Buganda, but a direct comparison of either of these with the British monarchy would be of very doubtful value.

This has one vital implication for social anthropologists. It is that

[1] Schapera, I., "Some Comments on the Comparative Method in Social Anthropology", *American Anthropologist*, Vol. 55, No. 3, 1953; Mair, Lucy, *Primitive Government*, Harmondsworth, 1962.

where social institutions are being compared from one culture to another, each must first be thoroughly understood in its own social context. To compare things implies that in at least some respect they are different, as well as that they are similar, and differences are only meaningful against comparable backgrounds. Anyone can tell a hawk from a handsaw, but to distinguish between two varieties of kingship requires a thorough understanding of each in its own proper context. This is the point of Schapera's injunction; it is more likely that social and cultural contexts will be fully comparable where the societies concerned are related or contiguous ones.

So comparisons of social and cultural institutions from contexts remote in space and time must be undertaken with caution, but it does not follow that they are always mistaken or useless. I have said that such comparisons are implicit in the language which we perforce use to describe other people's social institutions, and there is much to be said for rigorously investigating these comparisons and assessing their validity. For example, it is not impossible that light may be thrown on the working of certain historical societies in Europe and elsewhere by comparing them with existing societies of similar structural type in other parts of the world, or that our understanding of, say, ancient Greek ideas about divination may be advanced by the study of existing peoples who still practice similar techniques. Also, the plotting of similar culture-traits or usages on a world-wide scale, as has been done by the Cross-Cultural Survey at Yale University, is useful in providing a sort of ethnographic directory, provided always that the institutions taken to be the same are really so.

To be sure that they are, it is necessary for the social institutions being compared to be first thoroughly understood in their own social and cultural contexts. In the next chapter I consider how social anthropologists have tried to achieve this kind of understanding.

SHORT READING LIST

DURKHEIM, É., *The Rules of Sociological Method* (English translation), Glencoe (Ill.), 1950.

FIRTH, RAYMOND, *Elements of Social Organization*, London, 1951.

MERTON, R. K., *Social Theory and Social Structure*, Glencoe (Ill.), 1949.

NADEL, S. F., *The Foundations of Social Anthropology*, London, 1951.

PARSONS, TALCOTT, *Essays in Sociological Theory*, Glencoe (Ill.), 1949. *The Social System*, London, 1952.

POCOCK, D. F., *Social Anthropology*, London, 1961.

TOULMIN, STEPHEN, *The Philosophy of Science, an Introduction*, London, 1953.

4

Explanation in Social Anthropology: Social Function and Social Structure

(1)

SO EXPLANATION is putting things in contexts. Now there are different kinds of contexts into which social scientists may put their findings; I have already discussed one of them, subsuming things under rules, or classifying them. Thus we may explain certain features of the institution of bridewealth by pointing out that it is a case of the wider class of gift-exchanges, and that as such it must have certain characteristics, such as a reciprocating element. But what we really want to know is why this should be so, and no amount of generalizing can tell us this. If we are to add to our understanding, and not just to summarize or apply what we know already, we need some new synthesis, some hitherto unthought-of way of looking at things.

But what kind of synthesis? I stressed earlier that the notion of a social institution involves, on the one hand, a framework of action, and on the other, a framework of ideas, beliefs and values. Corresponding to this distinction, there are two broad types of explanatory synthesis used by social anthropologists. The first has reference to causes; the second to meanings. The two levels interact, and indeed explanation on either level requires some reference to the other. But they imply two quite different kinds of interests in the social institutions being studied.

Until very recently most social anthropologists, especially in Britain, have stressed the analysis of social systems as systems of action, that is, in causal terms. The most celebrated contributions of the past half-century deriving through Radcliffe-Brown and Malinowski from Durkheim and his predecessors, have been made at this level. This is not surprising. As we noted in Chapter 1, the key which opened the door to the systematic understanding of the simpler,

49

'primitive' societies was the organic analogy, which derived from French sociology. And the functioning of organisms, like the working of machines, makes sense without any reference to the states of mind (if any) of their constituent parts. Scholars on the Continent and in America, and a few social anthropologists in this country, have throughout sustained an interest in people's thoughts and ideas, both on their own account and as causally effective elements in systems of action. But the theoretical models most characteristic of modern social anthropology have been those which take societies as systems of action, and which either explicitly or implicitly invoke the organic analogy. It is only in the last few years that the study of social and cultural institutions as systems of meanings has again become a primary concern. In this chapter I discuss explanatory theory at the 'action' level, where causal connections rather than 'meanings' are paramount. In the next chapter I consider advances in the anthropological study of other peoples' ideas and values.

On the 'action' level, two different though associated kinds of questions can be asked about social institutions, both concerned with causes. The first relates to the problem of how things came to be as they are, and so is essentially historical. A certain existing state of affairs is better understood if it can be shown to have followed from some pre-existing state of affairs in accordance with principles of causation already familiar from other contexts. So if it can be shown (as of course it very often cannot) that a certain social institution is as it is because of certain historical happenings, social anthropologists take (or should take) note of these happenings, provided that there is sufficient evidence for them. And these happenings need not themselves be physical events on the 'action' plane of social reality; we know that ideas and values may play an important part in history. History is important for sociology not only as a chain of causes and effects running back into the past; from a different point of view it is also important as a body of contemporary beliefs about these events. Such ideas may be potent forces in current social attitudes and relations, and as such they are plainly the social anthropologist's concern.

But causal, temporal processes may be regarded not only as making up unique chains of antecedents and consequents culminating in the present; they may also be seen as current, habitual and repetitive. This provides the second and major dimension of the social anthropologist's interest in causes. For it is one thing to ask how a society, or a social institution, came to be as it is; it is quite another thing to ask how it works or 'functions'. This is the central difference between the historical approach and what has come to be called the 'func-

50

tional' approach in social anthropology. Both are concerned with causes, but the questions which one asks are aetiological or historical, while the questions which the other asks are operational or functional. An example of a historical question is 'did the kingship of the Baganda originate in conquest by an outside power?': an example of a functional or sociological question is 'what are the causal implications of the Ganda kingship for other institutions in the society, such as the economic system or the system of social control?' Both kinds of questions are concerned with causes, but in the second case, unlike the first, the causes and effects are thought of as repetitive or continuous in time and not as constituting a unique series. Also they are currently observable, or at least inferable, by the investigator.

These functional causal connections are not always obvious; they have to be looked for. So a characteristic of the functional approach is its concern to discover connections between things which at first sight seem to be quite separate. This is why functionalism as a technique of investigation had to await the development of intensive fieldwork. For to perceive causal connections between different social institutions in real-life situations it is first of all necessary to understand these institutions thoroughly; to know both how they work and what those who participate in them think about them (since their ideas may be causally effective). And this kind of understanding, at least in exotic and unfamiliar contexts, was impossible until intensive field studies of working communities began to be made. The chief importance of functional anthropology for modern fieldworkers is that it provides them with hypotheses about possible interconnections between institutions, and if and when these are established they afford reasonably adequate and satisfying explanations at the 'action' level. For example, witchcraft beliefs in a particular society may be shown to be closely connected with social control, since men may fear to invite either attack by witches or suspicion of witchcraft by socially disapproved behaviour. If this is shown to be the case, our understanding both of the social significance of witchcraft and of the maintenance of social order is much enhanced.

In Part 2 I record many instances of such functional interconnections. Durkheim's explanation of suicide statistics by demonstrating causal links with such other social factors as marital status and church membership is a classic example. Another instance is the type of explanation anthropologists give of the widespread institution of marriage-payment or bridewealth by showing how it is linked with other co-existing social institutions. Thus it may provide a means of legitimizing the status of children, or maintain certain kinds of relationships between groups of people. The pointing out of such necessary but not always obvious interdependences is the field-worker's most important task. Indeed, *qua* sociologist, it is difficult to see what else he could do, and as a fieldwork method there is not much more to functionalism than this. It has even been argued that there is no such thing as a specifically functional method, distinct from other kinds of sociological enquiry. The field sociologist's job, it may be said, is neither more nor less than to try to determine the nature of the social institutions he is studying, and the manner of their interconnections.

But there is a little more to functionalism than this. Causal connections between things can only be detected if the investigator has in mind hypotheses about the kinds of interconnections which he expects to find. And he is looking for consequences as well as causes. In this sense functionalism is forward-looking; and usually functional explanation involves either explicit or implicit reference to some end or purpose, which is seen—or presumed—to be served by the causal interdependences which have been discovered. Functional theory looms so large in modern social anthropology that I must say something here about these presumed ends or purposes.

Because it looks forward to some kind of end, and not backwards to a beginning, functionalism is evidently (in some sense) teleological. But the notion of teleology contains a fundamental ambiguity, and this has led to much confusion. In the first place, teleological explanation consists in showing that it is a quality of what is being explained to have certain consequences. But not just any consequences. To say, for example, that it is a quality of fire to burn things is not to offer a teleological explanation of fire, even though it certainly adds to our understanding of what fire is. For an explanation to be teleological it is necessary that the consequence should be for some sort of meaningful complex or system, which the investigator already has in his mind, whether it is precisely formulated there or not. This means that when the causal implications for that complex of what is being explained have become plain to him, he may say: 'so that is the point of it!' or, more naïvely, 'so that is what it's for!' In precisely this manner the functioning of the lungs is teleologically explained by pointing out that it provides for the reoxygenization of the blood and so for the maintenance of the life of the whole organism.

Thus teleological explanation is not just reference from a cause to an effect, the simple reverse of historical explanation or explanation by efficient causation, which refers an effect to an antecedent cause. Essential to it is the notion that what is explained has causal implications for some previously comprehended complex or system. And this complex or system possesses some kind of pre-existent interest, and so some kind of value, for the investigator. What is being explained is teleologically understood when it is shown how it contributes to the working or maintenance of that system. This is the strict meaning of teleological explanation; Herbert Spencer called it 'legitimate teleology'.[1] It can be seen that it does not necessarily imply either that what is brought about is somehow foreseen by somebody or something (other than the investigator himself), or that the causally effective agent is as it is because it has the consequences it does have. It involves no reference to goals or purposes as dynamic, causally effective agents.

But just as in explanation by reference to antecedent events the mind finds it hard to rest content with mere correlation in space and time but demands efficient causation, so in the case of teleological explanation efficient causation may be as it were reversed, and the factor to be explained understood to be as it is *because* it has the consequences it does have. This provides the second meaning of teleology; Spencer's 'illegitimate' teleology. The end brought about is thought of as somehow foreseen (by somebody or something), and the thing to be explained is understood when it is seen to be designed (by somebody or something) to bring about this end. That is 'why' it is there.

This second kind of teleological explanation is evidently appropriate to much human behaviour, for people do act teleologically, in that they try to bring about certain ends, at least some of the time. But it is very much less helpful in dealing with social institutions. Here is an example. It makes very good sense to say that a man is slaughtering a goat for the purpose of making a feast. It makes very much less sense, and in fact may be quite false, to say (for instance) that the purpose of sacrifice is to bring the members of a certain community together in mutual harmony—even though this may be a consequence of the institution. 'Whose purpose?' we may legitimately ask: the institution itself obviously cannot have an intention, as an individual can. It may be that the members of a community know that one consequence of their sacrificial institutions is to increase group harmony, and they may even sustain these institutions for this reason; but it is altogether more likely that they are quite unaware of it. By far the larger number of functional correlations identified by anthropological and sociological fieldworkers are implicit rather than explicit in the minds of the people they are studying, if indeed they are aware of them at all.

[1] Spencer, Herbert, *The Data of Ethics*, London, 1890.

Recognition of this has led to the formulation of the important distinction between those kinds of social consequences of which the members of the society are themselves aware, and those of which they are unaware, and which are identified only by the sociologist. Professor Merton has phrased this distinction as that between manifest and latent function. Of course there are difficulties about the notion of awareness in this context (for example what degree of explicitness constitutes awareness?), but the distinction is valid and important. It expresses an aspect of the distinction already referred to between the 'folk system', the social system as seen by its members, and the analytical system which the observer builds up in the light of his theoretical interests. I return to this theme in the second part of this chapter; what I am concerned to stress now is that there is an important difference between saying that a certain institution has significant implications for other institutions, and saying that this is *why* it has the character it has.

So we have here a 'how' question and a 'why' question. First, we may ask what happens; does such-and-such an event contribute to the working of a particular system of which we have already formed an idea, and if so, how does it do so? And secondly, we may ask the quite different question why it does do; how does it come about that things are as they are? Now this second question is really not a teleological one at all, for it expects an answer referring to some antecedent event, for example to someone's previous act of intelligence or will. An example of the first kind of question is: how are we to understand the form of a particular marriage institution? And a strictly teleological answer would be: by observing that it tends to produce or maintain a certain system of social relations, such as the integration of separate social groups. Once this is seen, the particular form which has puzzled us is, so far, explained. An example of the second kind of question is: why does that particular institution have the form it has—in other words, how has it come about that it is so conveniently adapted to the consequences by reference to which we explain it? This is really a historical question, for instead of looking forward to an end, it looks backward to a beginning.

Now in social anthropology, as in the other social sciences, the teleological approach which looks for the social functions served by institutions has proved to be most useful, but the attempt to provide genetic explanations of existing institutions in terms of somebody's purposes or intentions is much more rarely so. This is partly because social anthropologists have concentrated on the analysis of social institutions rather than on the study of the human individuals who have these institutions. And it is the individuals, not the institutions, that are motivated by ends, aims and purposes. Thus questions about intentions may, and indeed must be asked about the behaviour of human individuals; but they have little relevance to institutional analysis. And equally, questions which may usefully be asked about social institutions are often quite inappropriate in regard to individual people. It is entirely sensible to ask what are the social functions of an institution like marriage: it is very much less so to ask what are the social functions of particular husbands or wives. The frames of reference are quite different, but it is very easy to confuse them.

The existence of a certain institution and the fact that it contributes to certain socially significant ends may be due historically to any of a number of causes. It may be due to the conscious intention of past or present members of the society; it may be an unintended consequence of behaviour directed to quite different ends; it may be due to diffusion from elsewhere, or to some kind of social 'natural selection'. Or it may be, and most likely is, due to a combination of some or all of these factors. Where the answers to these historical questions are ascertainable they are of considerable interest to social anthropologists, especially if they are studying processes of social change. But usually in the case of simple, preliterate societies, we cannot know how social institutions came to be as they are, and then understanding in a different (if more restricted) dimension may be afforded by teleological explanation in its narrower and more exact sense. We can see the point of a marriage regulation or an economic institution when we have understood its causal implications for other aspects of the social system, even when we do not know how it came to be as it is.

So functional explanation in social anthropology does more than merely demonstrate that different, apparently independent, modes of social behaviour are causally connected in certain systematic ways. It looks also for their implications for institutional systems. This is the teleological content of functionalism. The accent is not only on the discovery of causal links, important though this is; it is also, and especially, on the part which one mode of institutionalized behaviour plays in a systematic and already conceptually prefigured complex of interlocking institutions. We are dealing with what may be regarded *analytically* as part-whole relationships. For example, the institution of vassalage is explained functionally (and teleologically) when it is shown that it contributes to the maintenance of the complex of social institutions which is usually called feudalism. And the institution of avoidance between certain relatives-in-law, found in some societies, is understood functionally when it is shown that by tending to obviate social conflict it makes possible harmonious relations in a broad range of contacts between the two groups concerned. We shall encounter many examples of this type of explanation in the second part of this book.

(2)

It is easy to see that functional explanation as I have so far described it is rather like what biologists do when they explain one part of an organism by reference to the contribution which its functioning makes to the life of the whole. But we must not allow this methodological resemblance to lead us to suppose that societies are something like organisms; they are not, and to suppose that they are may lead to serious error. An organism is a physical entity; you can put it on a table and dissect it. But a society, or a social institution, is not a thing at all. It is a concept, an abstraction from people's observed behaviour; and it exists only in the minds of the people who are concerned with it, whether as members of the society or as investigators of it. Of course there is 'something' there, but that something is not a single, living physical entity, like a frog or a jellyfish. It is simply a number of people who are related to one another and to their environment in innumerable ways. When we use the term 'society' in a strict sense we are not referring simply to this human collectivity (Emmet's 'social aggregate'); rather we are referring to the complex of institutionalized inter-personal relationships which bind them together, or to some aspect or aspects of this. The German sociologist Simmel put this point in a different way when he said that society is not a substance but an event—or, we might add, a series of events.

The mistake of thinking of societies as 'things' like organisms has led some anthropologists to speak of Society as having 'needs' (Durkheim) or, at a rather more sophisticated level, 'necessary conditions of existence' (Radcliffe-Brown). In fact, of course, it is people, not societies, that exist and have needs. It may sometimes be useful to ask what are the necessary conditions for the persistence of a particular social institution (a question which implies reference to other functionally related social institutions in the same society). But it is very much less useful, at least for social anthropologists, to ask what are the needs or necessary conditions of existence of any society considered as a whole, or of all societies everywhere. I return to this 'holistic' aspect of functionalism below.

The two most celebrated protagonists of functionalism in British social anthropology have been Malinowski and Radcliffe-Brown, and both of them claimed that their particular brand provided a key to the understanding of societies and cultures as wholes, as well as to the understanding of particular institutions. Malinowski held that human society and culture are best understood as an assemblage of contrivances for satisfying the biological and psychological needs of the human organisms which make up the society. In fact he found it necessary to supplement his list of needs with 'derived' and 'integrative' needs (not themselves strictly biological), but his central thesis was that anthropologists may best study human cultures as machines for satisfying men's organic needs.

Although the classification of human institutions in terms of the needs they serve (such as the provision of food, the propagation of the species, and the maintenance of physical security) provides a handy set of pigeon-holes for fieldworkers to use, few if any anthropologists today find this approach theoretically satisfactory. No doubt basic physical needs must be at least partly satisfied if human beings are to survive, and there can be no society without people. But it is not illuminating to analyse social institutions solely in terms of such needs. Their satisfaction is a condition of the maintenance of *any* life, not only of social life, so they can hardly throw any distinctive light on the latter. The sociologist is interested in the conditions of living *together*, not merely of living. And since fundamental human needs are presumably much the same everywhere, differences between social and cultural institutions can never be explained by them. Every society has to provide for mating and reproduction, but if we want to know why some societies are monogamous and others polygamous, we shall have to seek our explanation in terms other than biological ones. Although, as we shall see, Malinowski's contribution to modern social anthropology has been immense, his theoretical approach is not held in much regard today.

The second type of 'total' functionalism, which Radcliffe-Brown derived largely from Durkheim, has been more influential. It asserts that the function of any social institution is the correspondence between it and some general need or, in Radcliffe-Brown's phrase, 'necessary condition of existence' of the society. Radcliffe-Brown tended to think—or at least to write—of society as if it were some kind of real existent, and he thought that the ultimate value for any society is its continued survival. This, so his argument goes, can only be achieved through the maintenance of social solidarity or cohesion between its members. This means that they must tolerate, respect and co-operate with one another, at least to a sufficient degree. So social solidarity is the end to which social institutions are to be regarded as contributing, more or less effectively, and this contribution is their function. Radcliffe-Brown does say that functionalism is a hypo-thesis, not a dogma; his thesis is that social institutions *may* contri-bute to the maintenance of the whole society, he does not claim that they must invariably do so. Thus in his first and most celebrated book, *The Andaman Islanders*, he gives a functional explanation of certain of the ritual institutions of this preliterate and technologically simple people. What he does is to show that their rites express symbolically, and so help to sustain, certain social attitudes and values which are conducive to the smooth running of community life. Radcliffe-Brown thought of social function in the context of what he sometimes called 'the total social system', and he asserted that functional unity is achieved when 'all parts of the social system work together with a sufficient degree of harmony or internal consistency; i.e. without producing persistent conflicts which can neither be resolved nor regulated'.

The first thing to observe is how heavily this formulation leans on the organic analogy; it seems to imply that a 'total social system' is some kind of empirical entity to which definite attributes can be ascribed. He is still tacitly assuming that a society is something very like an organism. But we have seen that this view is no longer tenable. In recent years it has become clearer that the 'holistic' view of society which it implies is of little if any value in actual research. How, for example, could the lack of 'a sufficient degree of harmony' be proved, except by the physical destruction of the whole community? In any case 'society' is not something given in experience; as we saw, it is an intellectual construct or model, built up on the basis of experience, but not itself a datum. Society is a way of ordering experience, a working and for certain purposes indispensable hypothesis. If we impute substantial reality to it, we saddle ourselves with an entity which is more embarrassing than useful. Once this is grasped, the needs or necessary conditions of a society no longer appear to be analogous to those of a physical organism. Rather they appear as, at least in part, the logical implications of the particular theoretical model which we have constructed in order to advance our under-standing of those aspects of human life which we are most interested in. This is why explanations of particular social institutions by reference to the maintenence of the 'functional unity' of whole societies tend to be either tautologous or unilluminating, or just plain wrong. For example, if we explain the institution of communal feast-ing on certain occasions by saying that such commensality conduces to the maintenance of social cohesion, and if (as is very likely) part of what we mean by social cohesion is just such joint activities as eating together, our explanation amounts to little more than saying that when people are together they are together, or at best that the more they are together now, the more likely it is that they will be so in the future. The truth of this latter proposition is by no means self-evident.

So functional explanation which refers to society or societies as existent wholes has little practical value for social anthropologists. On the other hand the sociological functionalism of the 20's and 30's has added greatly to our knowledge by showing how social institutions may be interdependent with other, sometimes apparently distinct, institutions; how they 'fit together' in various institutional complexes, such as political, economic, or ritual systems. But it overreaches itself when it claims that societies themselves, regarded as some kind of existent wholes, can usefully be studied as totalities. 'Society' is better regarded, from this point of view, as the context in which the social anthropologist carries out his enquiries. As an empirical scientist, analysis of the concept itself is not an essential part of his task.

The organic analogy has led to error in one further respect. It implies, or has sometimes implied, not only that societies are empirically given systems, but also that they are harmoniously integrated ones, or should be if they are 'healthy'. These systems are then thought of as maintained in a state of equilibrium or 'homeostasis' by a set of smoothly interacting and somehow self-adjusting social institutions. In spite of the fundamental difficulty of determining with any degree of precision just what is a healthy integrated state of a social system, this model worked well enough in a rough-and-ready way in the early days of fieldwork, when most of the societies studied by anthropologists had not yet suffered with any intensity the disruptive effects of European contact. To all appearances these societies had continued structurally unchanged in any important way for many generations, though of course this is not to say that they were free from 'conflict'. But when social anthropologists came to deal with more complex groups such as the larger tribal societies of Africa, and also with more advanced communities in Western Europe and America, this simple 'organismic' prescription proved wholly inadequate. For it was only too plain that many such societies were very far from being harmoniously integrated systems. Their complexity and the multiple stresses and strains which they showed could not be adequately or even at all comprehended in so restricted a frame of reference. In some cases social institutions were changing radically; old types of political organization, of marriage, of economic production and exchange, were breaking down and being replaced by new ones, and the organic analogy could provide no means of understanding these changes. Evidently if a society is thought of as an integrated functional unit any change in the system must disturb this ideal equilibrium. At this point the classical functional model ceases to afford a valid (or indeed any) representation of what is going on. So earlier functional thinking, in terms of homeostatic, self-conserving systems, has had to be supplemented by analysis of the manifold expressions of social conflict, opposition and strain.

It is plain, then, that human communities are not really very like organisms, and that radical changes in social institutions have to be investigated historically as well as functionally. But despite its limitations, the so-called functional approach is the most characteristic method of modern social anthropology. It grew up in the context of fieldwork, and its results in the field studies of the past half-century have been immense.

Associated with the notion of social function is the idea of social structure. The distinction between function and structure is really that between process and form. When we speak of function we refer to the causal implications of certain kinds of events for other kinds of events, considered as systems. When we speak of structure we are attending to the formal, enduring aspects of whatever it is that is said to have a structure. So structure is a much wider concept than function. Whether any particular social institution has a function or not is a matter for investigation, but anything that can be comprehended at all, whether it be a concrete object or a set of ideas, can be said to have a structure. Poems have structures as well as atoms, and systems of beliefs no less than skyscrapers.

Of course there is room for difference of opinion as to which of the enduring characters of a particular class of entities shall be selected as structurally significant; the choice will depend on the interests and aims of the observer as well as on the nature of the phenomena. So it is not surprising that different anthropologists have meant different things by the term social structure. Radcliffe-Brown, who was one of the first to use the concept systematically in social anthropology, defined it as the complex network of actually existing relationships in any society. But this has proved far too broad to be useful, and others have adopted narrower formulations. Thus Evans-Pritchard, in his account of the Nuer, has preferred to restrict the term to those relatively enduring relationships which unite persisting social groups into wider units.[1] But however we define it, the essential idea is that parts or components are arranged in an orderly way to constitute what may be comprehended as some kind of systematic unity. This unity need not, however, be an empirically given one like a frog or a

[1] Evans-Pritchard, E. E., *The Nuer*, Oxford, 1940.

house; it may equally well be an analytical synthesis, constructed to unify experience and to advance knowledge. The structure of a system of ritual, or of a political system, is of this latter type.

Like our thinking about 'society', our thinking about social structure is peculiarly susceptible to the fallacy of misplaced concreteness. Some anthropologists have written as though there is something in every society called 'the structure', which can be revealed if one's investigations go deep enough. This onion-peeling view of structure is gravely misleading, for it projects into what is given something that is really only a particular interpretation of it. In fact any assemblage of data, social or otherwise, may reveal several different structures, depending on the observer's interest in it, though certainly some structural interpretations or 'models' will be more appropriate than others both to the material in question and to the kind of understanding the observer is seeking. Thus, for example, a particular complex of kinship relations can be structured jurally, economically, in terms of status and hierarchy, and in other ways. Structure is built up by the analyst on the basis of data, but it is itself not a datum but a construct. Most recent social anthropologists have been well aware of the dangers of reifying social structure. Lévi-Strauss has cogently attacked the view that structure is 'there' in the society; something that the anthropologist who uses the proper techniques may hope to discover and put on record.[1]

If, then, we wish to talk of social structures as 'facts', we must remember that they are facts of a very different kind (or at least imply a level of analysis so different as to amount to a difference in kind) from the raw data, real people actually doing things, which form our basic material. This is so even though it be conceded, as in a final analysis it must, that these lowest-level, 'raw' data, unpermeated by the conceptual organization of an apprehending mind, are in the last resort unknowable, even inconceivable. It is all a matter of degree. So when we speak of social structures, whether of political systems, kinship systems, legal systems or (very much less usefully) of whole societies, we are using models, not talking about concrete things. And the validity of scientific models depends not on their 'truth' (in the sense of their exact correspondence with some unknowable 'reality') but rather on their usefulness or strategic value in making sense of the given, in facilitating comparison, and in leading to new knowledge.

Here is an example. In many societies people's rights and duties depend very largely on their positions in kin groups based on descent in one line (that is, either through men or through women) from a

[1] Lévi-Strauss, *op. cit.*

61

common ancestor, and on the relationships in which their group stands to other similar groups. Now the structure of such a system may be expressed formally in a limited series of propositions about the way in which these groups are established and about the relations between them and between their members, and often it may be diagramatically illustrated. Such a structural statement does not tell us everything about the people in question and their culture, or even about their kinship system, and very often the facts are by no means as formal and consistent as they are represented as being. None the less, our structural model of the kinship system picks out and systematically orders certain key aspects of the social situation. It does this in response to certain questions. Some such questions are: 'what is the basis of group membership?' 'what are the categories of members?' and 'what are the rights and duties implied by the occupation of certain statuses in the system?' Essentially, the investigator's structural model should make sense of the data in terms of his interest in them, it should suggest new questions and problems, and it should make possible classification and comparison with other structures from elsewhere.

A model built up in this way may be quite unintelligible to the members of the society concerned, for they may not be capable of or interested in asking the kinds of questions which the anthropologist asks. Here we touch again on one of social anthropology's most crucial problems, to which in the nature of the case there is no parallel in the natural sciences. This is the question of the difference between a particular social system or institution as the anthropologist re-presents it for analytic or comparative purposes, and the 'same' system or institution as it is seen by the members of the society them-selves. I return in the next chapter to the problem of translation which this state of affairs involves. Here I want only to stress the importance of the difference; a social anthropologist studying an unfamiliar culture must be constantly aware of it. But even though the analyst's model (Lévi-Strauss's 'statistical model') may be too sophisticated or too general for the ordinary member of the society being studied to grasp, it must be at least ideally explicable to and recognizable by him, provided that he can be brought to share the outside observer's interest in his culture and to understand the questions he is asking. This is so because both the anthropologist and the people he studies are equally endowed with reason, however they may differ in edu-cation and cultural background; and because the anthropologist's 'structural model' is not (or at least should not be) pure fantasy. Its job is to make sense, in the light of certain interests, of 'facts' which are known to both observer and observed; facts, for example, such as that a man supports his kin in a blood feud, and that he owes specified obligations to his parents-in-law.

I conclude this chapter with a summary. The notions of social function and social structure have been the most important forces in British social anthropology during the past half-century. By the study of social function anthropologists have generally meant the study of the causal implications of social institutions for other social institutions and systems of institutions in the same society. By the study of social structure they have generally meant the definition of those enduring aspects of social institutions which have appeared to be most important in terms of their interest in them. Modern British social anthropology has sometimes been identified with what has been called the 'structural-functional approach'. Although there is much more to British social anthropology than this, it is true that these concepts have provided the operational framework for many field studies of high quality.

I noted that the structural-functional model derives much of its effectiveness from the analogy with organic systems, which it is useful to regard as complex wholes whose parts work together to ensure the harmonious functioning of the whole system. Though the analogy has proved useful, it has serious limitations when applied to communities of human beings, who differ from the mindless components of natural or mechanical systems in being themselves conscious, willing agents, sharing with the social scientists who study them the power of conceptual thinking, of representing their social and material universe to themselves, and of acting in accordance with these representations. The structural-functional approach sometimes took insufficient account of this fact, although its practitioners have recognized that people's ideas may be causally effective. If a human community is regarded primarily in its dimension as a system of action rather than as a system of ideas and symbols, then the distinction between the analytical system and the 'folk' system is unlikely to command much attention, any more than it does in the study of other causal systems, like biological or mechanical ones.

Indeed it may be said that despite the great advances in our understanding of the working of small-scale societies due to the development of functional and structural theory, this development has on the whole tended to distract attention from the equally important problem of how to understand other peoples' systems of beliefs and values. Of course these interested anthropologists long before the intensive development of structural-functional theory in the 20's and 30's, but it is only quite recently that the interests of a significant number of British anthropologists have returned to them. There has been a tendency to regard ideas and values as 'cultural' data, and for many years 'culture' has been regarded as at best a peripheral interest of structurally oriented social anthropologists. It is now more generally recognized that the social anthropologist is directly and legitimately concerned with both dimensions.

Systems of beliefs and values represent a distinct aspect of human social life, and their understanding calls for techniques different from those appropriate to the study of societies as systems of action. Social institutions have causal implications for other institutions, and the beliefs and values which people hold are important determinants of their institutionalized behaviour. But the mechanical, cause-and-effect model is inadequate to the comprehension of such conceptual systems in themselves. Ideas and beliefs do not 'cause' one another; their nature and interrelations must be investigated in other terms. It has recently been aptly remarked (by a philosopher, Peter Winch) that understanding a society is more like 'applying one's knowledge of a language in order to understand a conversation than applying one's knowledge of the laws of mechanics in order to understand the workings of a watch'. Social anthropologists would claim that both approaches are needed. In this chapter I have discussed other people's cultures as causal systems; in the next I consider how they may be comprehended as systems of symbols and meanings, understandable in other than causal terms.

SHORT READING LIST

EMMET, DOROTHY, *Function, Purpose and Powers*, London, 1958.

LEACH, E. R., *Rethinking Anthropology*, London, 1961.

LEVY, MARION, *The Structure of Society*, Princeton, 1952.

MCIVER, R. M., *Social Causation*, New York, 1942.

MALINOWSKI, B., *A Scientific Theory of Culture*, N. Carolina, 1944.

NAGEL, ERNEST, *The Structure of Science*, London, 1961 (Chapters 13 and 14).

POPPER, K., *The Poverty of Historicism*, London, 1957.

WINCH, PETER, *The Idea of a Social Science and its Relation to Philosophy*, London, 1958.

5

Beliefs and Values

SOCIAL ANTHROPOLOGISTS have always had to take some account of the beliefs and values of the peoples they study. Although functional theory has in some respects tended to distract attention from this field, in other respects it has greatly advanced our understanding of other people's ways of thought. It has done so mainly because of its emphasis on fieldwork, and on the necessity to understand the social institutions of simpler cultures 'in the round', and in the context of wider networks of social relationships in which they are embedded. This understanding implies reference to what people think, for as I have stressed, no human social institutions or relationships can be adequately understood unless account is taken of the expectations, beliefs and values which they involve. Nevertheless, with a few notable exceptions, systematic field studies of people's modes of thought, their values and beliefs, have only recently begun to be made.

For the earlier anthropologists problems about the modes of thought of so-called 'primitives' scarcely arose with any complexity. It was easy for the Victorians to assume that such thinking as they did was simple and 'childish' (this was one of their favourite adjectives); a very inferior version of their own. The intensive fieldwork which was to provide an intimate understanding of 'simpler' people's way of life and thought, and so to demonstrate the superficiality and inadequacy of such views, had not begun. So Victorian anthropologists are not altogether to be blamed for supposing that 'primitive thought', if not fundamentally different from that of civilized Europeans, was at least of a very inferior order. None of them had ever really got to know an unwesternized member of any of the simple cultures they wrote about so voluminously, so there was no way in which they could have known any better.

I referred earlier to the story, perhaps apocryphal, of Frazer's horrified reaction to the suggestion that he might have met one of the 'savages' whose customs he wrote about. It is not surprising that he supposed that the reason why 'primitive' peoples believe in magic is that they lack the capacity to distinguish between associations of ideas made mentally, and causal connections between things in the real world. Frazer thought that the Greek peasant's belief that jaundice could be cured by the application of gold was based on the erroneous conviction that because gold and jaundice were both yellow they are bound to interact causally. Similarly, he thought that the magical idea that a person can be harmed by destroying something that was formerly part of his body or in close contact with it (such as hair or fingernails, or a piece of his clothing), was based on the supposition that because these things and the person whom it was wished to injure had once been in close physical contact, a causal link between them must still persist. We shall see in Chapter 12 that this is a travesty of magical thinking, which is essentially symbolic thinking. No community, 'savage' or otherwise, could possibly survive if its members were quite unable to distinguish between fancy and experience, as Frazer suggested. E. B. Tylor was also much concerned with 'primitive' thinking, and devoted much time to discussing the kinds of misapprehensions, for example about the difference between waking and dreaming, from which the ideas of spirits, souls and ghosts could possibly have arisen. These scholars' interests were ethnological rather than sociological; they assumed that there was no great difficulty in comprehending the 'simple' modes of thought which they were discussing. So for them the really important problem was to determine how they could have arisen in the first place.

In France, in the early years of this century, the famous sociologist Émile Durkheim founded a school of social anthropologists which was called the *Année Sociologique* group, after the journal they founded. These writers devoted much attention to the study of the ideas which so-called 'primitive' peoples held about themselves and about the world around them, their *représentations collectives*. Like their predecessors, these scholars themselves did little or no fieldwork, so they were dependent for their information mostly on the reports of travellers and missionaries, which naturally varied a good deal in quality. Their studies are nevertheless of considerable interest and importance today. One reason for this is that they were more interested than their English predecessors and contemporaries in comparing not just isolated 'customs', but rather whole complexes of beliefs and 'meanings', so far as these could be reconstructed from the literature. Hubert's and Mauss's essay on Sacrifice, and Hertz's study of the representation of death, are typical products of this school, and have a surprisingly modern quality.[1]

This interest in 'primitive' ways of thought was further sustained in the present century in the writings of Lucien Lévy-Bruhl, who stressed what he called its 'pre-logical' and 'mystical' nature. Some of his critics have supposed that he meant by this that a capacity for rational thought was lacking in members of the simpler cultures. But what he really meant was that much of their thinking was symbolic and allusive, rather than scientific and logical. He did, however, somewhat overemphasize the 'irrationality' of primitive thought, while at the same time under-emphasizing the irrationality of much 'civilized' thinking. Nowadays we have learned from the psychologists that there are powerful and extensive irrational components in everybody's thinking, whatever his culture.

I return to some of these themes later; here I want to stress that it was only with the development of intensive fieldwork that the subtlety, complexity and, often, profundity of the ways of thought of pre-literate or only recently literate peoples began to be at all adequately understood. As soon as anthropologists began to live for periods of months and even years among the people they studied, communicating with them in their own tongue and sharing in their daily activities, it began to become plain that the old Western stereotypes about primitive modes of thought were quite inadequate, and often positively misleading. A landmark in the growth of this recognition is Evans-Pritchard's *Witchcraft, Oracles and Magic among the Azande*.[2] In this study the beliefs of this highly intelligent people of the southern Sudan are shown, not as a set of weird and irrational delusions about occult forces, but rather as embodying a mode of adjustment to the strains and frustrations of everyday life which, in the whole context of Zande culture, appears as eminently practical and sensible. The Zande system of beliefs, and others like it, provide both an explanation of misfortune ('why did this have to happen to me?') and a way of dealing with it; and in a pre-scientific culture there may be no other means of coping with such situations. Modern social anthropologists who are studying unfamiliar and 'unscientific' belief-systems of these kinds do not proceed by framing the ideas they involve in formal propositions about reality, and then trying to conjecture how a reasonable man (that is, the anthropologist himself) could possibly have come to accept them. This was the

---

[1] Hubert, H., and Mauss, M., *Sacrifice: Its Nature and Function* (English translation), London, 1964. Hertz, R., *Death and the Right Hand* (English translation), London, 1960.
[2] Oxford, 1937.

Victorian approach. What we do today is to attempt to understand these beliefs in the whole context of the culture of which they are a part.

Often when we translate the beliefs of a pre-literate, non-Western people into a European language, they seem not only irrational but nonsensical and self-contradictory. Here is an example from African ethnography.[1] Like many other African peoples, the Nuer of the southern Sudan have a particular regard for twins. One way in which they express this regard is by saying that twins are birds. They do not say that twins are like birds, but that they are birds. Now it would be a very naïve mistake (though a kind of mistake which anthropologists have often made in comparable contexts) to infer from this assertion that Nuer really think that human twins and birds are identical in all respects, so that a member of the Nuer tribe who was confronted with a human twin and a bird would be unable to say which was which. An anthropologist who is studying the Nuer needs to understand not only Nuer modes of thought about twins and birds, but also the Nuer language, the forms in which they express their ideas about the world. For these two things are inextricably bound together; one cannot be understood without the other.

Thus only by understanding the Nuer language and the way it is used can their assertion about twins and birds be seen to make sense. What they are really saying when they state that twins are birds is not that they are identical. They are asserting that twins come from God or Spirit, which is associated with the sky, the domain of birds. So for them there is a conceptual identity between twins and birds which justifies their speaking of the first in terms of the second. A Nuer's assertion about twins is not to be regarded as a scientific proposition, testable experimentally in the same way as, for example, the statement that water freezes at 32 degrees Fahrenheit is testable. It is rather the statement of an analogical or, as we might say, a poetical identity between the two concepts. Even though he overstated his case, Lévy-Bruhl was right in emphasizing the poetical, analogical character of much 'primitive' thinking. The predominantly scientific orientation of modern thought has much obscured the fact that peoples who are less concerned than Western Europeans are with scientific experimentation and logical method think about the world they live in in terms which are often symbolic and 'literary' rather than scientific. This is no less true of European peasant cultures than it is of remote African or Oceanic tribes. We do the grossest injustice to the subtle allusive and evocative power of language if we require all meaningful verbal expression to conform to the rules of

[1] Taken from Evans-Pritchard's *Nuer Religion*.

syllogism and inductive inference. Coherent thinking can be symbolic as well as scientific, and if we are sensible we do not subject the language of poetry to the same kind of examination that we apply to a scientific hypothesis.

We can put this aspect of the social anthropologist's concern with other cultures a little differently by saying that he is interested in symbols and symbolic thinking. The study of these is difficult, partly because in Western culture very much less importance is attached to this kind of thinking than to logical, 'scientific' thought. This means that most of us are unaccustomed to paying very serious attention to it. This is so even though Freud and his successors have shown how deeply the thinking even of 'enlightened' Westerners is shot through with symbolism, often implicit and unanalysed.

For the purposes of social anthropology, the first thing is to determine with reasonable clarity what we are to mean by the term 'symbol': for in some of its uses it is too wide usefully to denote a special field of enquiry. For example Radcliffe-Brown roundly stated that whatever has meaning is a symbol, the meaning being whatever is expressed by the symbol. But this is much too wide. Certainly symbols have meanings, in so far as they stand for or represent other things, but it is not useful to regard everything that stands for something else as a symbol. A green traffic light is a sign of something else, that is, that it is safe and lawful to proceed. But this does not make it into a symbol, even though there may be people for whom traffic lights, or the colour green, have symbolic significance.

It is therefore useful to distinguish between two different kinds of signs, of things that have meanings and which stand for something other than themselves. First there are signals, which give information about some state of affairs, past, present or future. What they do is to convey a specific message. Thus a red light signifies that it is dangerous or illegal to go ahead; a footprint signifies that Man Friday (or somebody else) has passed this way. Animals make frequent use of signals, but so far as we know they lack the capacity for symbolic thinking. Signs can be merely conventional, as in language; so far as we know there is no inherent reason why (for example) the sound 'man' in the English language should stand for the species *Homo sapiens*, and not some quite different sound, as in other languages. This is not the case with symbols, in the sense in which social anthropologists have found it most useful to use the term. For there is usually some reason why a particular symbol should be appropriate in a particular case; there is an underlying rationale which is at least ideally discoverable, even though it may be by no means obvious, and may even be quite unknown to the persons who use it. The rationale is, or seems to us, obvious in such examples as a serpent biting its tail as a symbol of eternity, an owl (large-headed and inscrutable) symbolizing wisdom, whiteness as a symbol of purity and virtue. It is perhaps less so in the case of a flag of a particular colour and design symbolizing a nation, or a totemic animal of a particular species symbolizing a clan. And the private symbolism expressed in dreams and in the behaviour of neurotics (which does not concern us here) may be wholly subconscious, though of course this is not to say that it does not possess a rationale or that this cannot be discovered.

The grounds on which a symbol's appropriateness to what is symbolized is based may vary. They may lie in some real or fancied resemblance between the symbol and what is symbolized, as in the first three examples above, or they may derive from some historical conjunction in the individual's or the culture's past. Some of the totemic symbols of certain African clans are chosen on these latter grounds. Thus one of the clans of the Nyoro people of western Uganda has as a totem a particular species of small bird; it is said that a bird of this species warned the founder of the clan that he was about to be attacked by a buffalo, and so saved his life. But whatever the ground of the association between symbol and referent, it will generally be found that it entails some kind of appropriateness. A social anthropologist studying an unfamiliar system of symbols will try to discover, if he can, their underlying rationales.

A second important difference between symbols and signals is that symbols commonly stand for or imply some abstract notion: they do not refer just to some event, or to a concrete entity. Nobody needs symbols for last Friday week, or for rocks, trees, cows or other objects, though such things may and often do *become* symbols. What we find to be symbolized in various ways in different cultures are more or less abstract notions like power, group solidarity, familial or political authority. Sociologically, this is the most important thing about symbols; they provide people with a means of representing abstract ideas, often ideas of great practical importance to themselves indirectly, ideas which it would be difficult or even impossible for them to represent to themselves directly. We sometimes forget that the capacity for systematic analytic thinking about concepts is a product of several millennia of education and conscious philosophizing. It is a luxury unavailable in cultures, whether 'modern' or 'primitive', whose members must devote all or most of their energies to procuring the minimum physical necessities of daily life. In his analysis of the religious life of the Australian aborigines,[1] Durkheim pointed out

[1] Durkheim, Émile, *The Elementary Forms of the Religious Life* (English translation), London, 1915.

that it would be difficult or impossible for members of this simple culture, most of whose time is taken up in wresting a living from their harsh environment, to represent to themselves in explicit terms the vital importance of mutual solidarity and support between the members of the groups in which their society is organized. But each group can express this common interest through its attachment to and practical concern for a particular animal or plant species, its 'totem'. This provides a convenient and comprehensible symbol for these essential group values. Other complexes of concepts and values, usually implicit (where they are explicit there is little need of symbols), underlie the attachment of members of more advanced cultures to their particular symbols, whether these be flags, old school ties, aspidistras, or opulent motor-cars.

So symbolism is essentially expressive; it is a way of saying something important, something which it is impossible or impracticable to say directly. What is said symbolically must be thought to be worth saying. This is a third important characteristic of symbols; what is symbolized is always an object of value. This means that people's attitudes to their symbols are rarely neutral; they are always more or less affectively charged. People tend to have quite, sometimes extremely, strong feelings about their symbols. This is because there is a tendency for the value which attaches to what is symbolized (patriotism, for instance, or mutual attachment within a group) to run over into the symbol (the flag or the totem), so that it, and not the implicit notion which it symbolizes, becomes the object of special respect and veneration.

I return to the subject of symbolism and ritual in Chapter 12. Here I consider only the interest anthropologists have in it, and some of the difficulties involved in studying it. The first of these is descriptive or observational: how are we to identify the symbolic element in behaviour? This is not always easy. It requires the clear formulation of a distinction which sociologists have drawn between what have been called the 'instrumental' and the 'expressive' aspects of human behaviour. Instrumental activity is directed to bringing about some desired state of affairs; it is oriented towards an end. Expressive activity is a way of saying or expressing something; usually some idea or state of mind. The instrumental aspect of any activity is understood by seeing what it is aimed at; its expressive aspect by understanding what is being said. So symbolism is a kind of language and it is appropriate to ask of any symbol what it means.

A difficulty is that much, probably most, human behaviour exhibits both instrumental and expressive aspects at the same time. A sorcerer acts instrumentally when he tries to kill an enemy, but the

71

means he uses (for example sticking needles into a clay model of his victim, or uttering incantations over a portion of his hair or clothing) may be essentially expressive or symbolic. Forms of behaviour which are basically instrumental and matter-of-fact—wearing clothes, for example, or wielding authority in a particular context—may come to have high symbolic significance. But even though these two aspects are often inextricably combined in real human behaviour, they can and must be analytically distinguished, for each needs a different kind of understanding. Instrumental behaviour must be understood in terms of the consequences it aims at and achieves; expressive behaviour in terms of the meanings, the ideas, it expresses. Serious mistakes have arisen from attempts to interpret types of behaviour which are primarily symbolic in intention as though they were mis-guided attempts to be practical and scientific. I have already referred to Frazer's attempt to explain the symbolism involved in magic as though it were solely instrumental in intention; this led him to a mistaken view of magic as a kind of inferior and erroneous science. There is an essential symbolic element in magic; it cannot be under-stood at all adequately if its expressive aspect is neglected. And the situation is further complicated by the fact that acts which are essentially ritual and symbolic are often taken by their practitioners to be causally effective just because of this very fact.

So symbolism must be studied on at least two levels. First, it has to be studied on the level of meaning. I have said that people commonly have symbols for notions which are in some way important to them; thus a community's values (I turn to this theme shortly) may often be understood by analysing their symbols. But symbolic behaviour must also be studied on the functional, 'action' level of analysis, for as well as having meanings it may also have social consequences. Radcliffe-Brown was chiefly concerned with these social consequences in his celebrated study of Andamanese ritual. He argued that the symbolic behaviour of these islanders expressed certain sentiments (or values, as we should say today), and that the maintenance of the social system itself depended upon a general adherence to these. His thesis was that their rituals kept these sentiments in the forefront of people's minds, and so tended to reinforce their effect. I noted earlier that hypotheses like these are useful in proportion to their specificity; holistic arguments which posit 'social solidarity' or 'social cohesion' as the end of all ritual activity tend all too easily to become circular. None the less symbolic behaviour often does have socially significant consequences, and it is an important part of the social anthropolo-gist's task to find out, if he can, what these consequences are.

Symbols express values. And social anthropologists are interested in the shared values of the peoples they study, both in themselves and because they may be important determinants of action. What, then, are values, and how can they be studied? First, they are not objective qualities that things have, like shape or colour; they are relational, that is they are values *for* someone. As the American philosopher Perry put it: 'value in the generic sense attaches to all objects of all interest'. Thus values are what people value, what they consider to be important and worth-while. The idea of value is a positive one, values afford incentives to action; what people value they desire. It is possible to speak of a negative value; that is, of something which is not desired. But this can be more precisely phrased in positive terms; strictly we mean that it is the absence of that thing, pain for example, which is desired. What is desired is always some condition of things, whether this be characterized positively or negatively.

To be very precise, we should say that what anthropologists are interested in are evaluations rather than values (in the sense of things that are valued). Evidently it is the fact that Masai attach a high value to cattle, rather than cattle themselves, that interests the student of Masai values. It is this interest in people's evaluations that we indicate by the phrase 'the study of values'. In the sense in which the term is used here values are states of mind; they are not 'things', or patterns of behaviour, even though they have to be inferred from patterns of behaviour, verbal or otherwise. Although they may not be precisely formulated (in fact they rarely are), they are concepts, thoughts about things, and not 'things' themselves.

The social anthropologist who is studying values is not concerned with all values. He is interested only in those that are institutionalized, and which are shared by all the members of a society, or by a particular group or category of persons in it. *Qua* social anthropologist, he is not concerned with values that are private and idiosyncratic to particular individuals, even though he recognizes that these may sometimes be socially important in the history of particular societies. He is interested in social values. But there is a difficulty here, for in a sense all values are social values. People grow up in a social world and not in isolation, and right from the beginning their thinking is conditioned by their contacts with their fellows. But the term 'social value' may be used in a more restricted sense, to refer only to values which are held *about* society, or, more precisely, about social institutions and social relationships. In this sense, a people's social values are their ideas, and ideals, relating to their kinship institutions, their economic relations, their political system, and so on. In every society most people share certain notions about the form that the various kinds of social institutions found in their society ought to take; they know how rulers should treat subjects, how subjects should behave to rulers, fathers towards sons, husbands towards wives, neighbours to neighbours. Indeed, as I have stressed, these various categories of institutionalized social relationships are not fully intelligible unless the expectations and values underlying them have been understood.

It might be suggested that as sociologists, social anthropologists should restrict their study of values to this narrower field; to the ways in which people regard their social institutions. But even if it were held to be desirable, such a restriction would be impracticable. First, values and beliefs are often linked in shared cognitive and moral systems, in terms of consistency or compatibility, and a particular value has to be investigated in the context of this system of ideas if its cultural significance is to be understood. The value which many peoples attach to commensality, for example, must be understood in the context of all of their ideas about food, about hospitality, about obligations to neighbours and strangers, and about the kinds of bonds that sharing food creates, before the full social implications of the practice can be properly investigated. Again, the ritual value attached by so-called totemic peoples to certain animal or plant species must be understood in the context of the whole range of such peoples' ideas about human groups, about nature, and about the relationship between men and nature, before the sociological significance of totemism can be adequately studied. Without this understanding, the institution whose social effects are being investigated may be quite misunderstood.

This is really another way of stating a point already made, that it is quite impossible to assess the relevance of particular values or systems of values to particular social relationships or systems of relationships until the values have been understood in themselves. A conscientious field anthropologist is bound to concern himself with the values of the people he is studying, without prejudging their sociological significance. Belief and action, values and social institutions, are inextricably bound up with one another, and I remarked earlier that social anthropologists have always given some account of the values and beliefs of the peoples they have studied. Where these have had clear relevance to social institutions the links have usually been pointed out. In his study of Zande witchcraft Evans-Pritchard shows how beliefs in witchcraft and oracles may have important implications for a system of political authority, and in his account of ancestral cult and social structure among the Lugbara of Uganda Middleton shows that the status of clan elders depends on how effectively (in the Lugbara view) they can invoke the ancestral ghosts. But we do not abandon interest where such precise links cannot be established; human cosmologies and religious systems are of interest to social anthropologists in their own right as well as in their relationships, if any, to systems of action. The social anthropologist's method of working in and through the culture he is studying peculiarly qualifies him for this kind of study, at least in pre-literate or only recently literate communities. Indeed it might be claimed that social anthropology's contribution to the understanding of other cultures has been at least as important in the study of beliefs and values, as it has been in the functional analysis of social systems.

Let us take this a step further. People's ways of thought may differ not only in the kinds of symbolism they use, and in the kinds of things they think important, but even in the very ways in which they represent to themselves the physical, social and moral universe they live in. It is an epistemological commonplace that people see what they expect to see, and the categories of their perception are largely if not wholly determined by their social and cultural background. The pastoral Nuer can distinguish, by reference to colour and shape of horn, between several hundred kinds of cattle, and they have names for all of them; to the agriculturalist a cow is just a cow. Distinctions are made in some cultures which are not made, or are made differently, in others. Here is a very simple example from kinship. A western European regards the brothers of both of his parents as relatives of the same kind, and he calls them all 'uncle'. But in many other cultures a man regards paternal and maternal uncles as entirely different kinds of relatives, and he calls them by completely different terms. We shall see in Chapter 7 that this usage is wholly consistent with a certain way of thinking about kin, in the context of which the European practice would seem absurd. Here is another quite different example. Western law makes a clear distinction between accidental death, and death caused by homicide or suicide—intentional killings. But in many cultures no such distinction is recognized; all deaths are thought to be intentional, whether the intention is thought to be that of a living person practising sorcery or witchcraft, or that of a ghost or spirit. Evidently such a way of regarding death must have important social implications.

So members of different cultures may see the world they live in very differently. And it is not just a matter of reaching different conclusions about the world from the 'same' evidence; the very evidence which is given to them as members of different cultures may be different. If in one sense all men everywhere inhabit the same world, in another and important sense they inhabit very different ones. And where these differences are culturally determined social anthropologists are centrally interested in them.

We can be more explicit. It has been argued that even such fundamental categories as 'time' and 'substance' may be very differently conceived by members of different cultures. From a study of the language of the Hopi people of the American South-West, and of the way they use it, the American linguist-anthropologist Whorf argued that Hopi do not imagine time, as we do, as a kind of continuum analogous with space, in which different events occupy different positions in an unending sequence of before and after. Rather they think in terms of immediately experienced duration—'earlier', 'later', 'now' —and they distinguish events by reference to their immediacy, their certainty, or their expectedness, not by reference to an objectified time-scale, embodied in a tense structure. Similarly, Whorf claims, Hopi modes of describing spatial relations do not postulate a sort of pre-existent 'space' which things are 'in' as eggs are in a basket; they imply only things and their positional interrelations.

So, according to Whorf, the linguistic forms of Hopi thought dispense with many unnecessary and non-existent 'entities' with which our particular language structure saddles us. Here is a further example. Where we say 'it's raining', thereby raising the quite unreal question: 'what is?', Hopi simply say 'raining!', or 'rain is happening'. In this way they eliminate a whole world of unknowable entities, and replace them by happenings or events. Whorf argued with a good deal of plausibility that a language of this kind and the ways of thinking about the world that it implies might well be more appropriate to the kind of thinking involved in modern physics than the Aristotelian substance-accident mode in which most Western philosophy and science have been cast.

But however this may be (and not all social anthropologists would go all the way with Whorf), his point that the ways of thought or 'collective representations' of members of other cultures may differ in quite fundamental and unexpected ways from our own, is crucially important. Innumerable difficulties and confusions, both theoretical and practical, have arisen because members of one culture have found it almost impossible to see things as they are seen by members of another culture. It is not just a matter of 'seeing the other fellow's point of view', essential though that is. The problem is the very much more difficult one of comprehending the unacknowledged and un-analysed standpoints from which his views are taken. Of course this can never be wholly achieved. We can enter in some degree into other people's ways of thought, and we can attain some understanding of their beliefs and values, but we can never see things *exactly* as they see them. If we did we should have ceased to be members of our own culture and gone over to theirs. But we can go a long way towards achieving this kind of comprehension, while still retaining a foothold in our own world. Perhaps social anthropology's chief claim to respect is that it has achieved some success in doing this.

Such success as it has achieved has been mostly due to the intensive fieldwork now regarded as essential. I now discuss some of social anthropology's characteristic fieldwork methods.

SHORT READING LIST

DURKHEIM, É., and MAUSS, M., *Primitive Classification* (English translation), London, 1963.
LANGER, SUZANNE, *Philosophy in a New Key*, Harvard, 1942.
LÉVY-BRUHL, L., *How Natives Think* (English translation), London, 1926.
LÉVI-STRAUSS, C., *La Pensée sauvage*, Paris, 1962.
PERRY, R. B., *General Theory of Value*, New York, 1926.
TEMPELS, P., *Bantu Philosophy* (English translation), Paris, 1959.
WHITEHEAD, A. N., *Symbolism, its Meaning and Effect*, Cambridge, 1958.
WHORF, B. L., *Science and Linguistics*, Washington, 1952.

6

Fieldwork

ADVANCE IN THE NATURAL SCIENCES often involves setting up experimental situations in the laboratory, and then seeing whether what happens confirms or disproves hypotheses previously formulated. Social scientists cannot usually test their hypotheses about human institutions in quite this way. Their laboratory is society itself, and where one is dealing with human beings other considerations besides the desire for knowledge, such as the general well-being, legal and moral standards, the national interest, must have primacy. For this reason it is rarely feasible in social science to set up experimental situations on the natural science model. It is even less feasible to arrange that such situations are repeated under conditions which are for all practical purposes identical, as natural scientists do.

Even where something approaching an experimental situation can be set up (as, for example, where a new cash crop is introduced in a peasant community, or, to give a recent instance from central Africa, where a whole population has to be moved to make way for a new water development project), the situation can rarely be subjected to strict control, as scientific experiments are. A much greater range of variables, including among other things the human personality and its decision-making powers, is involved, and for most of these we have no adequate techniques of measurement. Every human situation is unique in a sense, or at least to a degree, which is not applicable to the chemist's experimental set-up in the laboratory.

So, for the most part, social anthropologists must test their hypotheses about social and cultural institutions and their interconnections in the course of fieldwork in societies and situations which they have no power to control. Their tools are observation, interpretation and comparison, rather than experiment. But this does not mean that they can do without theory; they can no more dispense with it than any other scientists can. As we saw earlier, no sensible person undertakes a scientific enquiry without any idea of what he is

78

trying to do or of how he proposes to do it, and his statement of these things in his theory. As Nadel put it: 'every way in which facts are grouped in description involves theories, implicit or explicit, about the connections between things that are significant; and significance is a function of the kinds of questions to which the observer seeks an answer'. So it is pointless to debate whether a fieldworker should have theories about what he studies; he cannot fail to do so. The question is rather whether his theory is sound, articulate, and geared to current problems and interests, or whether it is merely unanalysed and implicit 'common sense'. Like any other scientific investigation, fieldwork is always an attempt to answer questions, and an investigator is more likely to give adequate answers to questions which he has clearly formulated, than to questions which he has not formulated at all.

Whether we like it or not social anthropology has become a specialist subject. It has its own theoretical equipment, some account of which has been given in preceding chapters, and it has by now a considerable body of comparative material to draw upon. No one who writes about the social institutions of a small-scale community without knowing anything about contemporary theory in social anthropology, and without some knowledge of the social and cultural institutions of comparable societies elsewhere, can nowadays hope to produce a scientifically adequate account. For he cannot know what are the most important things to look for, the most useful questions to ask about them, or the best techniques for getting the answers. In Victorian times there was no such *corpus* of sociological theory and comparative ethnography, so there was hardly any difference between the professional and the amateur. But today anyone who wishes to contribute significantly to the growing body of knowledge about the social and cultural institutions of small-scale and unfamiliar communities must acquire at least some theoretical training in social anthropology.

So the social anthropologist enters the field with a fairly comprehensive idea of the kinds of things he wants to find out, and of how he should go about doing so. As I said earlier, he does not want to find out everything about the people he is studying; life is too short and the range of human activities and of specialist knowledge about them is too large. In preceding chapters I have discussed the central interests of social anthropology; institutionalized social relationships, and people's beliefs and values regarding these and the world generally. But human social life is very much of a piece, especially in the conditions of simple, small-scale communities. This has meant that social anthropologists have generally found that to give a rounded picture of the social and cultural life of the people they study they have had to say something about such things as agricultural practice, tool-making, pottery, clothing, house-building, and many other matters not usually regarded as 'social'. In more advanced societies many such topics are matters for specialists, and this is true also of such more central concerns of social anthropology as economic relations, political organization, and systems of religious belief. An anthropologist who is working in a modern community has no qualifications to write authoritatively about, for example, transport systems, local government organization, or Christian theology, and he does not attempt to do so.

Why have social anthropologists written about extra-social, specialist aspects of culture in so-called 'primitive', pre-literate societies, when they would not have the temerity to do so in more advanced ones? There are two reasons for this. The first is that these matters are generally very much simpler and more readily comprehensible in such societies, where there are usually few if any full-time specialists. Specialist knowledge is carried in men's heads, not contained in libraries and archives, and usually it does not involve many years of specialized training and research in order to understand it, as it does in literate, technologically complex societies. This is not to say that expert knowledge is always to be easily learnt in simpler societies; sometimes it is difficult, even impossible to acquire it. But the difficulties lie in factors other than the extent or intellectual complexity of the knowledge itself.

The second reason why anthropologists write about specialist aspects of the cultures they study has already been mentioned; it is that the communities they study are often remote and difficult of access, so that there is no one else available to write about these things. So unless the anthropologist records them they are likely to go for ever unrecorded, for many such cultures are undergoing rapid change, and some have vanished altogether in recent generations. This is one reason why many of the earlier anthropological monographs covered a very much wider range of cultural topics than most modern ones do. Many of the communities nowadays investigated by social anthropologists are a good deal less 'primitive' and a good deal more complex than those studied a generation or so ago. For this reason contemporary fieldwork monographs tend to concentrate on the social and cultural topics discussed in the second part of this book. Indeed, often they concentrate on just one of these topics; kinship and domestic life, for example, or political organization, or the field of magic and ritual. Intensified fieldwork, theoretical advances, and the amassing of a great amount of comparative information have meant that there is a great deal more to be said about each of these topics than there used to be. In these specialist studies aspects of the society and culture other than those selected for special attention are not dealt with exhaustively, but only in so far as they are relevant to the chosen theme. But they are not disregarded, for the functional hypothesis that social and cultural institutions are, or are likely to be, interconnected is still fundamental in social anthropology.

An implication of the fact that social anthropologists take, or should take, some account of the whole social situation which faces them in the small-scale societies they study, is that when these societies are extensively affected by and permeated with Western norms and institutions then these latter, too, must be considered. In many present day 'native' communities in Africa and elsewhere, foreign district administrators, missionaries and, sometimes, traders and settlers play, or have played, important parts in the affairs of the community, and any social study which omits reference to them is bound to distort the reality. Every field anthropologist has to give an account of the traditional values and institutions of the society he is studying, so long as these are still viable factors. But he must be careful not to allow a vicarious nostalgia for a lost tribal past, or a personal distaste for the often disquieting implications of 'culture contact', to lead him to ignore the vital roles often played by agents of change. Sentimentality can be the field anthropologist's worst enemy, and the reader of anthropological accounts of some tribal peoples in Africa and elsewhere might well be astonished to learn that the people he is reading about have had European district officers, Western-type courts, European missionaries of several denominations, and retail traders, for half a century or more.

It might fairly be said that theoretical advances in social anthropology have in large part consisted in the development of increasingly sharpened criteria of relevance. Plainly the issue of relevance can hardly arise where the investigator is interested in everything he sees. But the more precisely his interests and problems are defined, the more must be excluded as irrelevant. Most social anthropologists today do not deal exhaustively with such topics as pottery, ironworking or agriculture in the societies they study. This is not because these are not highly interesting and important subjects in their own right; it is simply that they are not as a rule relevant to their selected interests. Where they are so relevant, their significance can usually be sufficiently demonstrated without detailed technological analysis.

What does the social anthropologist do when he first finds himself set down in the middle of an unfamiliar culture? Whether he is in a forest tribe of central Africa, a tiny Pacific island, or a peasant community in western Europe, what he sees to begin with are people doing things, conversing, probably in an unfamiliar tongue, coming and going. At first all is seeming confusion. The newcomer may be able to distinguish young from old, men from women, and he can identify such activities as eating, drinking, digging, cooking, fighting, when he observes them. He may, too, recognize that this man or group of men is, or appears to be, happy, that one angry, another grieving. But he does not know who is who, why these two are helping each other, those two quarrelling, what they are all talking about. At this preliminary stage, if the community and its culture differ very greatly from his own, the anthropologist feels utterly bewildered and confused. The experience is a daunting one, and it can last for a long time. Most anthropologists have known the feelings of frustration and despondency—even, sometimes, of desperation—which go with the early stages of fieldwork in an unfamiliar culture.

But slowly, often imperceptibly, this period passes. Living in hut or tent within the village, the anthropologist gradually begins to understand what is happening around him. As his knowledge of the language and his acquaintance with the community advance, things begin to make sense. An overheard conversation is understood; a pattern of behaviour is fitted to a learned social relationship. With luck he now has a few friends in the community, people who are willing to take time and trouble to explain things to him, to take him round the neighbourhood and to introduce him to others. From this point onwards the pace accelerates. The anthropologist gets to know most of the members of the community as separate individuals, differing in temperament and in social status (and in their degree of interest in his work). He learns their often intricate ties of kinship and marriage; he comes to understand what they think about one another, about the world they live in, and about him. He learns not only what are the appropriate questions to ask but of whom to ask them. He begins to feel 'at home' in the community, for he now knows it in many ways more thoroughly than he has ever known any community, even the one he grew up in. He has now made the breakthrough into another culture: as a field anthropologist, he has arrived.

For a Western anthropologist, probably born and brought up in an urban culture, this can be a vivid, almost traumatic, experience. The fieldworker who spends a year or more of his life as a member of a group of hunters and gatherers in Borneo, or of a tribe of African peasants or pastoralists, lives in more intimate contact with the basic conditions of human existence than has been possible for generations in the modern world. Birth, illness and death, the daily effort to win food from the environment with the simplest equipment, the smell of the hot earth, the wind and the rain—the urgent, first-hand awareness of these things is something new and yet somehow familiar to the visitor from a city culture. It is easy for anthropologists who have worked among such peoples (and of course not all do) to romanticize them, and many do. They have some excuse; the experience is an unforgettable one.

But whatever the type of culture, close and sustained observation is needed in order to understand what people are doing, to identify their most important social institutions, and to investigate the causal interrelationships between them. This must be guided by hypotheses which are continuously subject to review and reformulation, and it must be sustained over a long period; at least a year (in agricultural communities this will cover the annual crop cycle), preferably longer. The observer must live in and with the community he is studying; it is not enough to stay in a comfortable hotel or rest-house and to visit them for a few hours daily, or less often. Certainly something can be done in this way. Much can be learnt of a community's moral and legal standards, for example, or about other explicit aspects of its culture, through set interviews with selected individuals or groups. But this way of doing anthropology can only tell the enquirer what people think happens or should happen (or perhaps only what they wish him to think happens). It cannot tell him what actually happens, how the social and cultural institutions of the community fit together in a working pattern. To learn this, people's daily activities must be observed over a long period; the job cannot be rushed. Studies of other people's cultures carried out in a few weeks or months can be misleading enough when they are made in countries with which the investigator is more or less familiar; they are bound to be even less adequate when the culture is a totally strange one.

I have already made the point that adequately to describe an unfamiliar social institution we have to see it, at least to some extent, as its participants do. The relationship between a chief and a subject, for example, or between a sister's son and his mother's brother, cannot be understood as it really is in the society being studied unless the investigator knows what it means to be a chief in that society, and what categories of relatives people have in mind when they use the terms which he translates as 'mother's brother' and 'sister's son'. It is important to remember that the familiar categories of social status— 'ruler', 'subject', 'father', 'priest', and such like—are conceptual entities; they are not data somehow directly given in experience. Unless we understand how the people we are studying think about them, we simply replace their conception with ours. In certain circumstances (in a study of economic production, for example, or of the incidence of suicide) a fieldworker may disregard the people's own social categories, and go straight to what he may call the 'facts' of the situation. But he must remember that these 'facts' are not presented to him directly, stamped with some special kind of validity. They are simply his interpretations or models, constructed on the basis of his observations of actual speech and behaviour, but not the same as that behaviour. The members of the community concerned may see things very differently. But not absolutely differently. We noted earlier that the anthropologist's representation of the situation must bear some relation to the people's own actual (or potential) representations of it; it must be such that it could be presumed that if it were to be fully explained to a member of the society, he would recognize its validity. For in the last resort folk systems and analytical systems, mechanical models and statistical ones, relate to the same reality.

I argued earlier that the functional approach is pre-eminently appropriate to this 'action' level. Essential to this approach is the notion that certain institutions affect other institutions, and the observing and recording of such causal connections is an essential part of modern fieldwork. To give a simple example, it is a functional hypothesis that in those societies where bridewealth is paid at marriage by the bridegroom to the bride's kinsmen, the payment is not merely a purchase, but also has important implications for the status of the woman and her children. If repeated observation and enquiry have shown that wives for whom bridewealth has not been paid are looked down on and insulted by other women, and that the children of 'free' unions are constantly discriminated against in matters of inheritance, the investigator may consider himself to have validated (for the society he is investigating) a functional correlation between the payment of bridewealth, the domestic status of women, and the pattern of inheritance. Often such causal connections (which are of course sometimes very much more complex than in this example) are unknown to the people themselves, so that we are dealing with latent rather than manifest functions, in Merton's phraseology. When we speak in functional terms we are speaking of events and of their habitual implications for other events, whether these implications are generally recognized or not. This is why the connections which we arrive at must be at least ideally comprehensible and credible to anyone who understands and accepts that the events are of the kind they are.

It is plain that if the functionalist fieldworker's conclusions are to appear as more than mere impressionism and conjecture, he must support them with at least some quantitative evidence. Statistical methods, for the most part quite simple ones, are being increasingly used in anthropological fieldwork, and although they need to be used with caution this development is both desirable and inevitable. When statements are being made about social institutions and their causal interrelationships, we want to know what kind of evidence these statements are based on, and how adequate it is. The student who reads, for example, that among a certain people drunkenness is regarded as a ground for divorce, or that homicide is usually followed by a reciprocal killing, very reasonably wants to know how large the samples are upon which these findings are based. He wishes to know what proportion of all divorces is due to drunkenness, and how often homicide really is followed by a reciprocal killing. Most modern fieldworkers provide quantitative information of this kind, where it is appropriate and feasible to do so. Often they use household survey forms and questionnaires, not as a substitute for the intensive, qualitative investigation which is still central in the study of other cultures, but rather in order to provide evidence for their assertions. A systematic investigation of a sample of a hundred households, for example, or of five hundred marriages, may provide positive corroboration of the anthropologist's probably valid impressions about certain aspects of family life.

Such quantitative investigation may also, sometimes, have the equally important effect of showing that a pattern which the people themselves assert and even believe to be dominant (and which the anthropologist may therefore be inclined to accept as valid) is in fact not so. Further, properly carried out statistical surveys may suggest correlations which had not previously occurred to the investigator, who can then usefully follow up qualitatively the clues so provided. A marriage survey, for example, might show an unexpected correlation between, say, length of union and occupational rating. The research worker could then investigate this correlation by framing and testing hypotheses to explain it.

But there is some danger (though it can be exaggerated) that a too exclusive reliance on questionnaires and surveys may lead to an overformal and mechanical presentation of a community or a culture, at the expense of the intensive qualitative analysis which depends on first-hand knowledge and sustained personal contact. This is most obviously the case where people's ideas, beliefs and values are being studied. No amount of statistics will help us to understand a people's conception of spirit, for example, or their notion of substance, or even what they understand by marriage, or by their different categories of kinship. These can only be understood by an imaginative but none the less rigorous effort to define the concepts of the culture itself and to see the world in its terms. It has sometimes happened that the findings of statistically-minded fieldworkers have been vitiated by the fact that the material they have attempted to quantify, such as kinds of marriage or varieties of land-holding, has been insufficiently understood to begin with, so that important types have been misrepresented or omitted altogether. Quantitative studies of marriage stability in a particular society, for example, will produce very different results if certain types of temporary union habitual in that society are thought to be 'marriage' by one investigator, 'concubinage' by another. It has been found that questionnaires and other quantitative techniques have yielded the most useful results when they have been employed after the fieldworker has spent some time in the community, preferably at least a year, and so has a good working knowledge of its social and cultural institutions. It is certain that the quantitative approach in social anthropology has come to stay, and if social anthropologists' analyses of social institutions as causally interacting systems are to be taken seriously by other scholars, they must have at least a working knowledge of the simpler statistical methods.

The intensiveness of modern fieldwork, and the social anthropologist's increasing specialization, imply that he must become more and more dependent on other workers. In the communities which he studies nowadays there are nearly always at least a few people who can read and write, and most fieldworkers engage one or two assistants, sometimes more, and pay them salaries. These assistants may not only serve as permanent informants and advisers; often they can make useful local contacts as well as collecting information and carrying out surveys under the anthropologist's supervision. Also, the modern social anthropologist can, and sometimes does, benefit from collaboration with other 'outside' specialists in the field; such as agriculturalists, economists, and medical research workers. The difficulty is that generally there are no such specialists available in the field to collaborate with. But even if there are, social anthropologists cannot leave the areas to which their specialist knowledge applies altogether to them. Even if human societies are not the organic 'wholes' that the early functionalists thought them, they are still best understood as complex systems of interacting institutions and values. So to understand any component institution fully requires at least some understanding of other co-existing institutions. No division of labour can relieve the social anthropologist of his obligation to see the community and culture he is studying in the round.

I said earlier that the social anthropologist must participate as fully as he appropriately can in the everyday life of the community he is studying; he must live in it and get to know its members as people, as nearly as possible on equal terms. Evans-Pritchard claims that when he was studying divination among the Azande of the Sudan, he found it expedient to order his daily affairs by constant reference to the oracles, as Azande do. (He found this a less unsatisfactory way of making decisions than might be imagined.) Unless the anthropologist 'takes part' in the culture in such ways as this, he can never really hope to see it as its members see it. Only by at least some participation in community life can he hope to understand what people really think and how they really act, which are not always the same as what they say they think and how they say they act, when they are asked.

Where Europeans have for long been regarded as a powerful outgroup, as they have in many parts of Africa, claiming high status and remote from and indifferent, if not hostile, to the native community, it is often difficult for a European anthropologist to become accepted on terms of friendship and easy familiarity. Often it is essential for him to avoid being identified with one or other of the few categories of European hitherto recognized. In many areas all Europeans are believed to be either government officials or missionaries, and a European claiming to be neither may well be suspected of concealing his real identity and purposes for secret and sinister reasons. Often the field anthropologist has to establish a new category for himself. During the first stage of my fieldwork in Bunyoro, a native kingdom in western Uganda, I hoed and cultivated with my own hands a (small) field of sweet potatoes. My efforts, which resulted in blistered hands and very little else, were at first regarded with outspoken derision by my neighbours. But whatever I was up to, it soon became plain that I fitted into no preconceived category of European, and before long I was flooded with offers of help, which I gratefully accepted.

No foreign anthropologist can ever be wholly assimilated to another culture; he can never quite become one with and indistinguishable from the people he is studying. Nor is it desirable that he should. 'Stranger value' is an important asset: often people talk more freely to an outsider, so long as he is not too much of an outsider. Also, in a society where there are distinct social groups or classes, and especially when these are hierarchically arranged in terms of power and prestige, too close identification with one group or class may make easy contact with others difficult or impossible. This problem is particularly acute when societies like the caste communities of India are being studied, but it also arises in countries like Bunyoro and others in East Africa and elsewhere, where there is a marked difference between an aristocratic ruling class and the peasant population. One has to start one's intensive research at one level, and this may make it difficult later to achieve entry into the other. Plainly a great deal depends on the personality and temperament of the investigator. The ideal social anthropological fieldworker is adaptable, tactful, good-humoured, and possessed of a sense of proportion. Above all, he is patient and considerate. He is, after all, a guest (even though usually an uninvited one) in the community he is studying, and he must show the same respect and courtesy to his hosts as he expects to receive from them.

As well as living with and among the people he is studying, observing and participating in their activities, there are various other means of procuring and recording information available to modern social anthropologists. In addition to 'looking on' and asking unscripted questions, he and his assistants spend a good deal of time interviewing people, either singly or (nowadays more rarely) in groups, to elicit information on particular topics. Often it is useful to write down *verbatim* life histories and other material provided by old or particularly knowledgeable informants. Where some people are literate, a few of them may be persuaded, through essay competitions for school-children or adults, or directly for payment, to provide the anthropologist with written material. The obtaining of such 'texts', recorded in the informant's own words, is a very important part of modern fieldwork, for through them the people are enabled to speak for themselves. In this way an 'inside' view of the culture can be put on record, and the anthropologist can (to the degree that he knows the language and the culture well) learn how the members of the culture see their own institutions and traditions. Also, another scholar who reads the anthropologist's account of the culture is provided with a means of assessing for himself the validity of the interpretations offered. For the same reason, the provision of detailed case histories is important. It is not enough nowadays simply to report on people's social institutions in general terms; examples of actual social situations must be given from life, and in adequate detail. An anthropologist who reports, for example, that in such-and-such a society the traditional relationship of subordination and respect between men and their fathers is breaking down must give detailed histories of cases where it *has* broken down, giving a full account of all the circumstances, and of the behaviour and attitudes of the people concerned. Sometimes documentary material is available at first hand in the field, for example in the records of cases heard in native courts, and in the minutes of local council meetings. These may be a mine of valuable information about types of disputes and the means of settling them, sources of social strain, legal and moral ideas, political concepts and aspirations, and so on. The field anthropologist makes, or should make, full use of these sources. All is grist to his mill.

By all these means the field may be, as it were, brought back into the study. Something of the 'folk' system is directly communicated to the reader of the fieldworker's monograph. He is not left (as he often has been and sometimes still is) to take the anthropologist's word for it, and to make what he can of his often extremely abstract and sophisticated exposition of the society and culture studied.

This is not the place for a detailed discussion of the various mechanical aids to field ethnography. Sound recording and photography may provide valuable supplements to the written record, and air photography especially may save weeks of labour where such matters as the dispersal of agricultural plots or patterns of village settlement are important, as they nearly always are. But there is no substitute for the long and sustained personal contact upon which any comprehensive understanding of the community and its social and cultural life must be based.

In this chapter I have said something of the complexity of the task faced by a modern social anthropologist who is trying to understand, in the field, the social and cultural institutions of a small-scale community. He must learn to think simultaneously on at least two different levels. He is concerned not only with causal relationships, but also and no less importantly with the world of symbols and meanings. It is largely because of this latter concern that language has assumed its present importance in fieldwork, for different peoples have different ways of conceptualizing their social and physical universe, and concepts can only be comprehended and communicated through language. For this reason some knowledge of practical linguistics is essential for a modern social anthropologist, especially if he is working among a people whose language is unrecorded, so that he has not only to learn, but also to record, an unfamiliar tongue.

In any case the fieldworker, who has to convey to others through his own language what it is like to be a member of another culture, is faced with a crucial problem of translation. First he has to acquire, by a thorough knowledge of the language of that culture and of the ways in which it is used, an understanding of its basic categories, which in all probability differ radically from those of his own culture. Numerous examples of such category differences are recorded in later chapters. Then he must convey to people who lack his own first-hand knowledge of that culture and its language as adequate as possible an understanding of these basic categories and the ways in which they are used. Since he cannot write his books in the tongue of the people he has studied, this calls for a very careful and precise use of his own language. Unfortunately, skill in doing this is not automatically combined with a capacity for good fieldwork. So it is not surprising that some anthropological monographs fall uneasily between the Scylla of an excessive reliance on vernacular terms, often inadequately explained, and the Charybdis of a profusion of sociological jargon (since it is often easier to make up a new word for an unfamiliar concept than it is to find, or adapt, an old one).

There is no easy solution to this dilemma. It was rather less acute for the earlier functionalists, who were more concerned with consequences (the satisfaction of needs; the maintenance of the social system) than with meanings. But much recent and some older work has shown that a very high, if never quite complete, degree of success in resolving it can be achieved. Indeed, to give up hope here would be to abandon the belief that meaningful communication between all human beings is ultimately, and ideally, possible. Certainly failure in intercultural communication has been widespread, sometimes total, in the history of human affairs. But it need not be so, and there are no epistemological grounds for relapsing into sociological solipsism. In understanding other cultures, as in all human affairs, perfection is unattainable. A social anthropologist who claims that he has acquired a complete understanding of another culture or another language stands self-condemned. A year or two in a foreign culture is obviously quite an insufficient period for an undertaking which may occupy the lifetime of a member of that culture. But that is no reason for not trying. It is long enough for a trained social anthropologist to achieve some systematic understanding of that people's institutions, values and ways of thought. In the second part of this book I consider some of the spheres of social and cultural life in which social anthropologists claim to have made such advances.

SHORT READING LIST

BOWEN, ELENORE S., *Return to Laughter*, New York, 1954.
CASAGRANDE, J. B. (editor), *In the Company of Man*, New York, 1960.
ROYAL ANTHROPOLOGICAL INSTITUTE OF GREAT BRITAIN AND IRELAND, *Notes and Queries on Anthropology* (6th edition), London, 1951.
RICHARDS, A. I., in Bartlett, F., and others (editors), *The Study of Society*, London, 1939.
WINTER, E. H., *Beyond the Mountains of the Moon*, London, 1959.

PART TWO

7

Kinship

(1)

ACCORDING TO THE DICTIONARY, kinship has to do with relationships by blood, or consanguinity; affinity with relationships brought about by marriage. In social anthropology the two topics are very closely connected. All cultures distinguish various categories of kin and affines, and these categories, with their associated patterns of rights and obligations, make up what social anthropologists call kinship systems. In some societies every individual is, or thinks he is, related by kinship or affinity to everyone else: in others, including most Western ones, a man's kin and affines are limited for practical purposes to a few close relatives. But in every society some relationships of kinship and affinity are culturally recognized.

In this chapter I discuss the kinds of interest which social anthropologists have taken in kinship: in the next I consider marriage and affinity. Social anthropologists are sometimes accused of concerning themselves overmuch with the refinements and complexities of kinship terminologies, of indulging in what Malinowski called 'kinship algebra'. But there are good reasons for this concern. Very few of the interpersonal relationships which make up a Western European's social world are kinship ones. Kinship plays little or no part in his relations with his friends, his employers, his teachers, his colleagues, or in the complex network of political, economic and religious associations in which he is involved. But in many smaller-scale societies kinship's social importance is paramount. Where a person lives, his group and community membership, whom he should obey and by whom be obeyed, who are his friends and who his enemies, whom he may and may not marry, from whom he may hope to inherit and to whom pass on his own status and property—all these matters and many more may be determined by his status in a kinship system. Where everybody is or thinks of himself as being related to nearly everybody else, almost all social relationships must be kinship or affinal ones too. But even where kinship is less pervasive, it usually plays a much more important part than it does in modern urban and industrialized Western societies.

Why is kinship so important in small-scale societies? The short answer is that in all human communities, even the most technologically simple ones, the basic categories of biological relationship are available as a means of identifying and ordering social relations. This is so even though some of these categories may be differently defined in different cultures. Everywhere people are begotten of men and born of women, and in most societies the fact of parenthood and the bonds of mutual dependency and support that it implies are acknowledged. This leads to the recognition of other links, such as those between siblings (children of the same parents), and between grandparents and their grandchildren. So even in the simplest societies kinship provides some ready-to-hand categories for distinguishing between the people one is born among, and so for ordering one's relations with them. Apart from sex and age, which are also of prime social importance, there is no other way of classifying people which is so 'built in' to the human condition.

Of course biologically not only human beings but all animals have 'kinship'. But the vital point is that unlike other animals, human beings consciously and explicitly use the categories of kinship to define social relationships. When an anthropologist speaks of a parent–child relationship, or of the relationship between cross-cousins (the children of a brother and a sister), he is not primarily concerned with the biological connections between these kinds of kin, though of course he recognizes the existence of such relations. What he is concerned with are the *social* relationships between them; the fact that in the culture being studied they involve distinct types of social behaviour, and particular patterns of expectations, beliefs and values. Although he is interested in them as social relationships, he calls them kinship relations because that is how they are culturally defined, that is the idiom in which the people who have them think about them. They may not even be between biological kin at all, as in the case of adoption. I have stressed that from the social anthropologist's point of view an essential part of every social relationship is the way in which the parties to it regard it. And social anthropologists are concerned with kinship simply because in very many societies it provides the idiom for a great many different kinds of social relationships.

A consequence of the biological reference of kinship terminology is that to say that a relationship is one of kinship may convey no information about its content. To say of a relationship that it is political, economic or jural tells one at once which division of human affairs it is concerned with. But to say of a particular relationship that it is between, say, a sister's son and his mother's brother, or between cross-cousins, indicates only a presumed biological relationship; in itself it does not tell one anything about its social or cultural content. In fact, when social anthropologists deal with kinship relations they are really dealing with relations of a very different kind, that is, with social ones. These may be relations of authority and subordination, of economic exchange, of domestic co-operation, of ritual or ceremonial, and they may be affectively charged in various ways. Thus kinship relations are not a special *kind* of social relationships, like economic relations or legal relations. Rather the categories which kinship affords provide the context and the idiom for many different kinds of social relationships. It is the field anthropologist's task to determine, in the culture he is studying, what these are.

For practical purposes biological kinship provides only a limited number of categories for social use. This certainly makes things simpler for the anthropologist, but it involves a serious danger. For this common biological base provides a framework both for studying particular systems, and for comparing from one society to another the social relationships associated with particular kinship categories. It is still quite usual for anthropologists to present the kinship systems of the societies they study by means of a list of such biological categories. This has the advantages both of being readily intelligible to foreign readers, and of being easily comparable with (supposedly) similar data from other cultures. But there are grave defects in this procedure, if it is adopted uncritically. To begin with, a kinship system is not just a collection of distinct and mutually exclusive terms, each denoting a different kind of genealogical and social relationship. It is rather a whole way of life, and it can be understood only by a thorough investigation of the language, values and behaviour of the people who have it. Often the denotation of kinship terms is not fixed, but depends on the social contexts in which they are used, so that now one, now another genealogical relationship is invoked by the use of the same term. To give a simple example, in many cultures the term which we translate 'brother' may (though it need not) denote many relatives besides the son of one's parents; sometimes it may refer to people who are not biologically kin at all. What it does denote can only be determined in the light of a thorough knowledge of the culture.

Even the biological categories of kindred which are recognized, named and used for social purposes often differ radically from one culture to another. This means that it is often impossible to translate kinship terms directly from one language into another, for one may distinguish categories of kin which another does not. Attempts to translate the kinship terms of other cultures into English have sometimes led to serious misunderstanding. Here is a simple example. In many cultures relatives on the father's side and on the mother's side are terminologically distinguished (we shall see later why this should be), and are thought of as being quite different kinds of people. Where this is the case there are distinct terms for the mother's brother and for the father's brother, and these two relatives are very differently regarded. So to translate the term for either of them as 'uncle' is to conceal a vitally important social distinction. I remarked in the last chapter that there is no easy solution to these problems of translation; the important thing is to be aware of them. But we must avoid uncritically applying the prefabricated framework of our own kinship system to the social life of other peoples. The social anthropologist's task is to try to understand other people's kinship systems 'from the inside'; to learn to think in their categories, not to impose his own.

Kinship, then, may provide a guide to a very great many of the social relationships in which a person is likely to be involved in the course of his life. I consider some of the commoner of these relationships in the second part of this chapter. But over and above these, it is very commonly used for two important and related purposes. First, it provides a way of transmitting status and property from one generation to the next, and second, in some societies it serves to establish and maintain effective social groups. I consider first the question of inheritance.

In almost all societies, when a person dies he leaves something behind, whether this be status, such as headship of a family or local group, or moveable or immoveable property, like land, livestock or money. After his death these must pass to someone else, and in all societies there are rules for this transmission. In some societies it is equally possible to inherit position or goods from the father's side of the family and from the mother's side, but it is more usual for one line, either the patrilineal or the matrilineal, to be used for the transmission of particular statuses or types of property. Thus, in Western Europe, name and title almost invariably, and property usually, pass in the male line.

Most societies throughout the world have adopted a predominantly patrilineal mode of inheritance, but in some status and property are transmitted through women. In these a man's inheritance, instead of going to his son, passes to his sister's son. This is because in matrilineal societies no less than patrilineal ones, authority and property-holding are mainly (though of course not exclusively) the men's prerogative. And where descent through women and not through men is considered, a man's nearest matrilateral relative in the generation next after his own is his mother's daughter's child, that is, his sister's child. We can put this in another way by saying that in a matrilineal society property and status do not pass from women to their daughters (since men, not women, are the effective holders of property and status), but they do pass from the brothers of these women to the brothers of their daughters.

In some societies both lines of descent are used for purposes of inheritance, each in a different context. Thus the Yakö of Nigeria, described by Daryll Forde in *African Systems of Kinship and Marriage*, attach almost equal importance to both lines of descent. Where a man lives, the land he cultivates, and the ancestors he worships are patrilineally determined; but movable property like livestock and currency passes in the maternal line, as also does membership in a fertility cult. Even where one line or the other is of major importance for the transmission of status, rights, or property, some significance is almost invariably attached also to the 'submerged' line. Thus in a society so strongly matrilineal as that of the Ashanti of Ghana, it is believed that a spiritual principle called *ntoro* is transmitted patrilineally. And in many patrilineal societies it is believed that witchcraft or a propensity to it is inherited in the female line.

In many societies kinship is used to establish and define distinct corporate social units. In the conditions of most simpler cultures it is essential for everyone to be a member of a co-operating, closely-knit group of people, upon whose aid and support he can depend in such vital activities as hunting, agriculture and herding, and war. In such societies, the truism that no man can be sufficient to himself is plain to all: it is not obscured, as it is in Western culture, by a dependence on the impersonal forces of large-scale political and economic organization. In the conditions of many 'primitive' societies, unless a man can depend on a group of his fellows his life will be, as Hobbes put it, 'solitary, poor, nasty, brutish and short'. So men must form co-operating groups if they are to survive, and kinship is the means most readily and universally available for doing this. Always people are aware that they are related to a number of other people, beginning, usually, with the family circle of parents and siblings. But this group is rarely large enough to survive in isolation; remoter kin must be included in the group.

One way of forming larger than family units on the basis of kinship was that said to have been adopted by the ancient Teutons. For them, the group of people upon whom a man could count for help was called the sib. It included both maternal and paternal kin, so that one had certain rights and acknowledged certain obligations in regard to all relatives up to a certain degree of genealogical distance. The groups formed on this principle overlapped and intersected one another, since no two individuals (except full siblings) had exactly the same range of people in their groups or sibs. Thus a man's sib might be scattered over a wide area, and each of its members would have commitments of which not all were shared by the other members of his sib.

This way of organizing kin could not provide for the formation of territorially separate and distinct solidary groups, such that every member of the group was bound to every other member of it, and all shared the same set of obligations to the same set of people. Far more effective for this purpose is the principle of unilineal descent, which has been adopted in many parts of the world. The ancient Romans formed groups on this principle, and so did the ancient Hebrews. The Scottish clans were groups of this type, and many societies in Africa and in other parts of the world still form corporate groups of people in this way today. The central principle is that all the people who believe themselves to be descended in one line (either through men or through women) from a common ancestor a certain number of generations back, regard themselves, and are regarded by others, as forming a distinct group or association. They may form such an association for a specific purpose, for example for the performance of a religious cult. Or their mutual dependency and attachment may cover practically every aspect of their existence.

The term 'clan' is sometimes applied to groupings of this kind, though in some societies clan members form a category of people rather than any kind of closely-knit, co-operating group. Often they are widely dispersed, and engage in no corporate activity on a clan-wide scale. Sometimes they are unaware of the genealogical connections, if any, which link them with their presumed common ancestor and with each other. But they usually *think* of their interrelationships in kinship terms: a fellow clansman is always a brother, a father or a son, however remote he may be genealogically. Clansmen acknowledge mutual obligations on a kinship pattern, and often they share an attachment to a common symbol or totem. Where clan members are dispersed in this way, it is rather as though, in a Western European society, there were only a limited number of surnames, and everyone regarded all his namesakes as close kin (even when they were not), acknowledged definite obligations and claimed definite rights in regard to them, shared special religious beliefs with them, and thought of himself and of all with the same name as being somehow different from other people. In societies where clan membership is thought of in this way everybody *must* have a clan; clan membership is thought of as a quality that people have, like any other human quality. When I was carrying out fieldwork in Bunyoro I was often asked what my clan was. When I replied that we had no clans in Europe I was disbelieved, and soon I acquired honorary membership in a Nyoro clan. Other anthropologists working in similar cultures have had the same experience. Usually clans, even when they are dispersed in this way, are exogamous, that is, nobody may marry a member of his own clan. Important consequences of this are, first, that a man's affines (his relatives through marriage) are always members of a clan other than his own, and second, that a person's parents always belong to different clans.

When clans are dispersed, they do not, of course, form local, corporate groups. Where co-operating local groups larger than elementary families of spouses and their children are organized on the basis of shared descent in one line, anthropologists usually speak of unilineal descent groups or lineages. Thus a lineage is a group of people who not only think of themselves as descended in one line from a common ancestor, but who also claim to know what the genealogical links between them are. They may act corporately, on a relatively permanent basis, in such social activities as herding, hunting and raiding. This means that they must all live in the same area. Evidently where there are clans all the members of a lineage must also be members of the same clan. But the basis of their group attachment is lineage, not clan, membership.

Unilineal descent is used as the basis of local grouping and corporate activity in many societies which lack centralized government. It is easy to see that where co-operating groups larger than the family are needed (for herding, for example, or for war), and where at the same time there is little role specialization, and therefore few occupational distinctions upon which corporate associations might be founded, unilineal descent provides a very convenient means for establishing such groups. Where it does so, these groups may be of key political importance, as we shall see in Chapter 9. Here there are two important things to note about this kind of group organization. The first is that membership in the groups so formed is generally relative or situational, rather than absolute, and the second is that these groups have a constant tendency to divide or segment, a process which anthropologists call fission.

First a word about the relational aspect of unilineal descent grouping. It is evident that except for the very smallest and the very largest lineages or lineage segments, any given lineage will both contain smaller ones and be included in larger ones. Thus, for example, the lineage which is headed by my paternal grandfather includes the lesser lineages headed by my father and his brothers, and it is, with the lineages of my paternal grand-uncles, included in the larger lineage of my paternal *great*-grandfather. Thus any individual is at the same time a member of a number of distinct lineages, and the one in which his membership is relevant in any particular social situation will depend on his relationship to the other person or persons concerned in that situation.

Let me make this clearer. There are two possibilities. The individual concerned may be involved in relations (concerning a proposed marriage, say, or some dispute) with some person or persons with whom he recognizes no ties of lineage membership at all. In this case his position is quite simple. In theory at any rate, he can count on the support of all his patrilateral kin or agnates (if the society is a patrilineal one), that is, of all the members of the maximal lineage to which he belongs. As far as outsiders are concerned, the whole lineage group is a unit.

But the individual concerned may be dealing with a person or persons with whom he is (or believes himself to be) agnatically related. In this case, if the society is a patrilineal one, he and the other person or persons concerned share a common lineage membership at *some* generation level. In many societies—the Nuer of the southern Sudan, described by Evans-Pritchard, are the classic example—lineages are recognized which are many generations in depth, and so contain hundreds or even thousands of members. Where this is so, many of the men with whom a man is likely to have dealings in his everyday life will belong, at some level, to his own lineage. Now the problem is this: in any negotiation or dispute that may arise with one of his distant agnates, which of a man's patrilineal kin can he count on for support, and which of them will support his opponent? In a segmentary lineage system, the problem is easily solved. The lineage segment of which a man's membership is relevant is the largest one which is distinct from his protagonist's. This means that the point of division lies at the generation level next below that of the most recent ancestor shared by both parties; that is, at the highest point on their respective genealogical trees at which both of them can claim *different* patrilineal ancestors. These will usually be two brothers, sons of the same father, and, in the context of political relations, it is the lineages descended from these brothers that provide bodies of supporters for our two hypothetical opponents.

This is what is meant by saying that lineage membership is relative.

It is plain that in some situations men may find themselves aligned in lineage membership with men to whom, in other situations, they are opposed as members of different lineages. To give a very simple example, a man who quarrelled with his father's brother's son (his first cousin on his father's side) would count on the support of his brothers, that is, of the minimal lineage of which his father is the head, while his opponent would similarly count on the support of *his* brothers. But if our first protagonist should quarrel with his father's father's brother's son's son (his second cousin on his father's side), then both he and his former opponent would join forces as members of a two-generation lineage sharing a common paternal grandfather, in opposition to the lineage, of the same order, to which his new opponent belongs, descended from their paternal grand-uncle. Of course in real life the fission and fusion of lineages takes place at far higher levels of segmentation, but the principle involved is the same. For this mode of group attachment and solidarity can be, and often is, operative as far back as relationship can be remembered or presumed, often for seven or eight generations or more. When this is so, social and political relationships involving very large numbers of people may be organized on this principle.

Considered only in its relational aspect, lineage membership may be compared to some kinds of group membership in Western society. Thus an undergraduate at Oxford may think of himself as a member of his college as against a member of another Oxford college, but where relations with another University are concerned (the Oxford–Cambridge match, for example), college membership becomes irrelevant and both unite as Oxford men. Even members of different universities may combine, as against the universities of another country. But the most important difference between being a member of a localized descent group in a society like the Nuer and being a member of an Oxford college is that a Nuer's lineage membership, unlike an undergraduate's college membership, is vitally important for him in almost every aspect of his life. In Western society most people are members of a great many different associations and groups, all with different aims and different membership. But in smaller-scale societies organized in terms of unilineal descent, this one principle of organization forms the basis for practically all of a man's social relationships outside his domestic family.

I have already referred to the second important characteristic of unilineal descent systems, their fissive or segmentary tendency. This also distinguishes them from other forms of grouping more familiar in Western society. Just as, given a certain kind of economy and ecological background, there is a minimum possible size for an effective co-operating group, so also there is an optimum maximum size for it. For example, if it is too large its members may be too widely dispersed to be able to maintain corporate relations. With the passage of time new lineages are formed, as children grow up and acquire descendants of their own. Some descent groups may dwindle and die out, or perhaps merge themselves with stronger groups. But others will increase, until the point is reached at which a group has become too large to maintain itself as a corporate unit. Then such a group may segment into two separate lineages, perhaps as a result of a quarrel between its most senior members, perhaps because there is not enough land for cultivation or grazing available for everybody. It is rather as though an Oxford college, when its numbers reached a certain figure, were to split into two new colleges, each being still, as it were, a constituent of the old one. The two or more new lineages formed in this way might still combine or 'fuse' in certain social situations, in case of war, for example. These processes of fission and fusion are characteristic of lineage-based social systems.

In many societies, especially those which lack any kind of specialized or centralized political authority, the principle of unilineal descent may play a fundamental part in social organization. It is no wonder that in such societies attachment to and identification with the groups so formed is a major social value, for this attachment is vital to everyone.

In societies where unlineal descent is important it is not only one's own descent line which is seen pre-eminently as a group. Everybody in the society belongs to such a group. This means that many of a person's relationships outside his own lineage connect him with whole *groups* of people, and not only with particular individuals. In a patrilineal society, a man is linked through his mother and her brother with a whole group of people, the lineage of which his mother is a member. Although he is not a member of that group, he is bound to it by strong ties of attachment, and its members may reciprocate this attachment, and think and speak of him collectively as 'their' child.

Where everyone is a member of a unilineal descent group, the link with the group of that parent from whom one does *not* take one's lineage membership is very important. Like the links brought about by marriage, and by some other relationships such as those with grandparents, it may help to associate the members of the different descent groups as members of a single society. Without these and other extra-lineage bonds each separate descent group would be socially isolated, and there would be no sense in which one could speak of a 'society' in which these separate groups were included.

This is one reason why in patrilineal societies a great deal of importance is often attached to the relationship between mothers' brothers and their sisters' sons. For from the sister's son's standpoint, this is the vital 'man-to-man' link between him and the descent group outside his own to which he most closely related. So the relationship provides, in Fortes' metaphor, 'a breach in the agnatic fence' which surrounds individuals in such societies.

Unilineal descent, then, is the main principle of social organization in many societies. But even where other organizing principles are operative, for example government through chiefs, or an age-set system, unilineal descent and the associations based on it may still have some social importance, in the context of landholding, for example, or of ritual activity. It is very much a matter of degree.

Very often the kind of kinship terminology used expresses the importance of this 'group' aspect of unilineal kinship in many small-scale societies. The American anthropologist Lewis Morgan was the first to give a clear account of what he called the 'classificatory system' of kinship terminology, though the usage itself had been recognized before his time.[1] The essential point about it is that terms which are applied to lineal relatives (for example, father and son) may also be applied to certain collateral kin (for example, father's brother, brother's son). Sometimes the term thus applied to a collateral relative may be appropriately qualified, a father's brother being called 'little father', for instance; sometimes no such qualification is made. Basically what is happening here is that a group of siblings (for example, one's father and his brothers) are being thought of as a kind of unit. They are all, in a way, the same sort of relative, and so are thought of as being in a sense interchangeable with one another. Thus a man may have many 'fathers' and many 'mothers'. With his talent for identifying the essential elements in kinship relations Radcliffe-Brown called the principle involved here that of the 'unity of the sibling group'.

In a system of this kind, kin who would be reckoned as quite distant relatives in Western European terminologies may be called by the same terms as very close ones. For example, a man might call his father's father's father's brother's son's son's son (whom an Englishman would call his third cousin, if he recognized any relationship at all) 'brother', and so regard him. Evidently such a usage fits in well with the close bonds of mutual attachment which the members of an agnatic lineage are expected to sustain.

Often this mode of classification on the basis of descent cuts across

[1] Morgan, L., *Systems of Consanguinity and Affinity of the Human Family*, Washington, 1871.

the division between the sexes. Thus in many societies a father's sister is called 'father', with the qualification 'female' added, and a mother's brother is called 'mother', with the qualification 'male' added. This kind of usage seems at first sight very extraordinary to Westerners, for whom a relative's sex and the kind and degree of relationship involved are the important things, not his or her group membership. But where what matters most about one's relatives is the descent group they belong to, as is the case in societies based on unilineal descent, this way of naming relatives makes perfect sense. In a society organized in agnatic lineages, for example, the important thing about one's maternal uncle is that he is a member of the corporate agnatic descent group from which one's mother came, and with which therefore one has strong ties. He is not called 'male mother' because he is thought of as a kind of hermaphrodite, half man and half woman; he is so called simply because he is a member of the mother's group. The father's brother is not, and so he is called 'father'. For like one's 'real' father, he is a member of one's own group and of the generation next above one's own.

In such a society (Bunyoro is an example, and there are many others) a man thinks of the whole group of which his mother is a member as a unit, and so he thinks of it and of all its members as standing to him, in some respects, in a maternal role. Correspondingly, they all think of him as in some sense their 'child'. So there is no ground for surprise if, in such a society, a man refers to another man, perhaps much younger than himself, as his 'mother': all he means is that the person so referred to is a member of his mother's agnatic group. Of course he knows perfectly well that his mother and her kinsfolk are all separate and distinct individuals, related to him in different ways. But in many social situations what they have in common (membership in the same lineage) is more important than the differences between them, and this is what is indicated by calling them all by the same term. Radcliffe-Brown aptly identified the principle involved in these usages as 'the unity of the lineage'. But the question must be asked: what are the implications of terminologically unifying lineages in this way? And the answer is that in the societies in which it is done it implies, and is consistent with, strongly institutionalized attachment to social groups based on the principle of unilineal descent.

Almost a hundred years ago the English historian Sir Henry Maine noted the chief practical consequence of the classificatory way of naming and thinking about kin. Its effect, he said, is 'in general to bring within your mental grasp a much greater number of your kindred than is possible under the system to which we are accustomed'.[1] It does this because it places them all in a relatively small number of simple named categories—everyone is 'father', 'mother', 'brother', 'child', and so on. In a society where nearly everyone is a kinsman or an affine to nearly everyone else, the classificatory usage greatly simplifies social life and the social relationships which make it up. It provides the basis for an orderly system of social relations, for there are almost always appropriate patterns of behaviour, of expectations, rights and obligations, associated with each of the categories of relationship which are distinguished. Of course members of cultures in which relatives are divided into a few relatively simple categories on the classificatory principle are perfectly capable of distinguishing degrees of relationship within the categories so distinguished if they want to do so. And in fact a person's obligations towards a very distant 'father', for example (with whom contact is infrequent) are likely to be very much fewer and less intense than those towards his own father. None the less, in a real sense he regards all these people as relatives of the same kind, and the same general pattern of behaviour—respect, deference, obedience, friendliness, or whatever it may be, is held to be appropriate towards all of them. In a small-scale society in which a large proportion, if not all, of the people with whom a person comes into daily contact are kin, the classificatory way of categorizing them provides a ready-made set of behavioural categories, expressed in terms of kinship, for ordering and maintaining social relations.

(2)

So far I have been chiefly concerned with unilineal kinship, and with its social importance as a way of classifying people and placing them in groups. I now consider kinship from a slightly different viewpoint, that of the ordinary individual who sees his kinship system as a collection of interpersonal relationships in which he is, or may become, involved. So, bearing in mind the danger of uncritically comparing kinship categories from one culture to another, in the rest of this chapter I discuss briefly the following kinds of relationships: those between parents and children, between children and their parents' siblings (uncles and aunts, in Western terminology), between grandparents and their grandchildren, between siblings, between parallel cousins (the children of siblings of the same sex), and between cross cousins (the children of siblings of opposite sex). Often the categories of kin thus designated include other collateral kinsfolk and even non-kin, to whom they may be extended through the classificatory system

[1] Maine, H. S., *The Early History of Institutions*, London, 1874.

of kinship terminology, sometimes combined with a clan system. Of course other kinds of kin besides these are recognized in most societies, but the ones I have named generally comprise the more important categories of consanguinity which are recognized for social purposes.

I would stress that when we are discussing kinship we are concerned with social *relationships*, not just with categories of persons considered in themselves. There are always two terms (at least) to any relationship. Thus when we speak of parents we are speaking also of children, for parents are so only in relation to their children. And when we speak of a mother's brother we are speaking also of his sister's children, for each term has meaning only in relation to the other. If we look at kinship relations in this way, we can see at once that they, and the terms associated with them, fall into one or other of two broad types. First, there are those relationships the parties to which regard each other more or less as equals, so that each expects the same pattern of behaviour from the other. Relatives of this kind generally use the same term to address or refer to each other, like 'brother' or 'cousin' in English: terms like these are called 'reciprocating'. On the other hand, there are some kin relationships which are essentially unequal, so that the parties to them expect quite different kinds of behaviour from one another. Where this is the case, the terms used will probably be non-reciprocating, like 'father' and 'son', or 'mother' and 'daughter'.

I begin by considering the parent-child relationship. The first thing to note about it is the obvious fact that as the parents grow old and die, they and their generation are slowly replaced by their children. In many cultures the recognition of this is expressed in a certain constraint in the relationship between the two generations. In some patrilineal societies there are very strict rules about the way in which sons may behave towards their fathers. When the son grows up he may, if he is the heir, assume his father's status and take over his property. Thus his approach towards maturity may be seen as a growing threat to his father's dominant status in the family. So there may be a certain constraint between them, which sometimes seems almost to imply a latent hostility, and this may be expressed in certain formal rules. Among the patrilineal Tallensi a son may not look into his father's granary on pain of serious supernatural sanctions, for to do so would be to presume to his father's status. Among the Nyoro of Uganda, a youth may not shave his face, or begin smoking (both activities which typify manhood) before he has made a small payment to his father. In societies like these it is almost as though the son were committing an offence against his father simply by growing up, and must be punished for it, or must at least make token reparation. Again, often a son may not use or even touch some of his father's intimate personal property. Clothes, weapons, pipes, stools are often proscribed in this way, though other relatives may use them freely. This father–son opposition is an example of what Radcliffe-Brown has characterized as the opposition of adjoining generations. He contrasts it with an opposite principle, 'the merging of alternate generations' (that is, the grandparents' and grandchildren's generations).[1]

Since the ways in which parents and children regard one another are determined culturally rather than biologically, we shall not be surprised to find that in predominantly matrilineal societies, where a man inherits his property and status not from his father but from his mother's brother, the father–son relationship tends to be a good deal less formal and authoritarian. For in such societies, as I noted earlier, the son does not belong to his father's descent group but to his mother's, and her brother is the man in the generation next above his own to whose authority and property he may look forward to succeeding. So the relationship between men and their mother's brothers is commonly much more constrained and formal in matrilineal than in patrilineal societies.

In many cultures more stress is laid on 'social' than on physiological fatherhood, and the two are clearly distinguished. Often a man who is addressed and spoken of as 'father' is not the speaker's 'real' father at all, and everyone knows this. Adoption is such a case in Western society (and in many others), but more striking examples are to be found in those strongly patrilineal societies where such forms of marriage as the levirate and ghost marriage (discussed in the next chapter) occur. In the levirate, when a husband dies his place as spouse of the widow is taken by his brother or his son. There need be no new marriage; the new consort may simply take the place of his dead brother or father in a marriage which continues to exist. Thus any children who are subsequently born to the woman are socially regarded as the sons not of the new husband but of the dead man. Of course everybody knows that the late husband is not the physiological father of the children whom his brother begets, but for social purposes the dead man is their father and they trace their descent from and inherit from him, and not from their physical father.

Sometimes it is convenient to distinguish these two kinds of 'father' by the Latin terms *pater* and *genitor*: *pater* is the social father, who may or may not be the physiological father too, and *genitor* is the

[1] Radcliffe-Brown, A. R., and Forde, D. (editors), *African Systems of Kinship and Marriage*, London, 1950 (Introduction).

physiological father, who may or may not also be the social father. The distinction is particularly important in those segmentary societies where social groups are formed on the basis of unilineal descent in the male line. In such societies not only is it, as we have seen, of the very greatest importance that every man should belong, and should be seen to belong, to a specific descent group, but also, a very high value is attached to every man having a son or sons to carry on his line. The levirate, as well as some other types of union discussed in the next chapter, provides that even a man who dies childless may have social, if not physical issue. This matter is less important in those societies in which unilineal descent plays a less significant part. This is why leviratic and similar types of union are not commonly found in centrally organized, state-like societies. For in these, membership in groups defined by unilineal kinship is much less important (though it may have some significance). In them the politically significant groups are based on other principles, such as attachment to a chief or king.

It is not surprising that the father is the dominant figure in societies where descent and inheritance are normally from father to son, and where associations of agnates headed by their senior male members form a most important social grouping. The Roman *patria potestas* is a classical example. But in societies where descent and inheritance follow the maternal line the father–son relationship is structurally less important, and so in these it tends to be easier and more permissive. For in a matrilineal society a man's son belongs not to his line but to his wife's, and her brother stands in a position of authority over her children, who may inherit from him. Their father's authority, in turn, is not over them, but over his own sister's children. Sometimes in matrilineal societies the rival, though different, claims of a man's sister's children and his own children give rise to some ambivalence in the parent–child relationship. Anthropological writings about such societies (Malinowski's accounts of the Trobriand islanders provide examples) often describe how fathers attempt to secure for their children or their children's children some of the benefits which should in principle go to their sister's children.

Less need be said of the relationship between fathers and daughters. Almost always in non-Western societies (and until very recently in most Western ones too) women are taken to be of less account than men. In most societies it is only exceptionally, if at all, that women can inherit from their fathers, so the father–daughter relationship generally lacks the jural quality of the father–son relationship in patrilineal societies. In most such societies a woman moves out of her parental group when she marries, and so she is in effect lost to her own lineage, although, as we shall see, where bridewealth is paid the cattle received for her may enable her father and his group to obtain another woman to replace her. The mother–son relationship also usually lacks any substantial jural content, though it almost invariably implies a strong bond of affection. Since in most societies, whether predominantly patrilineal or matrilineal, women occupy a lower status and hold less property and authority than men do, relations between them and their menfolk are relatively unimportant in terms of the transmission of goods and status, though they may be highly important affectively. In most societies women do hold small amounts of personal and domestic property in their own right, and almost always such property may be inherited by a daughter.

I turn now to the relationship between parents' siblings and siblings' children, 'uncles and aunts' and 'nephews and nieces' in Western terms. The first thing to note is that where, as is widely the case in simpler societies, unilineal descent is an important principle of social grouping and marriage is exogamous (so that a person must marry outside his or her own group), then a person's parents' siblings fall in two different social groups. And very often this difference of group membership is the most important thing about them. In a patrilineal society a man belongs to a group which includes his father, his father's brothers and sisters, and his father's brothers' children. And his mother and her brothers and sisters belong to a different descent group, of which he is not a member; the group from which his father took a wife. And in a matrilineally organized society a man belongs to a group which includes his mother's brothers and sisters, and his mother's sisters' children. And his father and his father's siblings and his father's sisters' children belong to a different descent group, of which he is not a member; the group which provided a husband for his mother. Where unilineal descent is socially important, this group difference is most significant. A man finds security and status and a firm feeling of 'belonging' in his own group. But the group of the parent from whom he does *not* derive his group membership is not his group; he is outside of it, even though he may be closely linked to its members as their 'child'. I noted earlier in this chapter that the importance of this group difference is reflected in classificatory kinship terminology; father's brothers and even father's sisters may be called 'fathers'; mother's sisters and even mother's brothers may be called 'mothers'. In such cases the effect of the classificatory terminology is to stress the *group* membership of these relatives. For their group membership is much more important in societies organized on the unilineal principle than the actual genealogical links involved, even, sometimes, than the sex of the relatives concerned.

Attitudes to parents' siblings are usually consistent with this way of classifying them. In patrilineal societies a father's brother is usually thought of as the same kind of relative as a father (where the levirate is practised he may actually replace one's father if the latter dies), and the same kind of deference and respect that is owed to a father is due to him. Even one's father's sister may be thought of as a 'fatherly' kind of woman, rather sterner and more disciplinarian than a mother or a mother's sister. And, in such societies, one's mother's sister is regarded as a kind of mother, and her brother (who may be called 'male' or 'man' mother) is a relative with whom a much more friendly and intimate relationship is permissible than would be allowed with one's father or his brothers. In many patrilineal societies a boy can take liberties with his mother's brother and play tricks on him with impunity; tricks which he would be severely punished for if he tried them on his father.

This superficially free and easy relationship is sometimes called a joking relationship, since one or other (sometimes both) of the parties to it may take advantage of the other and abuse him jocularly without offence being taken. But sometimes, also, it involves certain formal restrictions and prohibitions, often of a ritual or symbolic kind. Thus among the Nyoro a sister's son may not squat on or near the hearthstones in his mother's brother's house, or touch anything new there; it is believed that if he does misfortune will befall his mother's brother. It is legitimate to infer from these restrictions that despite appearances there is an undercurrent of hostility in the relationship. To understand why this should be so we must recall, once again, the essentially group reference of kinship relations in many small-scale societies, especially where groups are formed on the unilineal descent principle. We need to remember, also, that in a patrilineal society the group with which a man is most closely linked through his mother's brother is the very group from which his father took a wife. His maternal group, that is, is his father's affinal group. Now where groups are exogamous, affines are in a sense strangers, 'outsiders'; they may be regarded as potential enemies, and a man's relationship with them may be characterized by respect, and even fear. In some cultures (Bunyoro is an example) something of this antagonism seems to be carried over, as it were, from father to son into the next generation; that is, into the mother's brother–sister's son relationship. But here it is qualified by the fact that the mother's brother's group, as well as being 'strangers' to the lineage of their sister's husband and her son, are also 'mothers' to their sister's child.

This means that affection and indulgence are prescribed. Thus there may be an ambivalent quality about the relationship. Where in human relationships there is ambivalence and potential strain, a common way of dealing with the matter is for strict rules to be applied in dealings between the two parties. This 'formalizing' of the relationship may imply special kinds of freedom and privilege combined with certain prohibitions (offence must not be taken; certain things must be avoided); or it may imply the prohibition of any face-to-face relations at all, as in the avoidance relationship between certain affines.

In matrilineal societies the emphasis is naturally reversed. One's mother's brother is a figure of authority and the man from whom one will inherit status and property; one's father's brothers, like one's father, are 'outsiders' with whom one's relationship is of relatively little structural importance. But whichever system of descent is used, it is plain that where grouping is based on the unilineal principle, father's siblings and mother's siblings fall on opposite sides of the fence. A man is a member of one group, but not of the other; and so they are thought of as entirely different kinds of kin. Plainly, in systems of this kind, nothing could be more misleading than to lump the siblings of both parents together in terms of generation and sex, and call them 'uncle' and 'aunt', without regard to their group affiliations. This would be a gross example of the fallacy already referred to, that of indiscriminately applying the categories of our culture in the context of another, a context to which they may be totally inappropriate.

In almost all societies the relationship between grandchildren and their grandparents is one of easy familiarity. Radcliffe-Brown has summed this up in his phrase 'the merging of alternate generations'. In a great many cultures it is said that grandparents spoil their grandchildren. They can afford to do so, for they do not have the responsibility, as the children's parents have, of disciplining them and bringing them up in accordance with approved social norms. Also, members of the grandparents' generation, unlike those of the parental one, do not feel their status to be threatened by the growing generation of grandchildren. They are already, as it were, 'out of the race', for they have already been replaced by their own children. For these reasons the relationship between grandparents and grandchildren is usually free and easy. In many Bantu—and other—societies a man and his grandfather may refer to each other reciprocally as 'brother'; and in some a man may jokingly refer to his grandmother as his 'wife', and so address her. This does not mean that he does or may marry the old lady, as some earlier anthropologists supposed. It

111

simply means that he looks on her as a kind of equal, a person from whom he may expect friendly affection, and who will cook a meal for him when he is hungry, as a wife would. It *can* mean in some societies (if he does not belong to the same descent line as she does) that he can marry into her lineage or clan. For in societies with a classificatory system of kinship terminology, just as all your mother's people are 'mothers', so all your grandmother's people (for example all the members of your mother's mother's descent group) may be 'grandmothers'. So the somewhat bizarre assertion that in some societies people may marry their grandmothers simply means that a man may marry a girl who belongs to his maternal (or paternal) grandmother's clan. All such women are therefore potential wives, and may be jocularly so addressed. In no society that I know of does it mean that a man can marry his actual grandmother or, as a rule, any near relative. The idea that it does derives from the mistake, now sufficiently familiar, of interpreting other people's linguistic and cultural categories in terms of our own.

Relations between siblings are very different in different societies, and, as we should expect, these variations are associated with differences in social organization. Thus in those patrilineally organized societies where membership of a corporate group of agnates is of vital importance, mutual obligations of co-operation and support between brothers are much stressed. 'Brotherliness' provides the idiom in terms of which the reciprocal obligations of clan or lineage membership are conceived. Often full and half siblings are socially and terminologically distinguished. For where marriage is or may be polygynous, as it is in many societies, a household often consists of a compound family of a man and his two (or more) wives and their respective children. The children of each wife, since they share a common father but have different mothers, are half siblings to each other. The difference, especially between full and half brothers, may be important. In a society in which social grouping is based on patrilineal descent, children of the same mother but of different fathers belong to different descent groups, while children of the same father but of different mothers belong to the same one. Conversely, in a society in which social grouping is based on matrilineal descent, children of the same mother but of different fathers belong to the same descent group, while children of the same father but of different mothers belong to different groups. And of course these differences of group affiliation significantly affect the kinds of rights and duties they acknowledge in regard to one another and to other kinsfolk. In any event, whatever the type of social organization, more stress is generally placed on the need for solidarity between brothers than between sisters. In many societies brothers form an important co-operating group throughout their lives, while sisters very often separate at marriage. And once a woman is married, her interests, at least in patrilineal societies, are usually subordinated to those of her husband and his group.

Relations between brothers and sisters vary from society to society from friendly intimacy to avoidance and respect. Sometimes they are complicated by the legal implications of the relationship. Thus in many African societies a man may expect to marry with the bride-wealth which is received from the man who marries his sister. In societies where the principle of local grouping is predominantly matrilineal, like the Ashanti and the Yao in Africa, the bond between brother and sister tends to be stronger than it is in patrilineal societies. This is because in the latter a man's sister and her children are, as it were, lost to her brother's group, while in the former a man maintains a continuing interest in and contact with his sisters and their children, for these children are reckoned as members of his descent group, and one of them will be his heir.

I turn, finally, to those relatives who in Western usage are termed 'cousins'. In many societies, and especially in those with unilineal descent grouping and a classificatory kinship terminology, parallel cousins and cross cousins are clearly distinguished and are regarded as quite different kinds of relatives. Parallel cousins are usually regarded as the same kind of relatives as siblings. Thus a person's father's brother's children and his mother's sister's children may be classified as (half) brothers and sisters, and be so thought of and addressed. This of course makes good sense in a system in which a father's brother is thought of as a kind of father, and a mother's sister as a kind of mother. Given this pattern, it follows that a father's brother's child is the same as a father's child, that is, a sibling, and a mother's sister's child is the same as a mother's child, and so a sibling too.

The cross cousin relationship is that between the children of a brother and a sister. Though the relationship is one, it looks quite different from either end. The brother's child's cross cousin is his father's sister's child; and the sister's child's cross cousin is his mother's brother's child. In societies based on unilineal descent the relationship between cross cousins is evidently an entirely different thing from the relationship between parallel cousins. For cross cousins *always* belong to different groups. In a patrilineal society your mother's brother's children belong to a separate group from your own; your mother's agnatic group, from which your father took a wife. And your father's sister's children always belong to a different group from your own; a group which has taken a wife from your group. In a matrilineal society, correspondingly, your father's sister's children belong to a separate group from your own, that is, to the matrilineal group of your father, from which your group received a husband. And your mother's brother's children also belong to a different group from yours; that is to a group to which your group *gave* a husband.

The essential group reference of kinship terms in many parts of the world throws light on what is at first sight a curious feature of cross cousin terminology in many classificatory systems. In a number of societies which are organized in exogamous, patrilineal groups, a person calls his mother's brother's children by the same term that he uses for his mother's brothers and sisters (that is, usually, 'mothers', male or female). And he calls his father's sister's children by a term which can sometimes be translated 'children', that is, he speaks of them as though he were their 'mother'. In a number of matrilineally organized societies this usage is reversed. A father's sister's children are spoken of as 'fathers', and a mother's brother's children as 'children'.

These two ways of thinking and talking about cross cousins are often referred to as the Omaha and the Crow systems of cross cousin terminology, because they were first recorded in the two North American Indian tribes so named, the Omaha being patrilineal and the Crow matrilineal. It looks as though their effect was to remove cross cousins from the speaker's generation and to put them into the generation next above or below. Earlier anthropologists were very puzzled to know how this curious usage could be explained. But it is really very simple when we remember how very important unilineal descent group membership is for a great many peoples. When grouping is agnatic, a man's mother, her brother, and her brother's children are all in the same descent group. Thus, as I noted earlier, they may all be regarded as in a sense 'mothers' to him. So to call his mother's brother's daughter 'mother', and his mother's brother's son 'male mother' (the same term that he uses for his mother's brother) is simply to give verbal expression to this recognition. The key principle is again Radcliffe-Brown's 'unity of the lineage'. The point is equally clear if we look at the relationship from the other end. If you identify yourself with your agnatic lineage as a whole, then a child of any woman of your lineage, your father's sister no less than your own sister, is 'your' child, and you, as a member of your lineage, stand to it as a kind of 'mother'. So to call your father's sister's child your 'child' is simply to give verbal expression to this way of looking at the relationship. This is so notwithstanding that such children are

114

plainly not the same as your own children. For they belong to a different clan, and usually there is a special term to distinguish them. But they are still your children, and may be so referred to. So the Omaha system of cross-cousin terminology makes perfect sense as soon as it is realized that for many peoples organized in patrilineal groups, generation membership is very much less important than group membership.

In a matrilineal society the position is simply reversed. Here your lineage identification is with your mother, with her brother, and with *her* mother and her brother, so that your mother's brother's child, and even your mother's mother's brother's child, is in a sense 'your' child, and you are its 'father'. And conversely, your father's sister's children belong to the same lineage as your father and so they are in a sense 'fathers' to you, and you are their 'child'. Odd though these usages appear to us at first sight, it is plain that they are entirely reasonable and consistent in social systems in which membership in a unilineal descent group is the paramount social value.

There is a great deal more to be said about the field of kinship studies than it has been possible to touch on here. In this chapter I have only attempted to demonstrate some of the main kinds of social importance that kinship may have in other cultures, and to discuss the ways in which social anthropologists study it. As I remarked earlier, they only study it because in a great many small-scale societies all or most of the important kinds of institutionalized relationships between people are conceived in kinship terms. We cannot begin to understand these societies, and the ways in which their members order their affairs, unless we understand the kinship categories by means of which they do so.

So, like a great deal of social anthropology, the study of kinship is centrally and essentially a study of other people's categories; of the ways in which the members of other cultures think about kinship and about other people. I have sufficiently stressed that social anthropology is not—and cannot be—concerned with human communities only as systems of action. It is concerned with them also and essentially as involving systems of ideas and meanings. The study of kinships is not just a study of what people do; it is also a study of what people think. For what they do is not fully intelligible until their modes of classification, their fundamental categories, are understood. Only then do their actual behaviour and its institutional implications make sense.

In this chapter I have shown that other peoples' ways of thinking about kinship are consistent and reasonable in their own cultural and social contexts. But they are often very different from those to which modern Europeans or Americans are accustomed. So, as I have emphasized, they cannot be understood by uncritically attempting to assimilate them to Western kinship categories. But this does not mean that kinship studies are exceptionally difficult or complex, or at least that they need be so. After all, even the least gifted members of societies with the most (to us) unfamiliar kinship systems manage to understand and operate them well enough. Here as elsewhere, the real problem for us is to apprehend, and to learn to think in, the totally unfamiliar categories of other cultures. Once this has been done, through the techniques of analysis and fieldwork discussed in earlier chapters, we can begin to understand these unfamiliar kinship structures as working systems, and we can attempt to convey something of this understanding to others. Like much of social anthropology an important part of kinship studies consists of problems of translation.

SHORT READING LIST

EGGAN, F. (editor), *Social Anthropology of North American Tribes* (revised edition), Chicago, 1955.

EVANS-PRITCHARD, E. E., *The Nuer*, Oxford, 1940.

FIRTH, RAYMOND, *We, the Tikopia*, London, 1936.

FORTES, M., *The Dynamics of Clanship among the Tallensi*, Oxford, 1945. *The Web of Kinship among the Tallensi*, Oxford, 1949.

LÉVI-STRAUSS, C., *Les Structures élémentaires de la parenté*, Paris, 1949.

RADCLIFFE-BROWN, A. R., and FORDE, D. (editors), *African Systems of Kinship and Marriage*, London, 1950.

RIVERS, W. H. R., *Social Organization*, London, 1926.

SMITH, W. ROBERTSON, *Kinship and Marriage in Early Arabia*, London, 1885.

8

Marriage and Affinity

(1)

LIKE EVERYONE ELSE, social anthropologists recognize that men and women must come together and have children if human society is to continue. They know too that unlike the young of most animal species, human children have to depend on adult care for many years, and that this usually involves some kind of more or less enduring family organization. But they are more interested in the social and cultural aspects of marriage than in its biological functions. In almost all societies marriage is an institutionalized social relationship of crucial significance. More than this, it is generally associated with a number of other important social relationships.

In this chapter I consider four connected aspects of the institution of marriage. First I discuss some of the different types of marital union found in human societies. I then consider the implications of these for relationships between and within groups of people. We shall not be surprised to find that the group aspect of marriage is generally much more important in small-scale, pre-industrial societies than it is in 'modern' ones. In the second part of the chapter I discuss the various regulations and prohibitions associated with marriage and sexual relations in various cultures. Finally, I consider some of the kinds of interpersonal relationships which marriage entails.

Marriage is almost always more than simply a legalized sexual union between a man and a woman, though it is almost always this, if we mean by 'legalized' socially acknowledged and approved. *Notes and Queries on Anthropology* gives a useful preliminary definition: marriage is 'a union between a man and a woman such that the children born to the woman are the recognized legitimate offspring of both partners'. This points to one important function of marriage in most societies; the fact that it confers acknowledged social status

117

on the offspring. This is evidently a matter of great importance in regard to such matters as inheritance and succession.

But there is no general definition of marriage which covers all of the kinds of institutionalized inter-personal relationships which it is convenient to include under the term. Here, as so often, we have to avoid the danger of uncritically assimilating other people's social and cultural institutions to our own. We shall see that it is sometimes hard to decide whether a particular kind of union in a particular society can usefully be called marriage. But although the names we give to the institutions we identify are important for the purpose of thinking and communicating about them, the first and most important thing is to understand their nature and significance in their proper contexts. In other cultures marriage may both mean something very different from what it means in Western culture, and have very different— and very important—social implications.

To begin with, a few broad distinctions must be made. First, marriage may be monogamous (one husband and one wife), or it may be polygamous. If it is polygamous it may be either polygynous (one husband and two or more wives) or—and this is very rare— polyandrous (one wife and two or more husbands). It is not surprising that although polygyny is an accepted form of marriage in very many societies, polyandry is much less usual. In most simple societies it is still true, as it was in pre-twentieth century Europe, that the human world is 'a man's world'. Also, in most human communities women outnumber men, a tendency perhaps accentuated in simpler cultures by the fact that men often engage in more dangerous activities than women, such as warfare and hunting. It has often been remarked that an effect of polygyny is to provide that all the women in a community can be married and so materially provided for. In many technologically simple cultures there are no means by which an unmarried woman can support herself. A spinster is a social anomaly; there is no accepted role for her or at best only a very restricted one. Also where a man's status and property pass to his own children, and where, as is often the case, his own reputation and his being remembered after he dies depend almost entirely on his having a large number of descendants, he has evidently a strong incentive to polygyny. A man with several wives can reasonably hope to have more children than a man with only one. But where a man's status and property pass on his death not to his own children but to his sister's children, this incentive may well be of less importance. Anthropologists sometimes distinguish sororal polygyny, in which a man is married to two sisters, and adelphic polyandry, in which a woman is married to two brothers.

Like a great many other aspects of marriage in pre-industrial societies (especially those in which the principle of unilineal descent plays an important part), these usages are best understood when marriage is seen not just as an arrangement entered into by two individuals, but rather as a relationship which essentially involves two groups. Like the group aspect of kinship, which I discussed in the last chapter, the group aspect of marriage is central. It is worth stressing at the outset that this is not just the anthropologist's idea. An essential part of any institutionalized social relationship is the way in which the parties to it themselves regard it. And it is a matter of ethnographic fact that in many patrilineal societies the members of an agnatic lineage, even including the women in it, often refer to a woman who joins their group as a wife to one of its members as 'our' wife. As they see it, the group as a whole, and not just the individual husband, has acquired a woman to work and bear children for it. In matrilineal societies, members of groups based on descent in the female line may regard, and refer to, the husbands of women of the group in a similar manner.

In many such societies the actual forms of the institution of marriage are consistent with this way of regarding it. I remarked in the last chapter that the form of union known as the levirate is characteristic of societies in which unilineal descent in the male line forms the central principle of social organization. The Bedouin of Arabia and North Africa, and the Nuer of the Sudan, are well-known examples of such societies. The ancient Hebrews had the levirate too; there is a concise description of the institution in Deuteronomy xxv, verses 5–6. In the levirate, if a married man dies, his widow may be taken over by his brother, or sometimes by his son, so long as the son is by another wife. But there need be no new marriage; the levir does not necessarily become the woman's husband, notwithstanding that she may be (as among the Nuer) in a sense 'wife' to the group as a whole. She may continue to be regarded as her dead husband's wife, and the children she bears to her new spouse are not reckoned as his, but as the dead man's.

The levirate is not the same thing as widow inheritance, an institution which is sometimes found in societies where unilineal descent is significant, but not of paramount importance. In widow inheritance also, the widow is taken over by one of the dead man's agnates, usually a brother or son. But she then becomes the wife of her new spouse, and any children she afterwards bears are his. The social importance of the levirate is that it enables a married man who dies childless, or at least without a son to succeed him and to continue his line, to be provided with one posthumously. Also, where there is

119

movable wealth such as cattle, it provides for the transmission of his property to his posthumous 'son'. The distinction between physiological and social paternity, referred to in the last chapter, is relevant here: for the child of a leviratic union, his social father and his physiological father, *pater* and *genitor*, are different people.

An even more extreme form of this institution, characteristic also of societies which attach a very high value to agnation and to membership of descent groups formed on that principle, is what has been called 'ghost marriage'. Among the Nuer, if a man dies before he has had a chance to marry and beget sons, it is a responsibility of a younger brother of the deceased to 'marry a wife to the dead man', or, as we should put it, to marry a wife in his name and on his behalf. The woman whom the surviving brother espouses in terms of this institution is not *his* wife. She is the wife of the deceased elder brother to whom she is 'married', a person whom she may never even have seen. And her children by her living spouse are not his children, but the children of their dead *pater*. Nuer would consider it improper for the younger brother of a man who had died unmarried to take a wife for himself before he had discharged this obligation to his elder sibling.

Marital institutions such as these evidently have important implications for the groups of agnates who have them. First, in a society in which every man is a potential lineage-founder, and where membership in a descent group is all-important, these usages visibly express and reaffirm this importance. Secondly, the mutual rights and obligations which they imply bind the members of the group more closely together. The levirate and ghost marriage imply the unity of the sibling group, for in these forms of marriage a man may, as it were, replace his brother. But they also and more importantly imply the unity of the lineage. That is, they serve to maintain the mode of grouping, based on unilineal descent, which provides the basic social units in such societies.

If we regard marriage as a relationship not just between individuals, but also, at least potentially, between groups, then an important distinction is that between endogamy and exogamy. The terms were first used by the Victorian anthropologist McLennan, and they simply mean that one must 'marry in' or 'marry out'; that is, inside or outside of a social group to which one belongs.[1] Since the terms are relative, it is necessary when using them to define the group within which, or outside of which, one must marry. Examples of endogamous groups are castes and sub-castes in India; in many of those very numerous societies in which unilineal descent provides the main principle of social grouping, clans or lineages are exogamous.

[1] McLennan, J. F., *Primitive Marriage*, London, 1865.

Endogamy is especially associated with the caste system. Caste implies not only that there are different 'kinds' of people, but that these kinds, often distinguished by the occupations they traditionally follow, are arranged in a hierarchical series. Any caste or sub-caste occupies a particular position on the ladder, with some below it (except in the case of the lowest) and some above it (except in the case of the highest). In societies so organized it is generally held to be very important that each caste or sub-caste should keep itself to itself, and avoid mixing with other castes, especially with lower ones. The rule of endogamy, often (in India always) associated with strongly institutionalized notions of purity and impurity, helps to ensure caste separateness: it also expresses the high value socially attached to such exclusiveness.

There are a very few societies in which unilineal descent provides the basic principle for the formation of social groups in which marriage within such groups is permitted: the Bedouin of North Africa are one. In such societies marriage within the agnatic group may be thought to strengthen the bond between related lineages; it may also serve to ensure that lineage property is not dispersed. Also, it may be considered safer to find a spouse among those whom one knows and trusts, that is, among one's own patrilateral kin. But throughout the world marriage in unilineally based societies is far more usually exogamous. In most societies where groups are based on agnatic descent you may not marry anyone who is a member of your own lineage or clan, however remote the genealogical connection may be, and even when, as in the clan systems of many Bantu peoples, no kinship link at all can be traced. It is rather as though, in Western society, no Jones could marry another Jones. Correspondingly, in most matrilineal societies it is forbidden to marry anyone to whom one is or believes oneself to be related matrilaterally.

The point of these rules of exogamy is not simply to prohibit marriage between close kin. In many patrilineal societies a man may marry quite close maternal kin, like the mother's brother's daughter, and in some matrilineal societies quite close paternal kin are acceptable as spouses. The effect of the prohibition is to ensure that people marry outside their own groups. Thus it is the group affiliations of the prospective spouses that are important, rather than the degree of consanguinity (if any) that connects them.

In societies consisting of a number of distinct groups of people, each centred around an agnatic lineage, and each related to other similar groups through ties of kinship and affinity (while at the same time conscious of and concerned to maintain its own separate identity), the rule of exogamy may have important social consequences. In such societies the separate groups are often mutually hostile. Sometimes, indeed (as in more advanced societies), the maintenance of an attitude of more or less permanent antagonism towards other groups of the same kind may be an important factor in maintaining the group's own internal cohesion. So often the rule of exogamy forces men to marry among their actual or potential enemies; it compels them to widen their social horizons, and to enter into more or less amicable relations with potentially hostile people outside their own group. 'We marry among those whom we fight', some peoples say. We shall see later that the potential hostility which may be latent in affinal relations in societies of this kind is often expressed in the ways in which affines think about and behave towards one another. Further, where the exogamous unit is a closely-knit, corporate group of kinsmen, the rule that its members must always 'marry out' helps to maintain the group's internal unity. For the jealousies and rivalries commonly associated with courtship are less likely to arise within the group when men must look outwards for mates, an arrangement which also ensures that conflicts with 'in-laws' are kept outside the group.

Although affines may quarrel they should, none the less, try to maintain good relations: affinal relations in one generation become kinship ones in the next. Thus a most important function of exogamy is to bind together, through affinal—and later kinship—links, the separate groups which taken together make up the social aggregate. Without these links these separate groups would be quite isolated from one another, and there would be no clear sense in which they could be said to make up one 'society' at all. The French social anthropologist Lévi-Strauss has stated the importance of the inter-group linkages brought about by exogamy in a vivid if somewhat gruesome metaphor (though the point had been made before). The rules of exogamy in patrilineal societies, he says, are 'the blueprint of a mechanism which "pumps" women out of their consanguineous families to redistribute them in affinal groups, the result of this process being to create new consanguineous groups'.[1] Thus (to change the metaphor from sewage farming to agriculture) groups are constantly cross-fertilizing one another. In this way the society itself is being continuously renewed, and at the same time, through an expanding network of affinal and kinship links, its members are being brought into relationship with one another in a variety of ways.

So regarded, marriage in very many societies can be seen as a kind of *exchange* between separate groups of men. One group receives a

[1] Lévi-Strauss, C., in *Anthropology Today*, Chicago, 1953.

wife; the other obtains something in return for the woman who is handed over. It is worth noting that in these transactions it is almost always men who do the exchanging; women are simply a commodity transferred, for a consideration, from one group to another. It is almost never the other way round. I remarked earlier that for obvious physiological reasons the social world which the members of simpler, small-scale societies inhabit is almost always a man's world. The primitive matriarchies about which some Victorian anthropologists liked to conjecture have no basis either in history or in ethnography. I return in Chapter 12 to the importance of exchange in creating and maintaining social relationships, and so in contributing to mutual interdependence and social cohesion. Here I note only that institutionalized exchanges do seem to have these effects, and that in very many societies marriage and the various transactions often associated with it may usefully be regarded as a kind of exchange.

These exchanges may be of different kinds. In some societies a woman in one group is directly exchanged for a woman in another; the simplest type of such exchange is sister exchange, when two men simply swap sisters. Some African peoples, like the Amba of Uganda, practise such exchange, or did so until very recently. In other societies the consideration may take the form of labour: a man who is given a wife by another group may have to work for her relatives for a specified number of months or years before he can take her to his own home. The story of Jacob and Laban's daughters provides a biblical example of this type of exchange. It is common in matrilineal societies, where the wife continues to live with her own group after marriage, at any rate to begin with. But in those pre-literate societies in which local grouping is based on patrilineal descent, and in which some form of negotiable property exists, the commonest form of exchange is for bridewealth. This is usually a payment of livestock or other goods, nowadays often money. The institution of bridewealth (it should be distinguished from dowry, which is best defined as a payment not from the man's side to the woman's side, but in the opposite direction) is so widespread and important that we must consider it in some detail.

Earlier administrators and missionaries, and some later ones, supposed that bridewealth was simply a purchase price; they thought that it meant that the husband was buying a wife, just as he might buy any other piece of property. So they condemned it as offensive to morality and degrading to womanhood, and did their best to suppress it. It is true that an element of purchase may sometimes enter into the transaction, especially nowadays when in many societies the traditional payment of cattle, beer or other consumable goods has been commuted to a cash payment. But to represent it as no more than this is to miss the whole point. In patrilineal, exogamous societies, where the bride leaves her natal group and is taken into the quite separate group of her husband, which may be some distance from her home, bridewealth does have the character of an indemnity. By the marriage the bride's group has lost a working member and a potential child-bearer, and the bridewealth paid for her is a kind of compensation for this loss. The group to which it is paid may use it to replace the woman they have lost: often a bridewealth is earmarked to be used to obtain a wife for a brother or other near relative of the girl on whose account it was received. Of course, in matrilineally organized societies bridewealth does not fulfil this function. For in these a woman retains her ties with her own group; she often continues to live in it, and her children belong to that group and not to her husband's. So in such societies if bridewealth is paid at all it is usually very small.

But even in patrilineal societies there is always more to marriage than simply paying bridewealth and taking over a woman. Usually there is some marriage ceremonial, often elaborate, and always there is a formal handing over of the bride from one group to another. Also, the transfer of goods which bridewealth involves is rarely a one-way process. Often return gifts have to be made by the bride's group, and often these exchanges continue for quite a long time after the marriage has taken place. Thus marriage may imply the initiation of a continuing series of exchanges between the two groups concerned.

Again, the payment does not imply the transfer of *all* rights in the bride to the husband and his kin, as it would if the transaction were an outright purchase. Marrying a wife is not like buying a slave. We noted that in matrilineal societies, even though the husband secures exclusive rights of sexual access to his wife, his children by her are attached to her brothers and their line, not to his. Even in patrilineally organized societies some rights usually remain with the wife and her group. The bridewealth may serve as security for his good behaviour as well as for hers. If the wife behaves badly her husband may divorce her and demand the return of his bridewealth. Her parents will normally be reluctant to repay it, especially nowadays when it is often paid in cash and may have been spent; they may accordingly put pressure on their daughter to behave herself so that they will not be called upon to refund it. But also, in many societies if the husband maltreats his wife or fails to support her she may leave him, and if he is found to be at fault his affines may refuse to return the bridewealth, so that he loses both property and wife. If bridewealth is purchase, it is certainly not unconditional.

124

But there is even more to it than this. Bridewealth is particularly important in establishing the legality of a marriage, and in validating the social status of its offspring. The overt transfer of cattle or other goods from one group to another is a manifest sign that the couple have been properly married. For very many peoples for whom marriage was traditionally ratified by neither church nor state but was simply the concern of the two groups involved, a union in which bridewealth had not been paid was looked down on as immoral, and the children of such a union had no recognized status in the community. Often both a man's and a woman's self-respect depended on the transfer of bridewealth. In Bunyoro, if a woman who is living with a man who has not paid bridewealth for her wishes to insult him, she may say 'and where have *your* cattle urinated, may I ask?' What she is implying is that he is too poor or too mean to have married her properly. Even today many members of patrilineal societies in Africa which have been largely Christianized still believe that if the marriage is to be really valid bridewealth must be paid. Men who have been married in Christian churches often arrange for bridewealth at current rates to be paid as well.

The payment of bridewealth, and the series of gift exchanges or 'prestations' which it often entails, not only provide for a continuing relation between groups, but they also may create and sustain relationships within groups. In many societies a man's kinsmen are expected to contribute towards the bridewealth needed for his marriage, the amount of their contribution depending on the kind and degree of their relationship to him. And they will expect to receive, *pro rata*, a share of the bridewealth received for his sister. Thus where cattle or other stock are transferred at marriage, as they are in many African societies, there is a constant movement of livestock both within and between the descent groups which make up the community. Writing of the Nyakyusa of Tanganyika, Professor Monica Wilson says that cattle are continually driven down the paths of human relationship.[1] We might go even further, and say that in fact they tread out these paths.

(2)

All societies have rules and restrictions about who may, or may not, marry whom. The 'primitive promiscuity' of the Victorians has no foundation in ethnography. Always there are certain categories of relatives with whom marriage is prohibited. Also there are certain categories of relatives with whom it is not permissible to have sexual

[1] Wilson, Monica, *Good Company*, London, 1951.

125

relations. Usually these two categories coincide, but they do not always do so. There are some societies, like the Masai and other Nilo-Hamitic peoples of East Africa, in which sexual intercourse is permissible between people who are not permitted to marry. Relations between prohibited kinds of kin are what we mean by incest, and as I noted earlier, sexual relations between the members of an elementary family (other than the parents) are universally regarded as incestuous.

There is one exception to this rule. In a number of societies—ancient Egypt, the Inca state, and certain interlacustrine Bantu kingdoms of East Africa are examples—sexual relations, even marriage, between rulers and their sisters ('real' or classificatory) were permitted or even prescribed. But they were never permitted to commoners, and an effect of the usage was to mark the distinctiveness and uniqueness of the rulers, who could perform acts unthinkable for ordinary people.

It is a common mistake to suppose that the incest prohibition rests simply on the idea of consanguineal propinquity. In many unilineally organized societies all relatives on one's own side, however distant they are genealogically, may be prohibited as mates, while marriage with quite close relatives on the other side may be socially acceptable and even preferred. Sometimes these prohibitions and preferences are associated with very varying ideas about the parts played in conception and gestation by the father and the mother respectively. Some matrilineal peoples think that the father's role in conception is minimal, if it exists at all: it may be thought that he only 'opens the door', as it were, or at the most shapes the growing embryo through intercourse. The Trobriand Islanders of Melanesia are said to hold such a view. For many patrilineal peoples, on the other hand, the father is seen as the real *genitor* of his child; the mother is merely the receptacle in which it is contained and nourished until birth. But however conception be regarded, there are always some relatives outside the elementary family of spouses and children with whom sexual relations and marriage are prohibited.

How is this universal incest taboo to be explained? Earlier writers spoke of an instinctive and universal horror of incest, and of a 'natural' repugnance to the idea of cohabitation with near kin. But there is little or no evidence for the existence of such instinctive emotional attitudes as these. If there really were such an instinctive aversion it is hard to see how incest could ever occur, as in all societies it not infrequently does. The grounds for the taboo's universality lie elsewhere. They derive rather from the ubiquity of some kind of family or other group organization, and from the fact that certain of

126

the social relationships which such organization implies are incompatible with the presence of sexual relations. The relationship which is appropriate between parents and children, for example, or that between siblings in the same elementary family, is totally different from and incompatible with the relationship between spouses. Thus there is no known society in which the father-daughter relationship could be assimilated to the husband-wife one; they serve entirely different social ends, and in every society they are regarded completely differently. It is significant that the Chinese characters which stand for incest can be translated as 'confusion of relationships'.

There is a further point. If the men of an elementary family were all competing for the sexual favours of the mother (as in Freud's celebrated fable) or of a sister, the unity of the family group would evidently be destroyed. And as we have seen, the maintenance of such family and group cohesion, especially in the conditions of most of the simpler societies, is of basic importance for everybody. These are the chief reasons why in every society some unions (and always those between siblings or parents and children in the elementary family) are almost unthinkable, and are regarded as grave sins when they occur. By threatening to confuse social relationships which should be kept distinct they threaten the very social order itself, and with it the security and even the survival of the members of the society.

As well as prohibiting marriages between certain categories of kin, some societies permit, or even require, certain kinds of relatives to marry. Where people are obliged to marry into specific groups or categories of kin, as in some societies of south-east Asia and Indonesia, and among the Australian aborigines, we may speak of prescriptive marriage systems. Sometimes there is a reciprocal exchange of women between two groups (there may of course be several such reciprocating groups in the whole community), and everybody must marry into the appropriate group and not elsewhere. Such marriages are usually defined by reference to the kinship relation which unites the two groups concerned. Thus often marriage with a particular cross-cousin (commonly a man with his mother's brother's daughter, and so a woman with her father's sister's son) is prescribed. In such cases it is important to remember, as I stressed in the last chapter, that in societies with classificatory kinship terminologies and in which groups are based on unilineal descent, specific kinship terms may denote, not just one specific kinsman or kinswoman but a whole category of relatives, of varying degrees of genealogical nearness and sometimes of different generations. Thus, for example, in some patrilineal societies the term which we translate 'mother's brother's daughter' may refer to almost all of the women who are members of one's mother's patrilineal descent group; in other words, to the daughters of all the men who are called 'mother's brother' or (more likely) 'male mother'. And these men may make up practically the whole of the mother's clan. Of course the women thus designated 'mother's brother's daughters' will include the relative whom we should call the 'real' mother's brother's daughter. But they will include a great many other and more distant relatives as well. In considering prescriptive marriage systems it is particularly important to keep in mind the essential 'group' reference of many kinship terms in cultures in which unilineal descent is important.

In societies in which social groups are formed on this basis, an important consequence of prescribed marriage of this type is the establishment of enduring relationships between the separate groups concerned, one group being bound to take, the other to receive, its women from the other. Where *all* marriages are prescribed in such ways, then the marriage system reflects the social organization of the society itself, and neither can be understood without reference to the other.

But in most societies there is no such obligation to choose a mate from a specific category of kin, though in some, including many African ones, marriage with certain categories of kin is socially approved, and may be practised to a greater or lesser extent. Where such preferential marriages do occur more or less widely they may have important social consequences. The Lovedu, a patrilineal Bantu people of South Africa, afford a good example of a preferential marriage system. Among them marriage between a man and his 'mother's brother's daughter' is very much approved. The Lovedu themselves see the situation somewhat like this. A man marries with the cattle which have been received from the marriage of his sister: since they were received for her, they are in a sense 'her' cattle. This gives her a sort of proprietory right over her brother's wife (who was married with 'her' cattle) and her brother's children by that wife. Because of this she can claim one of his daughters as a wife for her son. Thus her son marries his mother's brother's daughter, and the latter marries her father's sister's son. Seen in this way, what is stressed is the link between siblings, especially that between a man and his 'cattle-linked' sister.[1]

But structurally more important is the inter-group aspect of the relationship. If this kind of cross-cousin marriage is carried on over a number of generations, as it sometimes is, it must involve a more or less permanent relationship between the separate descent groups concerned. Thus any one Lovedu lineage will stand in one of two

[1] Krige, E. J. and J. D., *The Realm of a Rain Queen*, Oxford, 1943.

kinds of relationship to every other lineage with which it has affinal connections. To some it will be related as a group which gives away women and receives cattle for them; to others as a group which receives women and gives away cattle for them. And this relationship may be sustained for several generations. So cross-cousin marriage among the Lovedu may be seen as a means to the social integration of the whole Lovedu community. For it serves to create and perpetuate affinal alliances between the separate groups which make up the society.

In many matrilineal societies, too, cross-cousin marriage is approved or permitted. The Ashanti of Ghana are an example, as are the Trobriand Islanders of the Western Pacific. Here also it may have important social implications. Thus an Ashanti or Trobriand father, if he arranges for his daughter to marry his sister's son (who in a matrilineal society is his heir), provides that his daughter at least will have some share in the property he bequeaths. And if he obtains his sister's daughter as a wife for his son (who accordingly marries his father's sister's daughter), then his property and status, which by the rule of matrilineal inheritance pass to her brother (i.e. his sister's son), may in the next generation return to his grandson in the male line of descent. For his patrilineal grandson is also his sister's son's sister's son. This may sound obscure, but it can easily be seen by anyone who likes to work it out with pencil and paper.

This is the nearest I shall approach to Malinowski's 'kinship algebra'. I now say a little more about the different implications of marriage in patrilineal and matrilineal societies respectively. As I remarked earlier, the distinction between patrilineality and matrilineality is by no means a sharp one; it is very much a matter of emphasis. Although in a particular society one line may be the most emphasized, almost always some social significance attaches also to descent in the other line. The vital question is: what is one or the other line used for? And we have seen that either line may be utilized for such important purposes as the formation of territorial corporate groups, the organizing of associations for cult or other activities, and the transmission of property or status. I noted, also, that such institutions as the levirate and ghost marriage are characteristic of patrilineal societies. They are not found in matrilineal societies, for where a man's property and group membership are transmitted not through his son but through his sister's son, then his fecundity is less important to his own group. For the same reason polygyny is less usual in matrilineal societies except, sometimes, in the case of chiefs or other important people.

But the most important differences between marriage in patrilineal

129

societies and in matrilineal ones relate to the rule of residence on marriage. In societies in which the basic social units are exogamous agnatic clans or lineages, that is, where the kinship bonds that hold the group together are through men, it is usual for husbands to remain in their own groups after they marry, and for wives to leave theirs and join their husbands'. Thus after a woman is married, she tends to be more or less (though rarely completely) cut off from her natal group. She becomes instead a permanent member of her husband's group, and as we have seen she may continue to be so even after her husband's death. Such marriages may be called patrilocal (regarded from the point of view of the children of the marriage) or virilocal (regarded from the point of view of the spouses, since residence is with the husband and his group). This rule of residence is characteristic of most patrilineal peoples throughout the world. But in matrilineal societies a woman usually continues to live with her own matrilineal group after she marries, and her husband comes to live with her, or at least he spends a good deal of time with her. This kind of marriage may be called matrilocal, or perhaps better, uxorilocal, since the married pair set up house in the wife's group. But it is essential to such systems that the husband does not sever his connection with his own matrilineal group. For it is in that group that he is a person of importance, with authority over his sisters and their children, who may hope to inherit from him. Among some matrilineal peoples a rich or powerful man may take his wife home to live with him, and in others a man may be allowed to take his wife to his own place after a certain time, perhaps when his younger children reach adolescence. But in most matrilineal societies uxorilocal residence on marriage is the general rule.

In such societies this rule has important consequences for the status of the husband, and especially for the kind of relationship he has with his wife and with his sisters respectively. First, while a husband and father in a patrilineal, virilocal society has full authority (subject only to the overriding authority of *his* father or of another senior agnate) over his wife and her children, the position of the husband living uxorilocally in a matrilineal society is very different. Although he possesses some domestic authority over his wife and children, he generally has to share this with his wife's brothers, to whom his children really belong. In his wife's group he is a kind of 'outsider', admitted only on sufferance. His real authority lies not over his own wife and children, but over his sisters and their children in his home village. So a husband's position is ambiguous in such societies; the children who belong to his line and who will inherit from him, and the children whom he begets and (to begin with at any rate) lives with and cares for, are not the same, as they are in patrilineal societies. This dualism sometimes leads to conflict. Ethnographic accounts of matrilineal societies, like Malinowski's description of the Trobriand Islanders, sometimes refer to men's concern to favour their own children, to whom they ordinarily have close bonds of affection, at the expense of their sister's children, who are their legal wards. The matrilineal Dobuans of Melanesia, described by Fortune, aptly describe the husband as 'boundary man', for he occupies a precarious borderline between two different social worlds, in one of which he is master, in the other a distrusted stranger.

A further consequence of uxorilocal marriage in matrilineal societies is that the sibling bond between brother and sister tends to be much stronger than the husband–wife bond, while in patrilineal societies the reverse is very often true. This is because in a matrilineal society a man never really relinquishes his rights over his sister; even after her marriage she and her children remain subject to his authority. In a patrilineal and virilocal society, on the other hand, the wife is more or less completely cut off from her brother and other close kin, and she passes wholly under the authority of her husband and his agnates.

It might seem on the face of it that marriage in a matrilineal, uxorilocal society must be very much less stable than marriage in a patrilineal, virilocal one. All other things being equal, no doubt it would be. But all other things are very rarely equal, especially in human affairs, and the stability of marriage (however we define the terms 'stability' and 'marriage') is conditioned by many other factors besides the rule of residence and the pattern of domestic authority. It cannot in any case be assumed that in all societies there is one standardized relationship called marriage, which is sufficiently identical wherever it occurs to justify straightforward comparison from one society to another. We have seen in this chapter that there may be many and various forms of legitimized sexual relations. Cross-cultural comparison is perfectly legitimate and useful (indeed it is implicit in the very words we use to denote the phenomena we study), but it must be engaged in with caution. Nevertheless it does seem that in the nature of the case matriliny with uxorilocal marriage must imply a certain instability. For it divides between two sometimes opposed roles (that of the father and that of the mother's brother) a complex of rights, obligations and affections which in patrilineal societies are united in a single role, that of the father. And it is noteworthy that in many matrilineal societies there is a tendency for uxorilocal marriage to become virilocal—I remarked that chiefs and other important persons tend to marry virilocally in many such societies—while no marked contrary tendency has ever been recorded for patrilineal societies. It seems likely that most men, if they had a choice in the matter, would prefer to live in a patrilineally organized society and marry virilocally. It is significant that matrilineal, uxorilocal societies in fact form a small and decreasing proportion of the peoples of the world.

So far I have been discussing marriage, mainly in the context of small-scale, pre-industrial societies, as in various ways involving whole groups of people. Recognition of this essential group concern makes sense of certain kinds of union which at first sight seem strange to Western observers. We saw that even in matrilineal societies, in which women are not handed over from one group to another, group attachments may be highly important, although in such societies men's loyalties (though not women's) are divided between two groups. I now turn to consider in more detail some of the institutionalized relationships between particular categories of individuals to which marriage gives rise. In these relationships the fact that people are members of groups is, of course, still important. Indeed, strictly speaking there are no such things as relationships between groups, there are only relationships between individual people. The important point is that in these inter-personal relationships people's group affiliations may be more or less relevant. But we now slightly alter our focus. In the rest of this chapter I consider not the extent and kinds of group involvement that marriage implies, but rather the ways in which the various categories of affines concerned think of and behave towards one another. We shall see that these ways are very largely conditioned by the various kinds of group affiliation which I have discussed.

To begin with, what of the relationship between husbands and wives? First, in all societies known to us (but perhaps least in modern Western societies) the physiologically determined differences of role which distinguish men from women are associated with important social and cultural differences. Almost always there is a well-marked division of labour between the sexes; men do some kinds of work, women do other kinds. The fact that women bear and suckle children obviously tends to tie them to the home, so it is not surprising that in most societies child care, food preparation and, often, the cultivation of food crops are women's work. Correspondingly, the facts that men are usually physically more powerful and are not immobilized for considerable periods by childbearing and by the care of small children, usually means that such heavier tasks as hunting, fighting, the building of houses and stockades, as well as the tougher parts of cultivation like bush-clearing and the breaking up of new ground, and the care of livestock (where there are any), fall to them. The details of the division vary from culture to culture: for example in some pastoral East African societies women may milk the cows, in others they are strictly forbidden to do so. But always there are institutionalized role differences between the sexes, and always at least some of these are related to the physical differences between them.

Associated with these differences of role there are, usually, marked differences of status. Almost always, as far as interpersonal relations are concerned, a man claims superior status to his wife. He usually expects her to be (or at least to appear to be) submissive, humble and obedient, and in many societies he claims the right to beat her if she is not. Of course there are exceptions. In matrilineal, uxorilocal societies, although as a man a husband is his wife's superior, his power over her is limited by the rival authority of her brothers. And among some non-Western peoples (certain West African societies, for example) women have acquired considerable independence and power by participating in retail trade. Among the Ibo of Nigeria women have their own societies, manage their own affairs and hold their own property, which is quite separate from that of their husbands. If a man displeases his wife, for example by taking up with another woman, she may refuse to cook any food for him, and apparently there is little he can do about this. But this is an exception to the general pattern. None the less, as will appear in more detail in Chapter 14, the impact of Western ideas and in particular the advent of a cash economy are hastening the process of female emancipation in almost all of the simpler societies. But even so, in most of them the stress is still on men's rights over and in regard to women, rather than on women's rights over men, although in all societies she has some. I should add that I am speaking here only of those rights which are formally recognized and institutionalized. It is not only in Western-type societies where women have been emancipated that they have ways of making their influence felt.

It is always useful to consider institutionalized social relationships as involving, among other things, reciprocal rights and obligations. So regarded, the rights which husbands may have over their wives are of three kinds. First, there are domestic and economic rights, that is, rights to the products of a woman's labour. These rights are generally held by the girl's family, headed by her father or brother, until her marriage, at which point they are transferred wholly (in patrilineal societies) or partly (in matrilineal ones) to her husband. Secondly there are sexual rights, usually reserved, though not used, by the girl's parents or brothers until she is married, then conveyed to her husband. And thirdly, there are rights over the woman's offspring, actual or potential. This is plainly a different right from that of sexual access. In patrilineal societies a husband possesses both of these rights; in a matrilineal society he possesses one but not the other. In this context, as in other social contexts where rights over persons are in issue, it is sometimes useful to follow the Roman jurists in distinguishing rights over another person as a person, that is, to demand that he or she behave in certain ways (rights *in personam*), from rights in regard to someone as against all other persons, that is, rights over him or her as a thing or possession (rights *in rem*). Often in human relations both kinds of rights are associated, but sometimes one kind is stressed, sometimes the other.

I turn now to the relationship between co-wives. In those polygynous societies in which a man and his several wives live together in what has been called a compound family, relations between co-wives are often friendly and co-operative. But sometimes they are not, and it is obvious enough that the relationship is potentially one of conflict and rivalry. In such a situation women may see themselves as being in competition for their husband's affection and attention. Ethnographers have provided detailed reports of jealousy between co-wives from many polygynous societies in Africa and elsewhere. Professor Maquet says that the very word for co-wife *means* 'jealousy' among the Ruanda people of East-Central Africa.[1] In societies where a woman's most important social role is to bear and rear children for her husband and his lineage, and where barrenness, like other misfortune, is usually blamed on sorcery or witchcraft by one's enemies, it is inevitable that when one wife is childless and another not, grave suspicions of foul play often arise. Sometimes co-wives accuse one another of sorcery and witchcraft, and this may lead to ill-feeling, assault, even murder and suicide. Such cases have been recorded from many polygynous societies.

The disruptive potentialities of polygyny are institutionally recognized in many cultures. Sometimes, as among some Southern Bantu people, wives are hierarchically graded, a senior wife having much higher status than her juniors. This tends to make conflict less likely, since competition is only possible between people who think of themselves as in some sense equals. Very often different wives are maintained in different homesteads, perhaps some distance apart. Almost always each wife has her separate house and domestic equipment. It is a strict rule in most polygynous households that the husband must be careful to bestow his attentions equally and impartially among all his wives. So the potential instability of polygynous marriage is quite explicitly recognized in most societies

[1] Maquet, J. J., *The Premise of Inequality in Ruanda*, London, 1961.

where it is practised, and often there are institutionalized means to counteract it, or at least to reduce it. If these do not always work, this is a deficiency they share with all human institutions.

The relationship between a man and his parents-in-law, like that between a woman and her husband's parents, is almost always one of marked respect, often of constraint. This is understandable when the difference of generation is taken into account, combined (in societies where marriage is exogamous) with the fact that one's parents-in-law belong to a different group from one's own. Often, to begin with at any rate, they are regarded as strangers, perhaps as potential enemies. Yet at the same time a man should treat them as friends and benefactors, for they have provided him with the inestimably valuable gift of a wife. So the relationship, like so many social relationships, is an ambivalent one: although amity and mutual politeness are generally prescribed, often there is a strong undercurrent of antagonism.

One way of resolving this contradiction is to impose a degree of formality on the relationship, so that each party to it must conform to a strictly prescribed pattern of behaviour. This way of dealing with the situation is common in many societies: the rigid pattern of behaviour prescribed makes argument and disagreement less likely, and so reduces the danger of the relationship breaking down altogether. This is why in many patrilineal societies a man must treat his wife's father with extreme deference, and must constantly give him gifts and assistance of various kinds. Although he may be said to be 'like a son' to his wife's father, there can be no real intimacy between them.

The same considerations explain why in many patrilineal societies a man must avoid all direct contact with his wife's mother; he should not address her directly, and sometimes he should not even see her, although he may be allowed to communicate with her and to send her presents through a third party. There are even societies in which a man may not mention his mother-in-law's name, or even use any word the syllables of which resemble those of her name. The explanation of this is not that men dislike their wives' mothers, and do not wish to have anything to do with them (though no doubt this is sometimes so). In fact the avoidance is a way in which a man shows respect to someone who belongs to another group and who is of the opposite sex, but who is none the less closely connected to him through her daughter, whom he has married. Avoidance relationships both express this respect, and at the same time emphasize the separateness of a man from his wife's kin. It stresses especially his separateness from his wife's mother, who is not only in another

135

group, but is also in a different and often sexually prohibited generation. In its extremer forms, as in the name avoidance custom which I have just mentioned, we are dealing with ritual behaviour, and here, as elsewhere where symbolism is concerned, it is appropriate to ask what it is that is being symbolically said. In the case of the avoidance custom we have been discussing, it seems that what is being symbolically stressed is the fact that while mother-in-law and son-in-law are close, yet they are separate; and this separateness, no less than the affinal link between the two groups concerned, has to be expressed and sustained. But often, as the parties concerned get to know each other better, and especially after the birth of children, to whom both groups are kin, there is no longer any need for these precautionary avoidances. Thus in many societies the mother-in-law avoidance relationship declines in rigour with the passage of time.

Though a relationship of respect between men and their wives' mothers is usual in many societies, a rigorous avoidance rule is commoner in patrilineal than it is in matrilineal ones. This is because in the latter, unlike the former, a man must live at least for part of his life in his wife's mother's group. And sustained avoidance would be impracticable in the round of trivial contacts which make up everyday social life. And if we ask why we do not find a similar avoidance rule between a woman and her husband's father (we always do find that an attitude of respect is prescribed), the answer seems to be that for women an attitude of humility and respect for men, especially older men, is almost always demanded, while no such attitude is demanded from men towards women. Thus although a woman's relationship with her husband's father may be characterized by respect and even awe, it does not have that ambivalent quality with which the avoidance relationship between men and their wives' mothers is adapted to deal. Here as elsewhere in the context of marriage and affinity the differential status of the sexes emerges as an important factor.

When we turn to the relationship between affines of the same generation, a man and his wife's siblings and a woman and her husband's, we usually find the same kind of ambivalence, especially where local grouping is based on unilineal descent. On the one hand there is 'strangerhood' and incipient hostility; on the other good manners, affection and co-operation are usually demanded. But here the relationship is generally easier than in the case of parents-in-law and their children's spouses, for the parties to it are of the same generation and not of adjoining ones. So in some sense they are equals. In many, though not in all, societies a man can marry his wife's sister, and in some, as we saw, a woman may be taken over by the brother of her husband if the latter dies. Often in such societies there is a relationship of easy familiarity between affines of the same generation and opposite sex, for they are potential spouses. But this degree of equality may be modified when a son inherits his father's status as father-in-law. For then he must be treated with the respect and deference which are appropriate to the senior affine. So there may be a marked element of constraint in the relationship between brothers-in-law, who may be expected to treat one another with extreme formality and politeness, and to exchange gifts from time to time.

The ambivalent attitude towards affines often found in patrilineally organized societies is neatly summed up in the phrase used by the Nyoro to refer to their affines. They call them 'the people who make us feel ashamed'—ashamed, that is, if they behave with undue familiarity towards their in-laws, or fail to maintain the standards of formal politeness required. Similar usages are found in many such societies. I noted in the last chapter that this characteristically ambivalent and constrained relationship between affines is sometimes carried over into the next generation, where (in a patrilineal, virilocal society) it may also characterize the mother's brother-sister's son relationship. For although a man's mother's brother is his parent's sibling and so a close blood relation, he is also a member of another group, a group from which *his* group (that is, his father's group) took a wife. So, as a member of his father's lineage, a man may think of his mother's brother as being in some sense and in some degree what we should call an affine, as well as being a close matrilateral kinsman. Here is another case of the inapplicability of Western kinship concepts in many other cultures. We tend to think of kinship and affinity as mutually exclusive categories, but they are not so in all cultures. The anthropologist's task is to understand the relationships centring on kinship and marriage, like all other social and cultural institutions, in terms of the categories of the culture he is studying, not simply to impose his own.

In Chapter 14 I consider some of the ways in which the impact of Western values and institutions has altered traditional kinds of marriage. Here I have tried to show that in most non-Western societies marriage concerns groups of people as well as, perhaps sometimes more than, individuals. It may have been also thus in some Western societies not so very long ago. I have discussed some of the various forms which marriage takes in different cultures, as well as some of the social institutions associated with it, and I have tried to show that these forms could not be properly—or even at all—understood unless full account is taken of their group reference.

Many errors have arisen from Westerners' attempts to interpret so-called 'primitive' types of marriage in terms of modern Western ideas of what marriage is or ought to be. The kinds of marriage discussed in this chapter can only be understood if they are considered in the context of the societies and cultures in which they occur. Unless we see them as far as possible as the people themselves see them, we simply interpose our own unanalysed preconceptions between ourselves and the social reality which we are seeking to comprehend. And this leads not to understanding but to misunderstanding.

SHORT READING LIST

EVANS-PRITCHARD, E. E., *Kinship and Marriage among the Nuer*, Oxford, 1951.

FORTUNE, R. F., *Sorcerers of Dobu*, London, 1932.

GOODY, J. (editor), *The Developmental Cycle in Domestic Groups; Cambridge Papers in Social Anthropology*, No. 1, Cambridge, 1958.

HART, C. W. M., and PILLING, A. R., *The Tiwi of North Australia*, New York, 1960.

HOMANS, G. C., and SCHNEIDER, D. M., *Marriage, Authority and Final Causes*, Glencoe (Ill.), 1955.

KRIGE, E. J. and J. D., *The Realm of a Rain Queen*, London, 1943.

MAIR, L. P., *African Marriage and Social Change*, in Phillips, A. (editor), *Survey of African Marriage and Family Life*, London, 1953.

MALINOWSKI, B., *The Sexual Life of Savages*, London, 1929.

NEEDHAM, RODNEY, *Structure and Sentiment*, Chicago, 1962.

SCHAPERA, I., *Married Life in an African Tribe*, Oxford, 1940.

9

Social Control: Political Organization

(1)

THERE COULD BE no coherent social life unless the social
relationships which bind people together were at least to some degree
orderly, institutionalized and predictable. The only alternative to
order is chaos. To maintain an orderly system of social relations
people have to be subjected to some degree of compulsion; they
cannot, all the time, do exactly as they like. For often self-interest
may incite behaviour incompatible with the common good, and so
it is that in every society some rules, some kinds of constraint on
people's behaviour, are acknowledged and, on the whole, adhered
to. These rules and the means by which they are enforced differ
greatly from society to society, but always they more or less effectively secure some degree of social order. So a social anthropologist
who wishes to understand how a particular community works must
ask what are the norms, the rules, which on the whole sustain social
order, what is their range and scope, and how are they enforced?
By asking questions of these kinds in the societies they study, and by
seeking answers in terms of the theoretical interests discussed in the
first part of this book, social anthropologists have greatly broadened
our notions of how it is most useful to understand such concepts as
'politics' and 'law'.

There are many societies which lack rulers on the Western pattern,
but it would be a mistake to assume that their members live in a state
of anarchy; often there are no judges or courts which could be compared with those familiar in Western countries, but this does not
imply a state of complete lawlessness. Some sort of social stability on
a national or tribal basis may be achieved otherwise than through
constituted political authorities, and conformity to rules may be
sufficiently ensured by other means than the familiar Western
machinery of police-courts and judges.

139

There is not much point in distinguishing too precisely between the fields of political organization and law. As so often in social science, the distinction is not so much between 'things' as between ways of looking at things. Both politics and law are concerned with social control. When we speak of political organization we are thinking in particular of the maintenance of ordered relations between different categories and groups of people, over a social field wider than that which is implied by each of the component categories or groups taken separately. This wider social field may be what we call a society or (following Emmet) a social aggregate. Or it may entail relations between separate societies, whether these be tribal groups, nations or states. Thus the external social relations of any group which is being studied also fall within the sphere which it is useful to call 'political'.

Usually, though not invariably, the political unit can be defined territorially. So when we speak of a political system or a political organization we are usually referring to certain kinds of social relationships within a particular area, and this territorial reference is generally taken to be an important part of the definition of a political unit. When, on the other hand, we speak of 'law' and 'social sanctions' we are thinking primarily of the behaviour of individual people and of the relationships between them, and of the social factors which, by and large, ensure their conformity to the accepted rules of the society. So the difference between the two fields is mainly one of emphasis: political institutions must have a legal or sanctioning aspect, just as some rules of interpersonal behaviour and some social norms have political implications. But these two approaches to the problem of social control imply rather different interests, and raise separate problems. In this chapter I deal with political relations; in the next I consider the field of law and social sanctions.

I have suggested that the familiar categories of Western culture need re-examination before they can profitably be applied to unfamiliar social systems. This is so especially in the political sphere. So it will be useful to start with to say a little about the concepts of power and authority which political activity in particular implies. Although these two concepts are associated, they are not the same. The dictionary defines power as 'the ability to do something or anything, or to act upon a person or thing'. So conceived, power is a fundamental concept in social science, indeed in all human thinking, for the very idea of causality implies it. We commonly conceive of causes as producing their effects because they have the 'power' to do so. And we tend to think of this power as a kind of latent ability to alter the existing state of things, such as we are aware of in our own psychic experience. Thus (as Hume showed two centuries ago) power is not something we observe in nature; it is rather a projection into nature of a category which derives from our own awareness. In a very fundamental sense power is human power, and human power is the ability to produce intended effects, that is, to carry out one's will on oneself, on other people, or on things. Since it implies that the end which is brought about is foreseen, the notion of power is essentially teleological. When we say that a man has power we mean that he can do what he wants to do, and when we say that he has social power we mean that in any social relationship he can make another person do what he wants him to do. Thus social power is an aspect of very many interpersonal relationships; it is not restricted to those ordinarily called political, though perhaps it is specially characteristic of them. So we must seek other criteria besides the exercise of social power in order to delimit the special field of political relations.

Unlike power, authority implies right: a robber may have the power to rob, but he has no authority to do so. And right is a concept, an idea; it exists only in people's minds. It is something that people acknowledge, and it exists only by being acknowledged. So political authority is more than just the ability to exercise power; it implies also that the right to do so is publicly acknowledged. It therefore involves the existence of a shared system of values, which include the acceptance of the political and social institutions through which the authority is exercised. Since people generally accept things on some ground or other, a classification of these grounds provides a way of distinguishing different types of authority. The German sociologist Max Weber propounded such a classification; I return to it below.

The exercise of some form of legitimized or authorized social power, or the possibility of its exercise, appears generally to be a condition of the maintenance of social order. And usually an important concern of socially acknowledged authority is with the maintenance of orderly systems of social relationships. When I speak of social authority, then, I mean the right, vested in some category or categories of persons by all or most of the members of a society, to make decisions, issue orders and apply sanctions in matters affecting other members of the society. Usually such matters will either directly or indirectly concern the maintenance of social order.

It is even more difficult to give a clear and useful meaning to the term 'political'. It is usually defined as having to do with the state, the state being defined, for example by the Shorter Oxford English Dictionary, as 'the body politic as organized for supreme civil rule and government'. Like so many other social concepts which have grown up in the context of Western culture, this definition is too narrow to be useful when it is applied to some of the kinds of societies

141

which social anthropologists study. Peoples like the Australian aborigines, for example, or the Nuer of the southern Sudan, have nothing which could be any stretch of the imagination be termed a state. What we need are criteria for identifying certain kinds, or rather aspects, of social phenomena, and we know that these are found even where the body politic is not organized in this way.

Radcliffe-Brown's formulation, based on the classical definitions used by Max Weber and others, is more useful, though we shall see that it is not quite adequate either. In the Preface to *African Political Systems* he wrote that political organization is concerned with 'the maintenance or establishment of social order, within a territorial framework, by the organized exercise of coercive authority through the use, or the possibility of use, of physical force'. Now this definition employs two different criteria. First, reference is made to the end to which political activity is directed, the regulation and control of the social order within a certain territory. And secondly, the means whereby this is achieved are brought in; the organized exercise of authority, backed by force. Now social anthropologists can make good use of the first of these criteria. For some degree of social order is attained in every society, and social anthropologists are interested in finding out how this is done. That is, they are concerned to identify and analyse the social institutions through which order is maintained on a territorial or tribal basis and, we might add, through which relationships with other territorial or tribal groups are created and maintained. We need not be disconcerted by the fact that some such institutions, like the blood feud (which I discuss below) in certain societies, are not what we ordinarily think of as 'political'. After all, our interest is in the realities of social life, not primarily in the names we use to identify these realities; though we have to use words with care, lest the reality be obscured. Indeed, when we are discussing political phenomena in many small-scale societies, there is much to be said for speaking of the political *aspect* of certain social institutions, rather than of specifically political institutions. For often institutions which have political importance are socially significant in a number of other contexts as well.

But the second of Radcliffe-Brown's criteria, the organized exercise of authority backed by force, at once leads to difficulty when it is applied to some of the societies which anthropologists study. We can certainly speak of authority and force when we are considering centralized states like those with which most of us are familiar in the Western world, with their kings, parliaments, courts, judges and police forces. Many of the smaller-scale societies which social anthropologists study are of this type, though usually their political organization is less elaborate. But some of them are not. In such tribes as the Nuer, or the Tallensi of northern Ghana, there are (or were) no specialized political functionaries, and there is no organized structure of authority backed by physical force. (This is not to say that physical force is not exercised in such societies.) None the less, these societies do possess some sort of order and structural continuity; they may be shown to have a political structure. The facts that political authority may be widely diffused, for example among grades of elders or lineage heads, and that it may be backed by religious or magical sanctions rather than by organized physical force, do not mean that such authority is lacking, though it may be relatively unspecialized and very hard to identify.

Even where no political authorities at all can be found, as in some segmentary societies, the ends which I have defined as political may be brought about through the interplay of other institutions, not overtly political. We shall see later how this may happen. Here, as elsewhere, the classical conceptual apparatus of Western culture does not quite fit much of the unfamiliar social material which ethnography has revealed. In determining what we shall regard as political, we shall do best to retain as definitive the notion of the end attained, while keeping an open mind as to how it is attained. For in every society some sort of internal order is secured on a tribal or territory-wide basis, external relations are provided for, and decisions in regard to these matters are taken in accordance with generally accepted rules. The political problem is how, in a society being studied, these things are brought about.

It can only be solved by identifying and describing the various social institutions through which the ends which I have called political are accomplished. Where categories of persons with specifically political functions can be identified (as is not always the case), then the nature of the roles involved, and the bases upon which the authority vested in them rests, have to be investigated. Since societies vary greatly in regard to the means by which political ends are achieved in them, the first thing to do is to formulate some sort of simple classification which will enable us to distinguish between different types of polity.

In recent years typologies of increasing precision have been put forward, usually employing explicitly or implicitly three kinds of criteria. The first criterion is usually the degree of centralization: is there some central authority which (or who) is acknowledged by all the component groups in the society? Or is there no such head, the society consisting simply of a number of distinct groups or segments, the relations between which themselves make up the political system?

The second criterion is the degree to which political function is specialized. Is there a person, or are there persons, vested with specifically political authority, that is, with the right to issue orders and administer sanctions in a certain territory, such activity being generally directed, and seen to be directed, towards the maintenance of the existing social order, and being backed as a rule by the threat of physical force? Or are there no such roles in the society? This criterion is not the same as the first one. For it is possible to have specifically political authorities in a society which is non-centralized, in which there is no *over-all* political authority, and there are some societies in which ritual or religious authority is acknowledged on a tribe-wide basis, but little or no political authority is attributed to the central figure.

The third criterion concerns the basis on which political authority is allocated. It may be hereditary or elective, or a combination of the two: it may attach to membership in a particular line of descent, or to seniority in a lineage or an age set.

Now the trouble with these criteria is that, except for the first one, they do not permit of any rigid classification into classes that are mutually exclusive; it is very much a matter of 'more or less'. Specialization of political function is a question of degree, and in a given society authority may be allocated on more grounds than one, and to more than one category of person. Even with the first criterion it is by no means always plain sailing. Apart from the question whether it can always be said that the authority that is centralized is political (and not ritual), a great deal depends on the unit which is taken as definitive; what it is that one takes as constituting the society or the 'social aggregate'. Is a society consisting of a number of separate chiefdoms, each with its own internal 'centralized' structure but acknowledging no common head, a centralized society or an uncentralized, 'acephalous' one? There are many such societies in Africa. Plainly it depends on one's point of view. If one is thinking in terms of each political unit taken separately then they are 'centralized'; if one is thinking in terms of the whole tribal or cultural group, it is not. And, it may be asked, will even a slight degree of political ascendancy on the part of one of the constituent units change the whole into a centralized society, and if so *how* slight a degree?

These questions are important, but they are really questions about classification rather than about the nature of social organization itself. By and large the centralized–uncentralized distinction is a useful one, so long as it is remembered that one is not dealing with a simple dichotomy: the two types represent poles which allow for many intermediate positions; they are not mutually exclusive categories. It is broadly true that some societies do possess something approximating to a centralized government and executive, of which Western-type states are extreme cases, while others possess no such institutions at any level, and so may fairly be described as segmentary or acephalous. It is convenient here to consider first polities of the latter type, which in their various forms are the least familiar to Western readers. Centralized systems, which themselves may vary greatly in structure, are discussed in the second part of this chapter.

Very broadly, four types of these politically uncentralized societies may be distinguished. First there are those very simply organized communities, whose members usually live by collecting or hunting, in which the largest social units are co-operating groups of families or close kin, and in which there is no formal grouping of any kind above this level. From the point of view of political organization there is not a great deal to be said about such peoples, though of course there is much of interest to be learned about them and their way of life. Usually such authority as exists is vested in the senior members of these small family groups, and is of very limited scope. Examples of such societies are those of the South African bushmen, the pygmoid peoples of central Africa and South-east Asia, and the Australian aborigines.

Secondly, there are some societies which are made up of separate village communities, related to one another by various economic and kinship ties, but administered internally by more or less formally appointed councils. Whether it is useful to speak of political officials in such societies depends on the degree to which membership in these councils is formally based, and to which their members have specialized political functions. The grounds of eligibility to membership of such councils may vary; sometimes descent is relevant (for example membership of 'good family'), but more usually any kind of social pre-eminence, such as outstanding wealth or ability, forms an acceptable qualification. Such societies, which include several important and advanced West African peoples such as the Ibo and the Yakö, are often quite complex and show a wide range of economic specialization.

The third of our broad categories comprises those societies in which political control is largely conceived in terms of an age-set system. This type of organization is especially characteristic of certain East African peoples, but the allocation to older men of an increasing say in public affairs is common in many societies. The principle is given its most formal expression in societies such as those of the Masai and Nandi in East Africa, where an age-set organization is combined with the allocation of authority on the basis of seniority.

Such a system provides not only for the formation of co-operating groups and for relations between these groups, but also for the exercise of at least a limited amount of political authority over groups wider than those based on kinship. Let us see how it works.

The basic rule is that all the men born within a certain number of consecutive years are admitted into one set. The number of years during which men who have reached the appropriate age (this varies in different societies but is usually around adolescence) may be admitted to the same set varies; it may be as little as six or seven years or as long as fifteen. At the end of this period, recruitment to that particular set is closed, and recruitment to a new set begins. Admission to a set usually involves some initiation ritual, often including circumcision or other bodily mutilation. A chief effect of this ritual is to mark the individual's emergence from childhood, and his assumption of full tribal membership. These sets are named, and a man, together with a large group of his fellows of about the same age as himself, remains in the same set all his life. Usually the members of an age-set are bound together by a network of reciprocal rights and obligations, and they generally maintain close and friendly contact throughout their lives.

In most societies in which age-sets are important, every man is not only a member of a particular set, but also at any given time he occupies, with his age-mates, a particular grade. These grades are clearly distinguished from one another, so that a man can only occupy one grade at a time. A typical series of grades (after childhood) is junior warriorhood, senior warriorhood, junior elderhood, and senior elderhood. Specific rules are associated with each grade; thus warriors fight and defend the tribe from attack, elders settle disputes, make important decisions, and intercede with the ancestral ghosts.

The essential thing about this kind of system is that the sets move through the various grades as complete units. This means that a whole group of people—all the members of a particular set—change their grade, and so their social status, all at once. The transitions from youth to vigorous manhood, then to middle age, and finally to old age, do not form a gradual and imperceptible process, as they do in Western society: they take place in a series of 'jumps'. And people do not make these jumps one by one, as individuals; they make them as members of large and more or less corporate groups.

The system appears to have worked well in traditional times. But the suppression of tribal fighting by European governments and, often, their direct opposition to age-set systems, as well as the increased individualism consequent on the introduction of a cash economy, have led to its breakdown in most areas. What this type of

146

organization did was to provide for the establishment of effective, co-operating social groups, not on the basis of membership of a territorial chiefdom (such peoples do not have 'chiefs'), nor on the basis of unilineal kinship (descent is relatively unimportant in such societies), but simply on the basis of age.

The social importance of age-set systems can be summed up under four broad heads. First, they provide a means of establishing corporate groups, whose members while they are in the warrior grades may form a powerful standing army. Second, they provide for the formal transition of individuals from one clearly-marked social status to another. Such transitions, with appropriate ritual, are common in many societies (compare the graduation ceremonies, church confirmations, and so on of many Western countries). But where, as in societies organized in age-sets, the formal transfer from one grade to another is a matter of the greatest importance to everybody in the community, then they naturally assume major importance.

The third important function of an age-set system is to provide for the organized exercise of at least some political authority. Members of the senior grades sometimes constitute more or less informal councils of elders, whose importance as decision-makers may be backed by weighty sanctions. It may be believed that only they can intercede effectively on the community's behalf with the ancestral ghosts, upon whose goodwill the well-being of the whole group may be held to depend. Also, as a rule, the important decision as to when the next 'general post' is to take place can only be made by them. Fourthly, an age-set system provides a means of establishing social contact, even some sense of tribal unity and cohesion, over a wider range than would otherwise be possible. Often age-sets are organized on the basis of whole communities; they are not confined only to local groups. Sometimes they are even synchronized with the age-sets of neighbouring tribes with similar systems. In this way members of the same age-set may be scattered over considerable areas, and the network of mutual obligations which they acknowledge may be an important determinant of interpersonal behaviour, and so an effective agent of cohesion.

As we might expect, age-sets, which provide for the quick mustering of armed warriors, are especially characteristic of pastoral societies. For pastoralists, unlike agriculturalists, can move quickly from place to place with their property, and since this is naturally mobile it is particularly easy to steal and get away with. This is why an age-set system has developed so extensively among the pastoral Nilo-Hamitic peoples of eastern Africa.

The fourth broad category of uncentralized societies are those in

147

which political functions are effected through groups organized in terms of unilineal descent. In Chapter 7 we saw how quite large co-operating groups could be formed by means of this principle, either patrilineally (most usually) or matrilineally. There are no specifically political offices in such societies; there are no 'chiefs', although older men may exercise a limited amount of authority. The groups themselves may be in a state of what has been called 'balanced opposition'. This is to say, the members of a group defined by reference to a particular genealogical level of segmentation may express their group unity and identity, in a particular social context, by reference to other similar segments of the same order of segmentation. Thus all the members of a group descended agnatically from a particular man (say) five generations back may see themselves as a unit as against all the agnatic descendants of that man's brother. Often the groups so established maintain a relationship of actual or potential opposition to one another. This opposition is characteristically expressed in the institution of the blood feud. At the same time, as Gluckman especially has emphasized, these inter-lineage antagonisms are countered by other cross-cutting ties such as those of affinity and matrilateral kinship, so that almost always there are people in opposing groups whose interest it is to seek peaceful resolution of disputes between lineages.[1]

In some lineage-based societies the component lineages are combined in a single, all-embracing system, conceived wholly in terms of the principles of descent and of lineage segmentation. Then the whole community, or at least each of its major sections, can be represented as a huge, all-inclusive lineage. In this, the 'classical' type of lineage society (represented in Africa by the Bedouin and the Nuer), all inter-group relations are conceived in lineage terms. But in other societies organized on a lineage basis, the whole community may be made up of relatively small, distinct descent groups. Although the members of these may be closely bound together by kinship and affinal links and, often, by shared participation in common ritual, they do not think of their inter-group relations solely in terms of unilineal descent. Such systems lack the pyramidal, 'monolithic' quality of systems of the first type. Africa affords many examples of this second kind; among the best known are the Tallensi of northern Ghana, described by Fortes, and the Baluhya of Kenya, described by Wagner.[2] Among the Tallensi members of separate lineages are linked through common participation in earth cults, so that the

[1] Gluckman, Max, *Custom and Conflict in Africa*, Oxford, 1955.
[2] Fortes, M., *The Dynamics of Clanship among the Tallensi*, London, 1945; Wagner, G., *The Bantu of North Kavirondo*, London, 1949.

congregation which attends a particular earth-shrine may not coincide with any lineage group. Also, the bonds of clanship and kinship (which need not involve exact knowledge of genealogical connection) cut across the narrower ties of lineage membership. Sometimes, also, as among the Lugbara of Uganda, lineage heads or 'chiefs' emerge, generally the senior members of their lineages, and to them limited political authority may be ascribed. The point at which a lineage-based society in which specially political office has emerged qualifies for classification as a 'centralized' society is very much a matter of definition and of convenience; I return to this point below.

The institution known as the blood feud is characteristic of lineage-based societies of the former, 'classic' type, where the lineage organization is co-extensive with the whole society and almost all inter-group relationships are conceived in terms of it. It has been best described by Evans-Pritchard for the Nuer of the southern Sudan. By the blood feud anthropologists mean a more or less enduring relationship of violent hostility between two of the component groups in a society. It usually arises in consequence of an act of deliberate or accidental homicide by a member of one group against a member of another, and the primary aim of the injured group is to inflict a reciprocal homicide on the offending group. It is easy to see why the institution is characteristic of societies lacking any (or any effective) central political organization. Where there is an effective central government the feud tends to be suppressed, and inter-group disputes come to be dealt with by the Government, which *qua* government claims the monopoly of force in the territory it rules. The principle of self-help which the blood feud exemplifies is incompatible with the existence of an effective central administration.

Since the blood feud is essentially a group matter, it is plain that it can only occur where there is a high degree of group solidarity. And this is pre-eminently the case where local, corporate groups are formed on the basis of unilineal descent. Among the Nuer one of the most important implications of lineage membership is the obligation to assist one's fellow agnates in a blood feud. It is a further consequence of the group reference of the blood feud that it cannot arise in consequence of a quarrel between very closely related lineages, least of all between members of the same minimal lineage. For if it did both protagonists would have to call upon the same body of kin for support, and the result would be to set all the members of the group in opposition to one another, and so to destroy the very solidarity on which the whole system depends. This is why Cain's murder of Abel might lead to Cain's banishment or even to his death, but it could not lead to a blood feud, for that would destroy the kinship group (in this case the family unit) to which both belonged. Among the Nuer the members of closely related lineages are likely to live fairly near one another, and to depend upon one another for help in herding activities. So an enduring relationship of hostility between them would seriously interfere with the everyday business of life. If a feud did break out, there would be strong pressure to settle it without further bloodshed.

In its classic form, the blood feud is not the same as war, or even vendetta. Some degree of social control is always implicit. The *lex talionis* is always more or less strictly applied, so that a homicide should be avenged only by a reciprocal killing, after which the dispute is supposed to be ended, and reconciliation should take place. Of course, human nature being what it is, this does not always happen, and there is a tendency for feud to turn into vendetta (unrestricted killing between two groups in a society). Again, there is usually some means whereby a feud may be, as it were, nipped in the bud and settled by the payment of compensation instead of by a reciprocal killing. Sometimes cattle may be transferred; sometimes a person may be handed over to replace the person killed. Often, as among the Nuer, there are face-saving institutions through which such settlements may be achieved.

It is evident that in such societies the blood feud is not only effective as a social sanction (for the fear of incurring it may be a powerful incentive to good behaviour), but also it may have considerable political importance as the means through which intergroup hostility is expressed, and the essential values of group awareness and identity reinforced. When these values cease to be paramount, the blood feud decreases in importance and ultimately disappears altogether. There are many formerly lineage-based societies which through conquest, or through the emergence into dominance of one of its constituent lineages, have changed into more or less centralized ones. When this happens, as the central authority increases in strength, the blood feud may come to be at first permissive (that is, it may only be carried out with the ruler's permission), and then proscribed altogether. This has happened in the interlacustrine Bantu states of Uganda, in which it seems that centralized administrations have been imposed upon formerly segmentary communities.

To the question how political order is thought of and maintained (so far as it is maintained) in segmentary, lineage-based societies where there are no political authorities to make and enforce political decisions, there is no short and simple answer. For the maintenance of some degree of territorial order is a function of several different social institutions. Where unilineal descent provides the principle upon which corporate local groups are established, it provides also the idiom through which inter-group, even inter-tribal, relations operate, as we saw in the case of the blood feud. Where, as among the Nuer, lineage membership or non-membership is a relevant aspect of practically all social relationships, then lineage attachments and loyalties provide a framework for territorial relations also, and territorial grouping and lineage structure tend to show a rough-and-ready correlation. Even where other factors besides lineage membership play a significant part in many social situations, as among the Tallensi, the lineage organization is still of great importance. Once again, the matter is very much one of degree. The question is not so much whether such and such people 'have' lineages or not: in some sense of the term almost everybody 'has' lineages. The important questions are rather these. What kinds of social and political importance, if any, does unilineal descent have in the society concerned? If groups are formed on this basis how large are they and of how many generations do they take account? And what patterns of social behaviour and value are associated with membership in these groups?

(2)

When we turn to consider 'centralized' societies, we are faced with similar problems of identification and of degree. As Lucy Mair has recently pointed out, we cannot simply divide societies into those which have chiefs and those which don't; if we could, the classification of small-scale political systems would be much simpler. Two factors, especially, contribute to the difficulty of classification. The first is that lineage organization may still be of major political importance even in societies which have a titular head or king, and which may therefore be characterized as centralized. If, say, the segmentary Nuer were to acknowledge one man, or one lineage as ritually pre-eminent, while retaining their present segmentary social organization, should we have to say that they had a centralized political system? We should, rightly, hesitate to do so, and yet a common loyalty to a central head, however tenuous, and however restricted the authority allotted to him, certainly has political implications. So when we are considering so-called centralized societies we have to look very closely at the nature and scope of the political authority, if indeed there is any, which *is* centralized in such societies.

The second, more strictly taxonomic factor was touched on earlier.

151

It is that there are many societies or social aggregates possessing a common language and culture and more or less conscious of their tribal identity which have no central head, but which consist of a congeries of small, relatively independent units. These units may be based neither on unilineal kin groups nor on age sets; they may themselves be politically centralized statelets or chiefdoms, each centred on its own chief and politically independent of all the others. The important Sukuma and Nyamwezi peoples of Tanganyika form such groups. Whether we regard them as centralized or as segmentary societies depends upon whether we regard them from the point of view of their component units, or from the point of view of the whole social aggregate. On the whole it is most useful to speak of such societies as centralized, for unlike the strictly segmentary societies discussed in the first part of this chapter, their members do look to an individual head. His significance may be either ritual or political, or both, but his primacy is acknowledged over a wider social field than family or village. We shall do well to bear in mind, first, that centralization is very much a matter of degree, and of the point of view from which the social situation is regarded, and second, that centralization, however we define it, is only one of a number of criteria which it is useful to employ in classifying small-scale social systems.

The following are some of the more important questions which social anthropologists may ask about so-called centralized societies: the answers to these questions, either implicit or explicit, form the grounds for most of the classifications so far offered. First, it can be asked whether the authority claimed as 'political' is so at all, or whether the so-called king is merely a ritual or symbolic figure. If it is clear that political authority is being exercised, it can be asked, secondly, what are the range and scope of this authority. Thirdly, it can be asked what are the grounds upon which the authority is accepted, how and by whom is it acquired, and what restraints on its exercise, if any, are institutionalized in the society being investigated. Let us consider these points separately.

First, it is not always legitimate to assume that a person who is designated by a term which early European observers have translated as 'king' is necessarily an authority having secular power. It is necessary to determine whether he has authority to give orders to others, and means to enforce them within the territory he reigns over; whether, in fact, he is a political authority at all. Early European travellers in Africa and elsewhere sometimes made the mistake of supposing that the tribal 'chiefs' they encountered were potentates of the same kind as, if smaller in scale than, those with whom they were familiar from European history. Of course many of them were, but in a number of cases the king's significance for his people was wholly or mainly ritual. He was not the executive head of state, but rather an emblem, or symbol, of the whole community, a means through which they expressed their sense of tribal unity and identity.

Even though kings of this kind lack political authority, they are usually regarded with veneration, even awe. Often such a king is symbolically identified with his whole country, and it is believed that any physical injury to him must damage the country as a whole. So he has to maintain full physical vigour for as long as he reigns: if he begins to fail it is believed that he may be (or may have been in the past) secretly killed by his wives or ministers, so that the country he reigns over shall not share in his decline. Sir James Frazer's celebrated account of divine kingship refers to this symbolic kind of king. The point is not that the king is actually thought of as a god (though he may be so thought of), or even that he is thought of as specially near to God or the gods and so may intercede with them on his people's behalf (though this too is sometimes the case). It is rather that he is seen as somehow above and different from ordinary people, for in a sense he not only represents but *is* the whole country. So he is thought to possess a unique prestige and virtue.

The classical example of such a king is the Reth of the Shilluk of the Upper Nile, of whom Evans-Pritchard has written that he 'reigns but does not govern'.[1] The Shilluk people are organized in agnatic lineages similar in many respects to those of the Nuer, and order is maintained through 'self-help' rather than by means of any kind of centralized administration. Yet even though his political role is minimal or even non-existent, the king in societies of this kind still has political importance, for he is a visible expression of the unity of the people he reigns over, and their identification with him distinguishes them from other neighbouring peoples. Also, it may happen, as indeed it has happened in the case of the Shilluk, that a kingship whose primary function is symbolic, and which is traditionally associated with little or no political power, may become invested with such power in consequence of social change and the impact of foreign rule. For example, the availability of guns may enable a particular individual (and so his whole line if his office is hereditary) to establish a political as opposed to a merely ritual dominance, for which there is no traditional warrant. Also, an imposed European administration may, sometimes unknowingly, endow with the power to make political decisions persons who had formerly no right to do so.

[1] Evans-Pritchard, E. E., *Essays in Social Anthropology*, London, 1962, Chapter 4 (The Frazer Lecture, 1948).

Divine or ritual kingship is very much a matter of degree. Just as kings like the Shilluk king whose significance is primarily symbolic may none the less have, or come to have, some executive authority, so also kings who are traditionally rulers usually become the centre of much ritual. Just as ritual authority tends to become secularized, so also secular authority tends to become ritualized, often to an extravagant degree. We shall not be surprised at this if we remember that symbolism is a kind of language. The ritual in which symbolism is given overt expression is a way of asserting, and so reinforcing, values which the people who have the ritual hold to be important. In centralized societies ruled by a king or chief such values commonly include the validity of the ruler's claim to rule, his difference from and superiority to ordinary people, and the magnitude and extent of his power. Much royal ritual can be understood as expressing one or more of these themes. We may recall here Whitehead's dictum that 'symbolism, like the vegetation in a tropical forest, has a tendency to run wild'.[1] This tendency helps to explain the elaborate ceremony associated with some European monarchies, and also with the kingships of powerful non-European states like Ashanti and Buganda in Africa, and indeed with many states throughout the world. Such proliferation of ritual may range from a concern with emblems and insignia of office (crowns, sceptres, robes and such things), to rites like the immolation of subjects in order to 'strengthen' the king as in ancient Buganda and elsewhere. Very often royal ritual embodies reference to myths which ascribe a divine or quasi-divine origin to the ruling line. Such myths may be of great contemporary importance in validating the ruler's claim to rule; they provide, in Malinowski's phrase, a 'mythical charter' for the existing political and social order.

We may then conclude that in most of the simpler societies chiefship or kingship has both a ritual, symbolic aspect, and a secular, executive aspect. Sometimes, as in the traditional Shilluk kingdom, the latter is minimal, if it exists at all. But it seems that there is always a ritual aspect to kingship, whether (as in the case of the Shilluk) this is its whole *raison d'être*, or whether it is rather an embellishment to an authority which is already rooted in secular grounds.

If it be determined that political authority *is* being exercised in a particular case; that is, that the person who is designated an authority is able, at least in some contexts, to enforce his will in regard to matters affecting the maintenance of territorial order, then two further questions arise. First, what is the range of the ruler's authority?—that is, over what area is it effective? And second, what

[1] Whitehead, A. N., *Symbolism, its Meaning and Effect*, Cambridge, 1958.

is its scope, in other words, to what aspects of the subjects' lives does it apply? Its range, first of all, must be territorially indicated; in the area concerned everybody must acknowledge the ruler's authority in at least some matters, if we are to speak of political centralization. It is useful to retain the territorial reference of the term 'political'. For if we do not we shall have no means of distinguishing 'political' authority from that which is exercised in associations which are defined otherwise than territorially, such as families, churches, clubs and business concerns, which we do not commonly think of as by definition political (though they may have political significance). This is not to say that the area concerned is always precisely defined; very often it is not. Nevertheless when we speak of political authority we usually imply that this authority is exercised over all the people in a certain area, and it is important to say what this is.

When we consider the scope of political authority, that is, the extent of the social lives of the individuals subject to it over which they acknowledge the right of the person (or persons) recognized as an authority to impose his (or their) will upon them, we find very considerable variation. In fact it is often scope rather than range that anthropologists have in mind when they distinguish societies as more or less centralized. Thus the power of a central authority may be minimal, implying little if anything more than a claim to respect and to the acknowledgment of kingly status by all the inhabitants of an area. It may be restricted to sporadic demands for tribute or obeisance from the heads of outlying groups. Or, where there is a centralized administrative organization, it may cover very many aspects of the social lives of the members of the political unit. A social anthropologist who is describing an unfamiliar polity is, or should be, careful to say just what aspects of the subjects' lives are subject to political control.

In this connection the extent to which the use of force by private individuals or groups is prohibited or controlled by the central authority is especially significant. I noted earlier that the blood feud is characteristic of segmentary, lineage-based societies lacking any central authority. A centralized state, if it is powerful enough, will not permit the private recourse to violence that this institution implies. The well-being and good order of the political group are now the government's concern, and it claims a monopoly of force within its borders. Thus the blood feud often occurs in those states where, although there is a centralized head, his power is minimal: the Shilluk are an example. In states where a ruler or ruling group possesses a good deal of authority over a community in which segmentary organization is none the less still important, the blood

155

feud may be allowed, as we have noted, but only after the rulers have permitted the injured group to engage in it, and, often, subject to the payment of cattle to the ruler, or the acknowledgment of the ruling power in some other way. In strongly centralized and well-organized states the blood feud is totally prohibited. Homicide becomes a crime against the state and is no longer a matter for private settlement between the parties concerned. This is the position in most modern states, though the strength of the urge to private vengeance is shown by the gang warfare of Chicago in the 20's, and the activities of the Sicilian Mafia.

Sociologists sometimes express differences in the scope of a ruler's authority by means of the distinction between specificity and diffuseness. Thus in most modern societies those aspects of the subject's life which are subject to governmental control are specified (even if not always with complete clarity) by law and regulation. Everyone knows, or at least can find out, what the state requires of him, and in what matters his behaviour is of no concern to it. In some smaller-scale societies also, where the ruler's authority is minimal, it may be well known in which matters he has authority and in which he has none. But in a large intermediate range of centralized societies, particularly in those which have sometimes been loosely described as having a 'feudal' pattern and where political authority is, in Weber's term, patrimonial, the ruler's authority is often diffuse rather than specific. That is, its scope is not clearly, perhaps not at all, specified, and in consequence virtually every aspect of the subject's life is thought to concern his political superior. This is (or was) the case in many states in Africa and elsewhere. In these, rulers are interested in their subjects not only as taxpayers, or as manpower for labour or war. Of course they usually are so interested in them, but they are also interested in them as dependents, sometimes as relatives, always as individuals whom they know, or may know, personally. And in traditional states of this kind the subjects themselves expect this kind of interest from their chiefs, and they feel themselves neglected if they do not receive it. We shall see when we discuss social change that traditional expectations of this kind often survive into modern administrative contexts where they are quite inappropriate.

Political relations which are at the same time intimate interpersonal ones can only exist where the task of government is relatively simple. Usually in a single area one man, whether we call him chief or king, can assume sole political responsibility, and usually, too, the political unit is a fairly small one, so that personal relations between the ruler and at least a fair proportion of his subjects are possible. Very often these relations are expressed and reinforced through the transfer of goods and services between rulers and their subjects. The subjects may supply foodstuffs and other goods to the chief, who in turn provides feasts and sometimes help in need to his people. Thus both are, and see themselves to be, dependent on each other. But these conditions of inter-personal mutual dependency can no longer be met in a modern administration. The provision of up-to-date social services, and integration in a world economic system, demand literate, trained and specialist government personnel, and it is impossible for these officials to satisfy traditional demands. We shall see in Chapter 14 that the change-over from personal to impersonal political norms has caused social strain in many societies in Africa and elsewhere. Here I wish only to stress the personal, 'paternalistic' nature of political authority in many simpler, smaller-scale states, and to show that this is consistent with a type of social and political organization in which political authority is diffuse in scope, and involves no very high degree of specialization. Many societies in Africa and elsewhere still possess these characteristics, but they are now being rapidly and radically transformed.

What of the delegation and distribution of authority? It is a truism that in the conditions of simpler, small-scale states—perhaps in all states—a ruler cannot retain all his power for himself. He has to give some of it away, and naturally this considerably restricts both its range and its scope. Of course he can only do this if he *has* power to give away; where a king's main significance is ritual there can be no such delegation, and no pattern of subordinate political authority can be built up. But where there is such power, it is commonly delegated and redelegated, so that we have, typically, a pyramidal system of authority, with the king at the top, and a hierarchy of subordinate officials below. This may extend down to the level of village chiefs or headmen, perhaps through several levels of intermediate chiefs. All of these may have specifically delimited territorial authority, and each is subject to the ruler next above him in the hierarchy.

We now have to ask to whom rulers may delegate their authority in this way. Here two broad types of simple state polity can be distinguished, although they may be combined in various ways in the same kingdom. First, the ruler may distribute his power among his relatives, very often among his unilineal kin. In such states, the political system is, as it were, a family concern. The state may be said (in a sense) to be the family writ large, and often the ruler and his family are thought of as 'first among equals' rather than as being completely separate and distinct from all other groups in the kingdom. Some Southern Bantu states of Africa, such as the Swazi, are examples of this kind of polity. In the opposite kind of state the ruler distributes his power among subordinates who are bound to him not by kinship ties but by interpersonal bonds of loyalty and attachment. In such societies kinsmen are often regarded not as supporters but as potential rivals. So they may be excluded from political office, even liquidated, by the ruler and his immediate descendants. Thus it is said that princes in the ancient Ethiopian kingdom were incarcerated in caves for life. Ganda princes were sometimes also imprisoned by their successful brothers, and during at least one period of Ganda history they were killed. Similar attitudes to potential rivals, hardly less vigorously expressed, are not unfamiliar in Western European history.

In states of this second type, as in feudal and pre-feudal Europe, high value is attached to the expression of personal loyalty and dependence by subordinate to superior. Often the ruler's right to rule is validated by myth, and is expressed in elaborate court ceremonial which stresses his difference from and superiority to ordinary people. Extreme, even exaggerated, deference is expected from inferiors. But the loyalty and deference of subordinates has to be made worth while, for they are indispensable. So they are usually given a good deal of autonomy in the areas allotted to them, and they may derive considerable advantage from them in the form of tribute and labour. Very often in kingdoms of this kind special dignities such as titles or special insignia are bestowed by the paramount ruler, as a way of rewarding loyalty and good service.

But always rebellion is a danger. It is very common in such states for dependent sub-chiefs to be required to attend periodically at the king's court, and failure to do so is regarded as tantamount to rebellion. But in spite of this it is not unusual for segments to break off and assert their independence; this is how the interlacustrine Bantu kingdom of Toro came into being. In the conditions of these smaller-scale societies the power of the central authority may vary from a quite intensive control to a merely nominal authority, implying only occasional and token acknowledgment. When a social anthropologist is giving a sociological account of such a state, he has to specify not only the scope of the paramount's authority, but also that of the various grades of subordinate rulers. He must also specify the exact nature of the relationship between the two.

When in any particular case we ask what is the ground of political authority, we find that there are really two quite separate questions involved. First of all, on the level of action, we may ask how did the particularly system of institutionalized political authority with which we are confronted develop? And, second, we may ask what are the grounds upon which the persons subject to this authority accept and acknowledge it at the present time? The first question (if it is asked of any particular society and not about all societies in general) is plainly historical. And in many pre-literate societies there is insufficient historical evidence to answer it. But there is enough evidence to suggest that no 'monolithic' explanation of the development of centralized political authority will do. It is not true, for example, that all states are due to conquest, though undoubtedly some are. Even where we can be sure that the ruling line or group has come from outside the community it rules, it has not always established its ascendancy by war. Sometimes communities lacking any kind of centralized organization have actually invited foreigners with a reputation as rulers and law-givers to come and rule them, and to settle their disputes. The possession of a king and a royal court, however tiny, has often been regarded as a mark of prestige. In his account of the Alur people of western Uganda, Southall has described how centralized political authority may emerge, through peaceful penetration, in formerly uncentralized tribal groups. In this region this process has continued even into the present century.

But there is no doubt that many states in Africa and elsewhere have been established by conquest. Often small but militarily competent and well-organized groups have come from elsewhere and assumed control of populations much larger than themselves. Sometimes these populations have possessed a pre-existing central government of their own; sometimes they have not. African examples of such states are the Moslem Emirates of Northern Nigeria, and perhaps some of the interlacustrine Bantu states of the Great Lakes area of East Africa (though in the case of the latter the invasions took place so long ago that little can be said of them in detail).

Structurally there is usually a very great difference between those states which are founded in the domination of one people by another group culturally and socially quite distinct from them, and those which have arisen on the *primus inter pares* principle. In states of the former type the principles of political organization imposed by the rulers usually differ in kind from those implicit in the original tribal organization, which may still characterize social relations at the lowest levels. Thus there are often two societies as it were conjoined (sometimes uneasily) in a single unit, with relatively little institutionalized intercourse between them. The kinship-based community relationships of the peasant populations of states like Nupe in Nigeria and Bunyoro in Uganda differ in kind from the 'feudal'-type political relations which are associated with the government, and often the people themselves are quite conscious of the opposition between these two spheres. Nyoro make a clear distinction between the demands of the superimposed state and the obligations of local community membership, and they recognize that the two may sometimes conflict.

In states where the ruler and his people are of the same stock and culture, where the ruler is *primus inter pares* rather than *sui generis*, political relations throughout the society are often thought of in terms of a common structural principle. This principle may be unilineal kinship (as among the Swazi), or it may be (as in Ashanti) the military and political federation of ever larger but structurally similar units. In such societies there is likely to be a kind of structural homogeneity throughout all levels which is lacking in states of the conquest type. This difference becomes highly significant when the question of the degree of popular representation in government is being considered.

The grounds on which subjects themselves accept the authority under which they live may of course be quite different from the grounds upon which the political order was originally based. Max Weber distinguished three separate grounds upon which political authority might be acknowledged. He called the three types of authority thus distinguished 'traditional', 'rational-legal' and 'charismatic', but he was careful not to suggest that they were mutually exclusive. The political systems which social anthropologists have studied have mostly been of the sort in which political authority is accepted primarily on traditional grounds. But charismatic authority, which implies the acceptance of a ruler because of his personal qualities of leadership and magnetism, is also of concern to anthropologists. As Weber saw, it tends to become institutionalized, and so to become assimilated to the first of the types of authority which he distinguished. Rational-legal authority is based on the explicit recognition by the governed of the advantages of submission to a rule of law. This recognition is rarely explicit in most small-scale, preliterate societies, though sometimes it is expressed through myths and proverbs.

Most systems of political authority, especially simple, small-scale ones, derive at least some part of their validation from myth; that is, from accepted stories about how the system began. These stories should not be regarded simply as a kind of second-class history, or indeed as any kind of history, though they may sometimes have historical significance. They are rather a means of expressing attitudes and values which are current in the society which has the myths. These values usually include the existing system of authority, and stories about its origin provide a 'mythical charter' for it. In this

160

way myth may explain the inception of the existing system by reference to the ruling line's divine origin, to the magical powers of its
progenitors, or to imagined conquest in the past. Always its effect is
to validate the existing order, to show that it is right for the rulers to
rule and for the governed to be governed. And it is reasonable to
suppose that subjects may find subjection less irksome, and rulers
rule with more assurance, when all share the conviction that the
existing order is divinely inspired. Where this is accepted, to question
the rulers' right to rule is not only unseemly but impious. Sooner or
later in most societies such myths of authority come to be challenged,
and always grave oppresion and misrule may lead to rebellion, even
to revolution. But myth is politically significant in many cultures as
a means of stabilizing and rendering acceptable existing systems of
traditional political authority.

This brings me to the last of the kinds of questions which, I have
suggested, social anthropologists may most usefully ask about the
small-scale centralized political systems they study. That is, what are
the social institutions which have the effect of preventing rulers from
abusing their authority, from acting in ways (usually though not
always involving the exploitation of their subjects for their private
advantage) which are disapproved by the community which acknow-
ledges their authority? Earlier ethnographers in Africa and elsewhere
often wrote of chiefs and kings as having 'absolute' power. But it is
now plainer than it used to be that not only is a ruler's power always
restricted by the fact that he has to delegate some of it, but also there
are always important social institutions which tend to prevent him
from misusing such powers as he retains for himself. Of course they
do not always succeed in doing this; there have been despots in
simpler as well as in more complex societies. Nevertheless they tend
to do so, and often they are explicitly directed to that end.

Here are some examples. First, there are always rules governing
the transfer and exercise of political authority, and conformity with
these rules (in so far as they are conformed with) automatically precludes certain kinds of abuse. Thus in all states the manner in which
political authority is to be transmitted from one ruler to another is
governed by rule. In smaller-scale societies this is very often by
inheritance; to a brother or son in patrilineal societies, to a sister's
son in matrilineal ones. Less often, succession to political office is by
election or popular acclaim, in which case special account is taken of
the personal qualifications of the candidate for authority. In the case
of subordinate authorities appointment is usually by the superior
authority, who may (or may not) take account of popular opinion.
Often both ascribed and achieved criteria are combined, as when a

king must be succeeded by his son, but there is room for popular choice in determining which son shall succeed. In any case, these rules may not only help to obviate conflict at the critical phase of the transmission of authority from one ruler to another, but, often, they ensure that the best man succeeds.

Many rulers undergo ceremonies of oath-taking and admonition when they are appointed, and one effect of these is unambiguously and publicly to impress on them what is required of them. Busia describes how an Ashanti chief was admonished by his councillors on his accession: 'Do not go after women. Do not become a drunkard. When we give you advice, listen to it. Do not gamble. . . . We do not want you to abuse us. We do not want you to be miserly; we do not want one who disregards advice; we do not want you to regard us as fools; we do not want autocratic ways; we do not want bullying; we do not like beating. . . .'[1]

Most traditional rulers are advised by councils, which may consist of kinsmen, or of unrelated officials, or of a mixture of both. In many societies these councils have the power to reprimand and even fine a ruler; among the Swazi they may even depose him. In most societies, also, a subject who believes himself to have been unfairly treated by a subordinate chief has a right to appeal directly to the paramount ruler.

So long as they are regarded, these and many other institutions have the effect of ensuring that rulers conform with what is expected of them. But what happens if rulers none the less deviate from approved norms, as they sometimes do? Here a further set of institutionalized sanctions may come into play. Sometimes these sanctions are tied to specific normative institutions, as when the members of a council have the power to reprimand, fine or even depose a ruler if he does not follow their advice. But often the sanctions are independent of particular norms, so that any kind of misrule may bring them into play. An example of this latter type is the subject's ability to move out of the jurisdiction of a political authority: a ruler is only a ruler so long as he has people to rule, and in the conditions of most small-scale political systems he may lose them if he abuses his power. Again, often subordinate political authorities may be despoiled or deposed by the paramount ruler, and this is likely to be a powerful incentive to conformity among the lower ranks. The fear of sorcery or assassination by a disaffected subject may also be a factor in preventing oppression by chiefs. Finally, subjects or subordinate political authorities may in the last

[1] Busia, K. A., *The Position of the Chief in the Modern Political System of Ashanti*, Oxford, 1951.

resort revolt against intolerable misgovernment, with the aim of replacing a ruler by a more congenial one. In the conditions of most simple, small-scale political systems revolt takes the form of rebellion rather than revolution; it is not the system itself that is attacked, but merely the present incumbent of an office which itself continues to be acknowledged and respected. Today this is no longer the case in many parts of Africa and elsewhere; radical change and the adoption of new values are leading to the breakdown of old patterns of authority. It should be added, too, that the likelihood of popular rebellion is to some extent dependent on the likelihood of its succeeding. It is therefore more characteristically a feature of societies in which the ruling power has not acquired a monopoly of force in the society, for example through exclusive access to supplies of Western firearms.

In this chapter I have considered some of the many ways in which political ends may be achieved in relatively small-scale, pre-literate or only recently literate societies. We have seen that some measure of political order may be maintained even where there are no specialized political functionaries. Even where there are, their power and authority may vary greatly both in range and scope. I have stressed that in the societies which social anthropologists have mostly studied, political relations are pre-eminently face-to-face ones between people. These relations may be based on lineage or age-set membership, or on membership in a centralized and hierarchical political system.

These considerations explain why it is appropriate for social anthropologists, who are trained not as political scientists but rather as investigators of systems of inter-personal relationships, to study them. Social anthropologists are not, and do not claim to be, qualified to analyse the complex political interrelations of modern states, with their vast archives, complex technologies, and intricate communication systems. But they can and do contribute significantly to our understanding of the processes of political change and 'bureaucratization' which many of the more simply organized societies of the world have recently been and are still undergoing (as indeed all modern societies have done at some time or another). I consider in more detail in Chapter 14 some of the contributions which social anthropologists can make to the understanding of these processes. Meantime, it may be suggested that the usefulness of social anthropologists' analyses of the various kinds of political organization found in the simpler societies is not restricted only to the context of these societies. By studying at first hand the changeover from simple, inter-personal systems of authority to bureaucratic, impersonal ones, social anthropology may cast light on some aspects of the history of Western societies.

In the very broadest terms, social anthropology may add significantly to our understanding of the infinitely various patterns in which human behaviour may be politically organized, and of the ways in which these patterns may change. Whatever our culture, we are all members of the same species, sharing pretty much the same innate capacities and constitutions. We can, therefore, hardly fail to be interested in the various ways in which peoples of other cultures have dealt with the problem of maintaining social order. The problem, on a vastly larger scale, is an urgent one for all of us today.

SHORT READING LIST

BEATTIE, JOHN, *Bunyoro, an African Kingdom*, New York, 1960.

BUSIA, K. A., *The Position of the Chief in the Modern Political System of Ashanti*, London, 1951.

FORTES, M., and EVANS-PRITCHARD, E. E. (editors), *African Political Systems*, London, 1940.

LEACH, E. R., *Political Systems of Highland Burma*, London, 1954.

MAIR, LUCY, *Primitive Government*, Harmondsworth, 1962.

MIDDLETON, J., and TAIT, D. (editors), *Tribes without Rulers*, London, 1958.

RICHARDS, AUDREY (editor), *East African Chiefs*, London, 1960.

SCHAPERA, I., *Government and Politics in Tribal Societies*, London, 1956.

SOUTHALL, A., *Alur Society*, Cambridge, 1956.

WEBER, MAX, *The Theory of Social and Economic Organization* (English translation), London, 1947 (Chapter 3).

10

Social Control: Law and Social Sanctions

AT THE END of the last chapter I spoke of certain social institutions as sanctions against the abuse of political power. By a social sanction I meant, broadly, any institution a consequence of which is to incline persons occupying certain roles to conform to the norms and expectations associated with those roles. I now consider the sanctioning aspect of social institutions in relation not only to political authorities, but to all the members of a community. I remarked earlier that individual self-interest may often incite to behaviour which is incompatible with the common good. This implies that any social system must provide some institutionalized means of constraining individuals to at least some degree of conformity to accepted norms.

I distinguished above between norms and sanctions; that is, between institutionalized ways of doing things which themselves have certain implications for the maintenance of peace and good order in a society, and the consequences, themselves more or less institutionalized, which may follow from breaches of approved, normative behaviour. Consistently with the distinction between social institutions seen as systems of ideas and beliefs, and social institutions regarded as components of systems of action, sanctions themselves may be regarded from two different viewpoints. First they may be seen, at least in some degree, as the members of the society being studied themselves see them, that is, as the possible or likely consequences of deviance from socially approved norms. This is the sense in which they may be said to be (more or less) effective in preventing people from breaking the rules. It can be presumed that people will generally tend to avoid behaviour which they believe will entail painful consequences for themselves. So what is preventive is an *idea*, and this is so whether their belief is founded in past experience, either direct or vicarious, or on culturally dictated representations about the activities of gods, ghosts or witches, ideas which are

165

less susceptible of empirical verification. To understand social sanctions we have to conceive the social and cultural situations in which they operate as far as possible as these are conceived by the people concerned. Whether their conceptions are scientifically 'true' or not is irrelevant from this point of view.

Second and no less important, though calling for somewhat different methods of investigation, is the question what actually happens when norms are breached. As Llewelyn and Hoebel remark in their study of law in an American Indian tribe, 'it is the case of trouble which makes, breaks, twists or flatly establishes a rule, an institution, an authority'.[1] What new social activities (whether fully institutionalized or not—and we must remember that institutionalization is a matter of degree) are brought into play in such cases, and what consequences do these activities have? We shall see that sometimes these consequences are not foreseen or even thought of by the members of the societies concerned; none the less they may be very important. So the understanding of social sanctions, like the understanding of other social and cultural phenomena, requires analysis on two quite distinct levels. Sometimes these levels may overlap, but they do not always do so. In what follows I take account of both.

Although evidently social sanctions can only affect individual people, I am not here concerned with questions of personality or of psychological conditioning. Problems of education and 'acculturation' are evidently of very great importance, and the considerations which we classify as sanctions no doubt affect different people in different ways. But we assume that there is in general a normal, customary way of reacting within a given culture, and we are chiefly interested in the social and cultural institutions characteristic of that culture, rather than in the component individuals *qua* individuals. Of course the actual behaviour of individual people is our basic material, as it is of all the social sciences. But all scientists have to select, in the light of their particular interests, from the multiplicity of data presented to them. And the central interest of social anthropologists is in social and cultural institutions, and in the implications of these for one another. Individual case histories have an important part to play in social anthropology, but their importance lies less in their individuality and uniqueness than in the light they throw on the institutions, values and beliefs which all or most of the members of a community have in common, and on the social implications of these.

The question, then, is this: what are the kinds of social and cultural institutions which tend to prevent breaches of norms, and in terms of which action is taken when norms are breached? The first thing to

[1] Llewelyn, K. N., and Hoebel, E. A., *The Cheyenne Way*, Oklahoma, 1941.

be considered is how we are to phrase our problem. Is it useful to speak of this field as 'law' and to regard all such institutions as legal? Or is it better to speak of the whole field as that of sanctions, 'law' being merely one part of this field? The question is more than merely verbal, for by using terms which have well-known (if not always very exact) meanings in our own culture we may fall into what might be called the pathetic fallacy of social anthropology, the mistake of uncritically assimilating unfamiliar institutions to our own. When we speak in the Western world of law in its juridical sense, at least if we are speaking at all precisely, we imply the existence of rules which have been enacted by some authorized rule-making body or legislature, and we further imply that these laws are or can be enforced by the State (both through its judiciary and through a body of law-enforcement officers). Thus the jurist Roscoe Pound suggests that the term 'law' is best restricted to 'social control through the systematic application of the force of politically organized society'.

But this is not much help in the case of many of the societies studied by social anthropologists. When we speak of the blood feud, for example, or of the likelihood that peasants will withdraw economic services from an oppressive chief, we are certainly not speaking of anything that could be called law in this sense. In many such contexts the familiar distinction between criminal and civil law is even less appropriate. Thus among the Nuer there is nothing remotely resembling a central judiciary, so that all wrongs are wrongs against particular people or groups of people, not against the 'state', or against the 'law' as a formal body of enacted rules. In such societies people help themselves; they do not appeal to judges or law-givers. Here any distinction between criminal and civil law would be meaningless. Even where there are chiefs and courts, often offences against individuals and offences which affect the whole community are not explicitly distinguished, for sometimes the same offence may have both aspects. Many delicts (to use the term adopted by Radcliffe-Brown) have both public and private aspects, so that any distinction based on the opposition between criminal and civil law cannot usefully be applied to them. Sometimes too, as we shall see later, the primary aim of proceedings which we should classify as judicial is not to punish an offender, or even to recompense an injured party, but rather to restore good relations by re-establishing a disrupted social harmony. Where it is necessary to distinguish between offences which concern the whole community and those which are only the concern of individuals or groups within the community, we shall do better to follow Radcliffe-Brown in distinguishing between public and private wrongs or delicts. In this way we shall avoid bringing into our discussion of the maintenance of social control in other societies values and preconceptions which are appropriate only to more highly developed and complex legal systems.

In the study of social control in simpler societies, the contributions of Malinowski and Radcliffe-Brown have been particularly important. In his *Crime and Custom in Savage Society* (it was still customary forty years ago to speak of the simpler, smaller-scale societies as 'savage'), Malinowski discussed the maintenance of social order among the Trobriand Islanders. Although he tended to regard all factors of social control equally as 'law', an approach which leaves us with no sound way of distinguishing custom and convention from law, his intimate knowledge of the people he studied, combined with an easy and vivid style, bring home to us the reality of everyday life for these islanders. More than the figures in many anthropological monographs, they are real flesh and blood people. Malinowski's principal theme is that the chief foundation of social order, among so-called 'savages' as among ourselves, is the principle of reciprocity. Like other people, a Trobriand islander conforms to the rules which govern social relationships because he knows that if he obliges others they are more likely to oblige him. Putting it negatively, if you do not do what is expected of you in regard to other people, you are likely to find that others will not do as you expect and wish them to do in regard to you. This is the adage 'do as you would be done by' raised to a sociological principle. Malinowski illustrates it by reference to such Trobriand institutions as the mutual and obligatory exchange of fish and vegetables between coastal and inland Trobrianders, and the argument of his book is that primitive people are not constrained by blind obedience to conformity with custom and tradition, but that, like everyone else, they are moved rather by pragmatic considerations of self-interest and expediency.

Now there is no doubt that in most societies reciprocity, or the possibility of its withdrawal, is a very important social sanction. But it is only one of a number of sanctions (Malinowski himself discusses the importance of sorcery and of religious belief in ensuring conformity), and the author of *Crime and Custom* has been legitimately criticized for somewhat exaggerating its significance. He did this partly, perhaps, because reciprocal relations do seem to have been particularly important for the Trobrianders, especially in economic matters. But by erecting his Trobriand findings into a general principle he exposed himself to the criticism that he has illicitly drawn from this one field generalizations which he has then applied to all 'primitive' societies, a fallacy to which anthropologists, especially those whose main fieldwork has been in one culture only, are particularly prone. But, more importantly, Malinowski's emphasis was a reaction against the widely held view, still current at his time, that simpler peoples or 'savages' were kept in a state of slavish, almost automatic, obedience to tradition and custom, through fear of public opinion or supernatural punishment.

This view of the maintenance of order in simpler or 'earlier' forms of society had had a long and respectable history, and we are much indebted to Malinowski for exposing its inadequacy. The great Victorian historian Sir Henry Maine thought that unlike modern, 'civilized' societies, the earliest kinds of societies (which modern 'primitive' ones were supposed to resemble) were based on status relationships rather than on relationships of contract. He meant that in such societies people conformed to the rules because they occupied particular positions, usually hereditary, and not because they saw, as civilized people do, that a complex social system can only be maintained when different people base their interrelationships upon agreements mutually arrived at. Durkheim used the same idea in his book *The Division of Labour*.[1] In the earliest (and simplest) societies everybody did much the same kinds of things and produced much the same kinds of goods. Order was maintained through common submission to universally accepted rules, which Durkheim compared to the enactments of the criminal law in European culture. More advanced societies, on the other hand, are marked by increased specialization, so that different people do different things, and everyone depends upon very many other people for the necessities of life. So interpersonal relations are not determined by common obedience to a rigid code of law, but rather by the necessity for the mutual exchange of goods and services. These exchanges involve relationships of a contractual kind, and so they are amenable to something analogous to the civil law of civilized society.

Malinowski's point, and it was a good one, was that reciprocity and mutual interdependence are important in 'primitive' societies as well as in advanced ones, so that to represent the 'savage' as blindly subservient to custom backed by ritual and magic is to travesty the facts. But he went too far to the other extreme. There is no doubt that for the most part the members of simpler societies *are* more inclined than most modern Westerners are unquestioningly to accept customary rules and beliefs just because they are there and are prescribed by tradition. There is not, as there is in Western culture, a tradition of philosophic and scientific enquiry more than two thousand years old (even though not all Westerners partake fully in

[1] Durkheim, É., *The Division of Labour in Society* (English translation), Glencoe, 1933.

169

this tradition). So, in most simpler societies, there is little room for scepticism or dissent in regard to established usages. After all, peasant agricultural communities are notoriously conservative in all countries. Of course I am not saying that an analytical and critical temper is universal or even common in modern societies; it is plain enough that it is not. Still less am I saying that custom is never breached nor tradition criticized in simpler societies. But we shall see that in simple as in advanced societies conformity is ensured (in so far as it is ensured) by a variety of means other than the need for reciprocity, and Malinowski's somewhat one-sided approach tends to obscure this fact. Also, his rather imprecise use of the term 'law', and especially his application of the ideas of criminal and civil law to Trobriand society, means that his account, vivid though it is, lacks analytic usefulness and cannot readily be applied in other contexts.

Malinowski was the more brilliant fieldworker, but Radcliffe-Brown was the clearer and more systematic thinker, though he was sometimes wrong. His analyses of social sanctions and of primitive law have proved more useful than Malinowski's ideas in dealing with the very much wider range of sociological field material which has become available in the half-century since Malinowski carried out his fieldwork. Radcliffe-Brown defines a social sanction as 'a reaction on the part of a society or of a considerable number of its members to a mode of behaviour which is thereby approved or disapproved' (he does not say how a society could react otherwise than through its members). If a mode of behaviour is approved then the sanction is positive; if it is disapproved it is negative. Examples of positive sanctions are prizes, titles, fame, decorations for public service, and the good opinion of one's neighbours. They underline what one should do. Negative sanctions, on the other hand, underline what one should *not* do. And they always entail the idea that something unpleasant will happen, such as the imposition of a penalty of some kind, if one does what one ought not. Positive sanctions are sometimes important incentives to approved behaviour; but it seems that on the whole people are inclined to behave as they should rather because the consequences will be unpleasant if they do not, than because they will be rewarded if they do. At any rate, even though the same sanction may have positive and negative aspects (as the prospect of an examination may inspire in a student hope of success as well as fear of failure), in most societies the stress is on the negative rather than on the positive aspect. So in what follows we shall be chiefly concerned with negative sanctions.

Following Radcliffe-Brown, negative sanctions may be usefully distinguished as organized and diffuse. Organized sanctions are definite, regulated and recognized procedures directed against persons whose behaviour is socially disapproved: diffuse sanctions are spontaneous and unorganized, usually expressing the general disapproval of the community or of a significant part of it. Like so many sociological distinctions the difference is very much one of degree. For example it is not easy to say how the blood feud among the Nuer should be regarded. It is organized in so far as a recognized procedure is involved, diffuse in so far as there is no formal mechanism for each step in the procedures involved. But even if there are borderline cases, the distinction is important and useful. In modern societies the most important organized negative sanctions are those comprised in the criminal law. Where we have organized negative sanctions backed by a constituted authority with the power to enforce its decisions, we have legal sanctions, or 'law' in the strict sense. This is a much more useful way of employing the term 'law' than to distribute it over all, or most, social sanctions, as Malinowski did. Strictly, then, there is law only when there are courts, and where there is an organization for carrying out the court's decisions. The American jurist Seagle wrote: 'In human societies there exists one institution which is conceded authority over all other institutions in that society. This speaks as the whole community, and its commands are recognized as law'.[1] But what when no such institution exists, as it does not in many societies? Strictly, such societies have no law. But, paradoxically, this is not to say that they are wholly 'lawless'. They have systems of social sanctions, and Radcliffe-Brown offers us a way of analysing and classifying these.

There are other organized negative sanctions besides law. Bodies which do not represent the whole community but only particular associations within it, for example, such as churches, clubs and professional groups, may have organized ways of dealing with breaches of accepted rules, and these may form effective social sanctions. For a doctor to be struck off the Medical Register, or a solicitor from the Rolls, may be a far severer penalty than a court conviction. Also, often in simpler societies there are tribunals or 'courts' which although they do not command the backing of physical force, nevertheless do express the consensus of a community. Their decisions may be more or less effectively backed by diffuse sanctions expressing public opinion. Sometimes (as in many ex-colonial African territories) these tribunals co-exist with legally established courts, operating at the lower, 'face-to-face' level of community relations. Thus in Bunyoro disputes between fellow-villagers are often settled by an

[1] Seagle, W., *The Quest for Law*, New York, 1941.

171

informal group of neighbours, who have the traditional right to impose a penalty on the party judged to be in the wrong, but lack any formal means of enforcing their judgments. The penalty imposed is always a payment of meat and beer, which must be brought to the successful litigant's house on an appointed day. There it is consumed by both parties to the dispute, as well as by those neighbours who were concerned in the settlement (and anyone else who happens to drop in). It is plain that the object of this procedure—which does not always work, though it often does—is not so much to punish a wrongdoer as to reconcile the disputants and to restore a disrupted village harmony.

There are a great many negative sanctions which are more or less unorganized or 'diffuse', in the sense that even though they involve more or less institutionalized patterns of behaviour they do not imply action by officially constituted bodies or authorities. Almost always they are expressions of the public opinion of the community. Ostracism and house-burning are types of diffuse negative sanctions. There are numerous borderline cases, where there is *some* degree of organization. Thus the Kamba of Kenya used to have a custom, called *king'ole*, whereby with the approval of the elders an incorrigible thief or sorcerer might be put to death by a group of fellow-villagers assembled for the occasion. By all acting together the possibility that the death might give rise to a blood feud was avoided, for responsibility was shared by the whole village, and not attached only to a particular clan or lineage within it. There is an old (southern) Spanish custom called the *vito*; similar customs exist in other Mediterranean countries. This is a way of bringing home to a person who has offended against the standards of the community the public opprobrium in which he is held. A party of villagers visit his house at night, make a great din and shout abusive songs, and submit their victim to other annoyances, to such an extent that often a culprit finds it expedient to leave the area. Here what Radcliffe-Brown calls the 'satirical sanction' may come into play. The fear of being laughed at, and especially of being subjected to public mockery, is a powerful social sanction, especially where honour and shame are important values, as they are in most Mediterranean cultures, and also, in one form or another, in many other societies.

Witchcraft and sorcery beliefs often act as powerful diffuse negative sanctions. For a disagreeable and anti-social sort of person is likely to invite the enmity of others, and it is believed in many cultures that this may be expressed in reprisal by witchcraft or sorcery. Also, a surly and bad-tempered man is likely himself to incur the suspicion of being a witch or a sorcerer, with possibly most

172

unpleasant consequences. Sometimes the negative force of public opinion is expressed symbolically. The Nyakyusa people of southern Tanganyika, described by Monica Wilson, have a concept which they call 'the breath of men'. This is thought to be a power which although it is associated with witchcraft is not in itself evil, and it is believed that people who have it (who generally include the headman and other important members of the community) can cause a person whose behaviour is generally disapproved to become ill.[1]

This brings us into the field of what Radcliffe-Brown calls 'ritual sanctions'. Strictly speaking, these are not 'social' sanctions in the sense that the other sanctions I have discussed are. Although, like them, they depend for their efficacy on the ideas that people have of the likely consequences of their actions, in their case the consequences which are foreseen are not reactions by other living people, by 'society', but instead the action of ghosts, spirits, and other non-human forces and powers. So while the sanctions hitherto considered act both on the level of idea and, in the case of breach, on the level of action, ritual and religious sanctions owe their effectiveness mainly to the systems of belief in which they are incorporated. Thus the belief that certain kinds of disapproved behaviour may cause ancestral ghosts to injure the delinquent is a ritual sanction; for it is the belief, and not the actually experienced activities of ghosts, that tends to ensure conformity. On the other hand, the belief that anti-social manners may cause others to suspect one of being a witch or a sorcerer is not a ritual sanction. For such suspicion may, and often does, entail social action of a very vigorous and (for the suspect) painful kind, as the social history of Europe and America—to look no further afield—amply shows.

So understood, ritual sanctions include the many forms of religious belief, whether these imply reference to a god or gods with the power to punish, either in this life or after it, or to the power of ancestral or other ghosts which may visit injury on living persons who act in disapproved ways. Among many African people the ghosts of dead lineage ancestors are believed to attach high importance to the maintenance of good relations among the living members of the lineage. In such societies illness is often diagnosed as being due to the failure of brothers to live near one another as they ought, or to lineage members neglecting to assemble at appropriate intervals for sacrifice to the ancestors. Almost always it is believed to be a condition of successful sacrifice that the participants should be on good terms with one another, and that none should be harbouring feelings of hostility or resentment. In this way joint participation in sacrificial ritual may

[1] Wilson, Monica, *Good Company*, London, 1951.

be an important ritual sanction for good mutual relations between the members of a lineage group.

Radcliffe-Brown suggests a further division of social sanctions, cutting across the organized—diffuse dichotomy, into primary and secondary ones. Though the terms are a little misleading, it is hard to think of better ones. Primary sanctions are those which involve action by the whole community (whether the action is 'organized' or not) or by its authorized representatives. They thus include the sanctions of the criminal law. Secondary sanctions are those which involve only the action of a particular person or group of people in regard to another person or group of people, within a society. But though this action is in a sense private, since it is primarily the concern of the persons or groups concerned, it is nevertheless carried out with the general approval and concurrence of the community as a whole. For everyone recognizes that the action taken is appropriate and correct in the circumstances. So these sanctions no less than primary ones involve the moral approval of the community, but only in a secondary sense, for they are primarily the business of the individuals or groups concerned, who may initiate action without regard to higher authority. The civil law, as this is understood in Western societies, is a secondary sanction, for a civil case is not usually initiated by the community or its official representative (the State); primary action is taken by the injured party. But he can only do so with the State's agreement. And, in Western countries, the State can if necessary bring certain primary sanctions to bear on a defendant, such as distraint or imprisonment.

So secondary sanctions are concerned with private rather than public delicts. Societies differ greatly in respect of which delicts they regard as 'private' and which as 'public', or rather—since the same wrong may be of both private and public concern—in respect of the emphasis they give to the private and public aspects of delicts. Where there is no centralized authority, and specialized political and judicial offices are lacking, most wrongs have to be treated as private delicts and dealt with by the injured party without reference to higher authority. I noted in the last chapter that homicide affords a test case. In fully centralized states like those of Western countries homicide is entirely a public or state concern; it is treated as a public and not as a private delict. But in some traditional states in Africa and elsewhere homicide has been regarded as having both aspects. Thus in pre-European Buganda a group which had suffered the loss of one of its members through homicide by a member of another group could undertake a blood feud against the group which had injured it, but it could only do so with the chief's permission, and if compensation were agreed to, a part of this would have to be paid to him. Even in recent years, the members of many African communities have regarded it as strange and unreasonable that European administrators should take away a homicide and kill or imprison him, without concerning itself at all about the matter of compensation for the group which has lost a member. To deprive of another member a community which has already lost one member by death seems to them the reverse of common sense. For them homicide is still pre-eminently a private delict, even though it is of public concern.

The blood feud is a characteristic secondary sanction. The danger that a man may involve his kin in unwanted hostilities may serve to restrain him from homicide, and, if it fails to restrain him, institutionalized action will ensue to restore the *status quo*. The principle which the blood feud expresses is the *lex talionis*, the law of like for like. Only one life should be taken for one life, and in some societies, such as that of the Berbers of North Africa, the requirement of exact equivalence demands that the person killed in revenge must be of the same standing as the original victim. So if a man in one group kills a woman in another, the object of the injured group will be not to kill the murderer, but to kill a woman on their opponent's side.

It is evident that what is sought in the blood feud is not to punish a guilty individual, but rather to restore a disrupted balance. In the Berber case just quoted the actual killer is technically immune from revenge (though of course outraged feelings may lead to attempts against him). It is consistent with this that the first killer's intentions are irrelevant; in some societies an accidental homicide no less than a deliberate one may lead to the reciprocal killing involved by the feud. But almost always there are institutionalized means for settling the dispute without recourse to a further homicide, even though these means may not always or even often be adopted. Among the Nuer a feud may be settled by the payment of compensation, through the mediation of a ritual authority called a leopard-skin chief. It is this institutionalized provision for settlement, together with the strict adherence to the *lex talionis*, that distinguishes the blood feud from war (involving hostilities between societies or within a whole society) and vendetta (involving hostilities between two groups within a society), for in these types of conflict there are no, or fewer, rules, and there is usually no socially acceptable means for final settlement. When, in the blood feud, the injured party accepts some form of compensation, it often does so with some show of reluctance, for it is usually held to be ignominious to agree tamely to accept property

in lieu of a further life. Hence the importance of face-saving inter-
mediaries in such contexts, like the Nuer leopard-skin chief.[1]

Where compensation is accepted it may assume various forms. In
some societies another person is handed over to replace the one who
was killed; a man for a man, a woman for a woman, and a child for
a child. Sometimes a woman is handed over, to bear children for the
bereaved group to replace the person lost. Where there is movable
wealth in the form of livestock, as among the Nuer and the Bedouin,
payment of a prescribed number of cattle or camels may be acceptable. This may be thought of as a means to obtain a wife and child-
bearer for the group which has lost a member. As I have shown, the
blood feud relationship is always between groups rather than between individuals as such, and always its object is not punishment,
but the restoration of a disrupted equilibrium. It may be an important
social sanction in those societies which have a strong group organization but are incompletely or not at all centralized; indeed it is characteristic of such societies.

Other secondary sanctions which involve or may involve the use of
physical force by private parties are the duel, once a familiar institution in Western society, and what has been called the expiatory
encounter, engaged in by certain aboriginal Australian tribes. This
provides that a person against whom an offence has been committed
may throw spears at the offender until he succeeds in wounding him,
after which the matter is supposed to be closed. Secondary sanctions
which do not entail recourse to physical force include the 'singing
duel' of the Eskimos, among whom a dispute may be settled by the
parties publicly singing abusive songs about one another, the one
whose abuse is the most potent and convincing being adjudged the
winner. Among the Trobriand Islanders, described by Malinowski,
a person who believes himself to have been injured by another may
shout out his accusations and his contempt for the offender from
within his house in the middle of the night, so that the whole village
hears his complaint. A person thus charged would be unlikely to stay
in the village unless he were very sure of his own rights in the matter,
and Malinowski records several cases of suicide arising from the
feeling of shame thus engendered. Whether the satirical sanction is
invoked by an injured party or, as a primary sanction, by the community at large (as in the case of the public obloquy to which people
who have earned the community's disapproval are subjected in some
societies), it can be a very potent one, especially, as noted above,
where honour, and shame when honour is breached, are important.

Economic reciprocity, much stressed by Malinowski, is un-

[1] Evans-Pritchard, E. E., *The Nuer*, Oxford, 1940.

176

doubtedly a very important secondary sanction. In the conditions of most small-scale societies mutual co-operation is an essential condition of survival, so the possibility that co-operation may be withdrawn is a powerful inducement to conformity. Malinowski was right in claiming high importance for this sanction, although, as we saw, in his anxiety to prove that 'savages' are not slaves of custom he rather overdid it. In its very broadest sense, indeed, 'reciprocity' expresses the fact that men are dependent on one another and that no one can live for himself alone. I consider the wider importance of this fact in the next chapter; here I stress only that the possibility that reciprocity may be withdrawn is an important inducement to good behaviour in a wide range of social relationships.

This summary account of some kinds of social sanctions shows that many social institutions, not all of which may usefully be called law, may contribute to the maintenance of social order. We are especially indebted to Malinowski for having shown that social order is not maintained only by the repressive force of an embryonic criminal law, and we are indebted to Radcliffe-Brown for seeing clearly that the categories of Western jurisprudence are inapplicable to the institutions of simpler societies, and that only confusion can result from their indiscriminate application to them. We also owe to him a typology of modes of social control, based on foundations laid by earlier thinkers. Even if this typology is less than perfect, it does enable us to classify and distinguish with reasonable clarity the kinds of social control which have been described by ethnographers, as well as by historians and sociologists in Western cultures. Here, as elsewhere, Malinowski's and Radcliffe-Brown's contributions to social anthropology are complementary rather than antagonistic. The brilliant fieldwork of the one, combined with the analytical skills of the other, provide an indispensable framework for a comprehensive, comparative approach to problems of social control in small-scale societies.

I have stressed that our understanding of the institutions of other cultures has often been obscured by over-facile interpretation of them in terms of our own institutions. This is especially so in the study of breaches of norms, or delicts. Westerners, with their emphasis on the individual and on personal moral responsibility, tend to think of a large range of delicts in terms of sin and guilt. Simpler cultures are by no means without these concepts or ones analogous to them, but often they apply in very different kinds of contexts. I noted above that the blood feud, for example, is not directed only (sometimes not at all) to the punishment of a guilty individual, but to quite other ends. And the aim of many apparently judicial activities, often too readily identified with Western court procedures, is not primarily to convict and punish a wrongdoer; it is rather to restore good relations when these have been disrupted. Certainly many non-Western societies have had written or unwritten criminal codes, and have imposed punishments on offenders, often very severe ones. But almost always these have been in centralized and relatively advanced societies. When the first Europeans reached the court of the king of Buganda, for example, they were shocked at the savage penalties meted out for what appeared to be trivial offences; death and mutilation were commonplace occurrences.

It may seem odd that such punishments are not found in the simplest and most 'primitive' societies, but only in more 'advanced' ones, with organized systems of government. But evidently punishments like these cannot be inflicted unless there is some person or group of persons with the physical power to inflict them, and there is no such power in most simpler, uncentralized societies. Also, and most important, punishment may be said to be, among other things, a means of expressing the whole community's reprobation of certain types of behaviour. As Westermarck wrote: 'the immediate aim of punishment has always been to give expression to the righteous moral indignation of the society which inflicts it.' And such expression, if it is to be organized, requires the existence of authorized representatives who can act punitively. This expressive aspect of punishment, which Radcliffe-Brown also stressed, is crucial. Nowadays we tend to think of punishment as primarily instrumental: thus we may represent it as deterrent (though modern evidence suggests that it is less so than is commonly supposed), and as reformative (though regarded solely in this aspect it can hardly be called punishment). Almost always it expresses the sense of outrage and indignation felt by the community (or part of it) in the face of behaviour which conflicts with its most cherished values. The primacy of this expressive aspect is plain from the punishments which our ancestors solemnly imposed on animals and even on inanimate objects, for it cannot be supposed that these were aimed at deterrence or reformation. Like other rituals, the rite of punishment expresses a value which, often, the people who hold have neither the desire nor, sometimes, the capacity to express in analytical, rational terms. When this is realized it is possible to understand why certain sections of modern Western opinion still strongly support such penalties as flogging and hanging, although there is no evidence that such punishments are either more deterrent or more reformative than less brutal ones would be.

The importance of regarding punishment as an expression of the moral opprobrium of the whole community or a significant part of it becomes plain when we consider how such crimes as sorcery, witchcraft and incest are regarded and dealt with in many societies. All of these offences have themselves, it may be noted, a ritual or symbolic component, and all of them are thought to be injurious not only to particular individuals, but to everyone in the social group concerned. Thus often in such cases the whole community or its representatives take action against an offender, while homicide and theft, for example (unless habitual) are taken to be the concern of particular individuals or groups, and are often settled by private vengeance or by compensation. The public concern is also especially manifest when offences against the ruler or state (where such exists) are in issue. Treason is always regarded as especially heinous, and is punished with particular rigour. For in a sense the king *is* the state; usually he embodies the central values of the whole community, so that an injury to him is seen as an injury to all.

It seems that in all cultures delicts which are regarded as in some way injurious to the community as a whole are thought of as involving a real change for the worse in the person or persons concerned. This is not necessarily a matter of personal morality, though it may be; a man may enter unwittingly into such a state, and if he does special ritual may have to be performed in order to restore him to normality. I discuss these concepts of ritual status in more detail in Chapter 12. Here I wish only to mark the important difference between (in our terms) crime and sin. A crime is an offence against a man-made law, but it need not involve the deterioration in ritual status that the term 'sin' implies. Thus in the modern world it is a crime to fail to submit a correct return of income to the Income Tax Commissioners, but not all of us would regard it as a sin. On the other hand, fornication is not a crime in European countries (provided that it is between consenting adults), but many people regard it as a sin.

So sin, unlike delicts which although wrong are not sinful, is thought to involve a change in the actual condition of the sinner; it is believed that he has suffered a decline in what Radcliffe-Brown called his ritual status. In very many cultures this condition is represented not only negatively (as implying a loss or diminution of such status) but positively, as implying the presence of an actual quantity or 'thing'. I have noted before this universal human propensity to turn qualities and relations into real things. Sometimes this may be personified as an evil spirit or 'devil', which can be exorcised by appropriate ritual. This idea is common in many cultures (including Western ones), and spirit mediumship cults to deal with such 'devils' are found in many parts of the world. Sometimes

179

it is conceived rather as a kind of diffused substance, a sort of contagion which may spread and infect others if it is not controlled. In this sense it merges with the ubiquitous purity-impurity dichotomy. The Hebraic institution of the scapegoat provided one way of getting rid of this contagion. Often the idea of expiation is involved, and sacrifice is required, with its implication of symbolically yielding up a part of oneself to a god or gods conceived to be offended. In any case, the persistence of this condition is believed to imply a continuing danger, and ritual action to end it is obligatory.

Although we may not recognize the identity, notions similar to these survive in the rite of punishment in Western society. I noted above that in so far as punishment is aimed neither at deterrence nor at reformation but is regarded as justifiable for its own sake, its significance is expressive rather than instrumental. And when we think of 'guilt' as a kind of existent, and of the guilty as somehow deserving of punishment regardless of consequences, we are reifying what is not a thing but an aspect of social relations no less than simpler peoples are, with their devils and scapegoats. It is partly because in modern Western societies the deterioration in moral status involved in wrong-doing is conceived in terms of guilt rather than in terms of spirits or of ritual pollution that punishment is still so strongly institutionalized in them. But there are contributory factors. One has already been mentioned; it is that where societies are organized in strongly centralized political communities, as is necessarily the case in complex modern states, the principle of self help must give way to centralized control. This means that most delicts tend to become public delicts or 'crimes', to be dealt with by the community through its constituted judicial organs, and not directly by the injured parties. Thus the state punishes, where the individual or local group might have rather sought redress or the restoration of good relations. A second factor is the development of the notion of individual as opposed to group responsibility. Although today men are more dependent on their fellow men than ever before, this dependence is now often at many removes. We are no longer, like the Australian aborigines, dependent for our very existence on the constant support of a small group of people with whom we live all our lives in close, face-to-face relations of mutual interdependence. If we were, we too would identify ourselves closely with the group we belonged to. But where every man is for himself, then he, not a group with which he is closely identified, must accept responsibility for his actions, and he and not the group must suffer if he breaks the rules. And, thirdly, the promulgation of the universalistic systems of ethics associated with the great religions, and in particular with Christian-

180

ity, has broadened the sphere of personal responsibility and so of potential culpability. When it is claimed that interpersonal obligation extends beyond the family, the kin, the tribe and even the nation, to humanity as a whole, then moral obligation becomes (in principle at least) universal, and involves all human relationships. This is so notwithstanding that the final step is still a long way from being taken.

Here such large themes as these can only be touched upon. In this chapter I have attempted to show that conformity to approved norms may be achieved (in so far as it is achieved) through a variety of social and cultural institutions, and that only a few of these can properly be regarded as consciously and explicitly directed towards social control. I have suggested that when we are considering the maintenance of social order we are thinking primarily on the level of action, rather than on the level of ideas and beliefs (though the theme of the last few pages makes it plain that we cannot deal adequately with either level without taking the other into account). Our central interest in this chapter has been in the consequences of people's behaviour, whether these consequences are foreseen or not.

We have been mainly concerned with what Merton called latent functions rather than with manifest ones. I did not say that Nuer practise the blood feud because they believe that to do so will ensure some degree of conformity to the necessary conditions of a common life, nor that Trobriand islanders attach high importance to reciprocity because they see it to be a condition of orderly social existence, nor that the Azande believe in witchcraft because an effect of their ideas about witches is, in some contexts, to constrain them to socially approved behaviour. Sometimes people appreciate the social implications of their institutions, but more often they do not, and even where they do not these institutions may have major social significance. My central question was 'how is social order maintained?' not 'how do people think that social order is maintained, if they think about the matter at all?' It would be yet another example of the pathetic fallacy in social anthropology to suppose that all of the institutions I have discussed in this chapter are aimed, like the criminal law of Western society, at suppressing crime by punishing offenders. Often they are aimed at very different ends.

SHORT READING LIST

BOHANNAN, P. J., *Justice and Judgment among the Tiv*, London, 1957.

GLUCKMAN, MAX, *The Judicial Process among the Barotse of Northern Rhodesia*, Manchester, 1955.

HOEBEL, E. A., *Law of Primitive Man*, Harvard, 1954.

HOGBIN, I., *Law and Order in Polynesia*, London, 1934.

MAINE, SIR HENRY, *Ancient Law* (with notes by Pollock), London, 1906.

MALINOWSKI, B., *Crime and Custom in Savage Society*, London, 1926.

RADCLIFFE-BROWN, A. R., *Structure and Function in Primitive Society*, London, 1952 (chapters 11 and 12).

SEAGLE, W., *The Quest for Law*, New York, 1941.

WESTERMARCK, E., *Origin and Development of Moral Ideas*, London, 1906.

11

Economic and Property Relations

(1)

I REMARKED in an earlier chapter that it might reasonably be
held presumptuous in social anthropologists to discourse confidently,
in the contexts of the societies they study, on subjects which in
advanced cultures are the preserves of specialist scholars. Economics
is such a subject, and few of the social anthropologists who write
about 'primitive economics' are professionally trained in that
discipline. But the presumption is more apparent than real. Professional economists have chiefly studied the complicated economic
institutions of Western societies, with their complex monetary
systems and their wide-range organization of production and distribution. The investigation of these indeed requires specialist training
and knowledge; they are no fields for amateurs. But though the
systems of production and exchange in the small-scale communities
which social anthropologists chiefly study are often complicated
enough, they can generally be adequately understood (as the people
themselves understand them) without the help of the categories of
advanced economics. In fact these categories are inappropriate to the
economic life of most small-scale, technologically backward communities, which either lack money or use it only for restricted
purposes, and in which most economic relationships are also inter-
personal ones. In this chapter I show how economic ends may sometimes be achieved by means very different from those familiar in
Western countries. It will appear also, as the 'functional' model discussed earlier might lead us to anticipate, that institutions which are
apparently economic may also, and perhaps more importantly, serve
other ends besides utilitarian ones. Further, it is just conceivable that
the investigation of the working of small-scale economic systems may
suggest some new ways of looking at the more familiar economic
institutions of Western society.

The study of the economics of simpler societies falls into two main divisions, and I deal with these separately. First, there is the question how people manage to extract the physical necessities of life from their environment; here we are concerned with the means by which resources are exploited and the kinds of social activities involved in production. Second, there is the question what is done with the goods after they are produced. In the end of course they are (mostly) consumed, but often quite complex mechanisms of distribution and exchange are involved, and not all of these can be understood simply in economic terms.

A first and most essential requirement for any human community is to feed itself, and in some of the very simple societies this is everybody's main preoccupation from childhood to death. It is a truism that everything we eat, whether animal, vegetable or (occasionally) mineral, comes either directly or indirectly from the earth. But this is much less obvious to the modern man who lives in a world of processed foods and supermarkets, than it is to a member of a peasant community, living at or near a bare subsistence level. As well as food, the environment has also to produce shelter, clothing and essential tools. Anthropologists have usually distinguished three main methods by which these necessities have been chiefly secured, and in the eighteenth century and later it was usual to rank the communities which practised them in an evolutionary order of 'progress'. The very simplest communities subsist entirely by, as it were, directly raiding the environment; these are the hunters and collectors, sometimes they are also fishermen. They obtain their livelihood, often with remarkable ingenuity, by gathering wild fruit, roots and so on in season, and by hunting and trapping. The Eskimo are such a people, who have achieved a remarkable command over a very harsh environment. Tropical forest peoples like the pygmies of equatorial Africa and South East Asia have a far simpler technology, and a less rigorous environment to cope with. Dwellers in arid regions like the territory of the South African bushmen and the Australian aborigines have developed delicate adjustments to their sparse environment. It is obvious that the conditions in which such communities live impose certain limits on the size and complexity of their social organization: the territories they occupy, given their simple means of exploiting them, can rarely support more than a very sparse population. So the effective social unit is usually a small group of not more than a few dozen members, who live, for at least the greater part of the year, in relative isolation from the other similar groups which make up the society. It is evident, too, that most such communities must be constantly on the move; as the natural resources of one region are used up fresh areas to exploit must be sought. In consequence material goods are few and easily portable, and often there is no over-all tribal organization over and above the level of the small family groups which compose the effective economic units. It is natural that in such conditions the very highest value is usually attached to the solidarity of these small groups, for every one is dependent on the support and co-operation of his fellows.

At some time in the unrecorded past men began to domesticate wild animals. With the domestication of such important species as cattle, goats and sheep it became possible for human communities to sustain life on the produce of their flocks and herds. Though many societies, including the most 'advanced' ones, have a mixed pastoral and agricultural economy, the emphasis differs widely from society to society, and there are still many peoples who subsist wholly, or almost wholly, on their herds. Some nomadic peoples of the Asian steppe fall—or fell—into this category, as do the Nilo-Hamitic Masai of East Africa. Traditionally the Masai lived exclusively on the meat, milk and blood provided by their cattle; they rejected vegetable foods and despised those who dug the earth to produce them. This way of life also imposes certain restrictions on those who practise it. They must have adequate supplies of grazing and water for their stock, and often this means that they cannot stay for very long in the same place. Sometimes they are transhumant, which means that they make seasonal movements from their base in search of water and grass: sometimes they are strictly nomadic, that is, they are for ever on the move to pastures new. A pastoral way of life also imposes limits on possible population density; a herding population is of necessity somewhat thinly scattered on the ground (though usually not so thinly as hunters and collectors), and this usually precludes any very intensive or highly centralized administration. It is often said of pastoral people that they are independent and resentful of authority; it is easy to see why this should be so. It is easy to see, too, why their social systems are so often adapted to raiding and warfare: unlike some other forms of property livestock are easily stolen and transported, and raiding is a common diversion in many such societies.

Agriculture makes possible a more settled way of life. Although in many parts of the world cultivation is of the shifting 'slash and burn' type, whereby new ground is cleared for planting every few years and old gardens allowed to revert to bush, this mode of subsistence does permit relatively long residence in the same area. It also entails a very different attitude to land from that commonly held by hunters and herders, for whatever the system of land holding (I discuss land tenure below) cultivators, whether as individuals, families or lineages, have a very specific—if rarely exclusive—concern with the plots of land they cultivate and from which they hope to harvest. This is not the place to discuss the growth of the first great civilizations from the early cultivators in the great river valleys of the Middle East and elsewhere. But certain consequences of an agricultural way of life may be noted. First, the greater population density possible, combined with the relative stability of agricultural populations, readily enables wider-scale political units than family or clan to be established. In some fertile areas such as West Africa (to say nothing of the early riverine civilizations), it has also made possible urban concentrations of considerable size, with all the administrative complexity that this implies. Another consequence of the adoption of agriculture has been the emergence of a leisured class and, often, of some form of aristocracy. This is because in good conditions and with suitable crops a cultivator, unlike a hunter or a herder, need not give all his time to food production. Also, a surplus may be produced which can be used to feed non-cultivators, who may thus be freed for other forms of productive activity.

Whatever the predominant type of subsistence production, it demands co-operation. Even in the simplest hunting and collecting economy people must combine for certain purposes, though the range and scale of their co-operation may vary. There is no society known to us which lacks some form of domestic co-operation, for preparing food and rearing children. No man can live for himself alone, least of all in the arduous conditions of many of the simpler societies, and the bonds of economic co-operation may form the very foundations of social life. This reflection has led social anthropologists to consider the different kinds of co-operation possible.

This type of analysis was first systematically undertaken by Durkheim in his famous book *The Division of Labour*. Characteristically, his primary concern was sociological rather than economic. He wanted to know just what are the forces which bind men together into communities; what are the bonds of social cohesion? He concluded that social cohesion could be sustained in two ways. The first is through what he called mechanical solidarity. This is a state of affairs in which all or most of the members of the co-operating group, be they hunters, herders, cultivators or something else, carry out the same kinds of tasks. Thus conformity to a common set of rules is the paramount value, and Durkheim thought that this conformity was achieved through the fear of punishment, either secular or supernatural. As we saw in the last chapter, Malinowski showed the inadequacy of this model if it be taken to represent the way in which any 'primitive' society actually lives. To this kind of solidarity

186

Durkheim opposed, as a later and more civilized type of co-operation, what he called organic solidarity. Here the bonds lie not in conformity to rules (though of course there are rules and conformity is required), but rather in individual or group specialization, so that some people produce some kinds of goods or services, and other people other kinds. These are then reciprocally exchanged, so that, like the constituent members of an organism, every man is dependent on the activity of other men, their joint activities contributing to the smooth running of the whole community. Durkheim thought that in such a system repressive sanctions tend to be replaced by restitutive ones; the fulfilment of contractual obligations and not conformity to rules is the cement which binds society together.

Although Durkheim may have distinguished too sharply between these two types of economic co-operation—for obviously both must occur in some degree—the distinction is valid. It was foreshadowed in Maine's distinction between societies based upon status and societies based upon contract: for Maine, as for Durkheim, the simplest and earliest societies were characterized by relationships between people who acted as they did because they occupied the statuses they did, usually statuses defined by position in a kinship system. But in later and more advanced societies performance becomes more important than hereditarily determined status, and interpersonal relations come to depend more on what people do and how well they do it (for example as specialist producers or rulers), and less on the statuses they occupy regardless of individual performance. This means that 'contractual' agreements freely entered into between persons or groups who produce different things, all of which are needed by everybody, become the key to social relationships.

We can admit the usefulness of this distinction, while rejecting the naïve evolutionary hypothesis that there were at one stage societies in which all social relationships were based upon 'status', or on mechanical solidarity, and that these were somehow succeeded by societies in which all relationships were based on 'contract', or organic solidarity. Modern sociologists are using essentially the same distinction when, with the American anthropologist Linton, they distinguish between 'ascribed' and 'achieved' status, that is, between attitudes to people which depend on what they *are* and those which depend on what they *do*. The sociologist Talcott Parsons has built the distinction into his system of 'pattern variables', a list of some different ways in which people may regard their relationships with other people.[1]

[1] Linton, R., *The Study of Man*, New York, 1936; Parsons, T., *The Social System*, London, 1952.

In describing the means of production in simpler societies, modern social anthropologists have made use of these distinctions. Malinowski echoes Durkheim's classification when he distinguishes what he calls communal labour from organized labour. In communal labour the same kinds of tasks are performed by a number of people in association; in organized labour several socially and economically distinct but related tasks are performed by separate individuals or groups of individuals. An example of communal labour is the shared activity of a hoeing party or a group of berry pickers; an example of organized labour is the building of a house, where one man collects building-poles, another grass, and a third does the actual building. In one sense, what is happening here might be appropriately called the addition of labour rather than its division; it depends on whether it is regarded from the point of view of the component tasks or of the whole enterprise. Obviously very much more complex organizations of productive labour are found in advanced—even in 'simple'—societies. Firth also uses this distinction, but he rightly suggests that 'simple' and 'complex' combinations of labour are better terms than Malinowski's. For any labour combination is communal if the community or some members of it participate in it together, whether the tasks concerned are similar or diverse. Even when they are similar, some organization of the activities involved is usually necessary.

Malinowski has stressed the psychological advantages of simple combinations of labour; the part played by emulation, the feeling of 'oneness' with the group, the spur to concerted effort provided by rhythm of either movement or song. All these aspects of such joint activity are very evident to anyone who has watched, say, an African hoeing party working in unison. The social advantages of specialization, which is implied by complex combinations of labour, are sufficiently obvious. The rich and varied life which can be enjoyed—if nowadays a little precariously—by at least some members of advanced cultures implies an almost complete dependence on other people, mostly total strangers, for the necessities of life. It is a truism that there is no point in specializing unless there is a possibility of exchange; there must be some means whereby all may be enabled to avail themselves of the special products of each. This calls for some degree of social and economic organization.

The social anthropologist who is trying to understand how a particular community functions is interested in both simple and complex combinations of labour, but naturally the latter gives rise to the most interesting questions. For where different kinds of employment are engaged in by different kinds of people (whether these employments be regarded as contributing to the same end or not), the question arises: on what principles is the differentiation made? First, it is useful to ask whether the division of function is temporary or permanent. Although the difference between a temporary combination and a permanent one may be a matter of degree, there is obviously a considerable difference between an organization consisting of a number of professional specialists, and one in which specific tasks for a particular job are allocated among a number of individuals, any one of whom might be allotted a different task on a subsequent occasion. It is only in the former case, or in cases approximating to it, that we can usefully speak of specialization. Considering, then, relatively permanent combinations of different kinds of tasks, we have to ask both what the tasks concerned are (this is a matter of informed ethnographic observation) and, more importantly, what are the grounds on which they are allocated to one individual or group rather than to another.

There are various grounds upon which different kinds of tasks may be allotted to different kinds of people, but four differentiating criteria are particularly important. These are sex, age, ascribed social status, and aptitude or special skill. In all known societies certain tasks are regarded as appropriate for men, others for women. Some of these, such as women's role of suckling and caring for children and carrying out tasks that can be done at home, like cooking and house maintenance, and men's role of hunting, fighting and performing heavy manual labour, are associated obviously enough with physical differences between the sexes. But others are determined socially and culturally, not physiologically, and so they vary from society to society. Among some pastoral African peoples, for example, women may and should milk the cattle; among others they are strictly prohibited from doing so: which rule prevails depends upon how cattle and women are regarded.

The division of tasks on the basis of age is also physiologically determined in some degree. Some tasks, like the herding of small stock, can be carried out by children; others, like fighting and hunting, call for the full strength of able-bodied men; others, like the settlement of disputes and the making of important decisions affecting the whole community, call for special wisdom and experience, and are performed by older men. This age division of labour may be highly institutionalized, as it is most strikingly in the age grade systems of the Nilo-Hamites and some neighbouring peoples of East Africa. But always there is some differentiation of tasks on the basis of age.

Thirdly, status differences affect the distribution of tasks in almost

189

all societies. In very many cultures, including most Western ones, class distinctions affect the kinds of occupations in which a person may engage. Although such restrictions are less rigid than they used to be in many European societies, they are still a factor to be reckoned with. The caste system of India, based on ascribed rather than on achieved qualification, is the most celebrated example of this kind of division of labour—though of course the caste system is very much more than merely a mode of organizing labour. In it a man follows a particular trade or profession not because of sex, age or aptitude, but because he happens to have been born as a member of a certain caste or sub-caste. The symbiotic relationship between the pastoral Bahima and the agricultural Bairu in the Ankole kingdom of western Uganda affords another example. Among these people, the Bahima or superior class do not cultivate; that is the task of the Bairu peasants. None the less the Bahima claim some part of the produce of Bairu labour.

The fourth ground on which labour may be allotted is ability or achievement. Where, for example, a man shows a particular aptitude for pottery he may become a potter (provided that pottery is not the prerogative of a special class to which he does not belong). But almost always other social factors besides aptitude and ability enter into the matter. Obviously no one, however talented, can become a potter, a painter or a physician if he is allowed no access to potter's clay, paint or physic. More important, the various criteria I have mentioned are usually combined. Thus a particular task may be allotted on ascriptive grounds only to a person who belongs to a particular caste or class, but a choice may be made on grounds of achievement from among the persons so qualified. As so frequently in social science, we are dealing here with differences in proportion and degree rather than in kind. It is legitimate, with regard to any particular community, to enquire to what degree the allocation of economic roles is dependent on sex, age, status or aptitude. But it would not be helpful to attempt to distinguish societies from one another solely by reference to the presence or absence of one or other of these principles of division.

As well as asking how labour is divided, that is, who does what kinds of tasks, we must ask how the task force is organized. For example, who is responsible for the allocation? Are the tasks done individually, or are they done collectively, by a group working together? If the latter, is the group unsupervised or does it work under the supervision of a foreman or a leader? If there is someone in charge of a group of workers, we may ask whether the supervisor is a fellow-worker, himself a member of the group, or a foreman who comes from outside the group and is not himself a worker. The leader,

as opposed to the foreman, is typically associated with undiffer-
entiated 'simple' groups of workers: the foreman with complex,
specialist groups. This is because in the former case the same task
is by definition obligatory for all; no one can be readily detached
from it, and all are equally workers. But in the case of more complex
combinations of labour this is not so; every member of the working
group has his special task to perform, and he cannot be taken away
from it in order to lead the group without disrupting its joint activity.
All of these various types of organization can be found in the societies
which social anthropologists study, and they have to be identified and
distinguished.

It is plain that questions of these kinds are much easier to answer in
small-scale, technologically simple societies, than they are in the
large-scale modern industrial ones. But this does not mean that they
are practically unimportant. For one thing, a great part of the
world's agricultural production comes from small-scale peasant
agriculture, and it is essential for those whose concern it is to make
such production more efficient to have some understanding of the
principles and values involved in it. Also, the increasing participation
of people throughout the world in large-scale industrial activity
raises problems of small group integration and efficiency, and some
light may be thrown on these by the investigations of simpler
combinations of labour made by field anthropologists.

I have considered some of the basic ways in which human populations exploit the physical world they live in. Now the effective use of
these resources requires that the claims that different individuals and
groups may have in them should be, on the whole, mutually compatible. So the next question to be considered is the manner in which
different peoples determine and adjust their rights in their social and
physical environment. First, I say something about the kinds of rights
that are commonly held in the land itself, the first and most indispensable necessity of human life.

A people's interest in land is determined both by what they use it
for and how much of it there is. For a hunting and collecting community, for example, the land is just 'there', a commodity free for
everyone like air. Such groups are of necessity widely dispersed, so
they are unlikely to come into conflict over land, although certain
areas may come to be regarded as the preserve of one or other of the
small groups in which such societies are generally organized. On the
whole the same is true of most pastoral societies, upon many of which
sparsity of water and grazing imposes a nomadic or at least a trans-
human way of life. Here again, however, particular areas may come
to be regarded as the preserve of particular herding groups and

191

jealously defended. As with other commodities, the scarcer grazing and water are, and the greater the competition for the use of them, the more explicitly rights and obligations relating to them are formulated.

In primarily agricultural communities, where cultivators have a special concern with the pieces of land which they have tilled and from which they hope to harvest, ideas about land rights are inevitably more specific and clearly defined. The degree to which they are so depends to some extent on how permanent the cultivator's attachment is to the particular piece of soil he cultivates at any one time. In many parts of the world soil infertility and its slow rate of regeneration, combined with simple technology, mean that a particular piece of land can only be cultivated for a few years. After this it is exhausted, and a new piece of land must be cleared from forest or bush, the used one being left to regenerate over a period of years. There are many variations on this pattern, which is sometimes called shifting cultivation; it is common in almost all the underdeveloped areas of the world. Where it is found, almost invariably the land is not regarded as the private property of individuals, but rather as vested in social groups, whether these be tribes, clans, lineages or extended families. Always individuals have the right to cultivate and to enjoy the produce of the land they till, but their rights in a particular piece of land are conditional. They depend, usually, on the community's acceptance of them, also on actual residence and cultivation. If a cultivator leaves an area which he has been living on and cultivating, after a time his rights in this piece of land lapse. (This has created problems at the present day, when with the impact of a cash economy and new opportunities for earning, peasants in Africa and elsewhere have left their holdings to seek temporary employment on mines and estates.) Very often the allocation of cultivation rights is the responsibility of a lineage or clan head, or of a village headman. But the person who exercises this authority is not thought of as 'owning' the land; rather he administers it on behalf and in the interest of the community he represents.

Even where soil fertility and agricultural technique make possible the continuous exploitation of the same fields over long periods, rights in land, at least in traditional systems of land tenure, tend to be vested in groups rather than in individuals. In many parts of West and some parts of East Africa, the attachment of a lineage group to its land is expressed by reference to the ancestral graves or shrines which are maintained on the land, and it may be believed that both the dead ancestors and their living descendants share an effective joint interest in the lineage territory. In West Africa especially, for example among the Tallensi of northern Ghana, there are shrines not only for the ancestors but for the earth itself. But however the land be regarded, in the simpler, technologically undeveloped societies it is rare to find that there is any notion of its being owned by any particular individual. Failure to recognize this led to grave mis-understanding in some parts of Africa, where Europeans supposed themselves to be buying land outright from chiefs who, as custodians of the land, meant only to allot it for temporary use. We shall see in Chapter 14 that the idea of private ownership in land has gained ground increasingly in recent decades.

There are some centralized societies in Africa and elsewhere in which a 'feudal' type of land holding has grown up, whereby large areas of populated land have been held as grants from a chief or king by an upper class of royal relatives or favourites, or condition of homage, service and the payment of tribute. Where this has happened, as it has in some of the interlacustrine Bantu states of East Africa, rights over land and political rights over people have tended to fuse, so that neither the political system nor the system of land tenure can be properly understood without reference to the other. But even in such systems tenure does not amount to ownership. Rights are held subject to well understood conditions, and they can be revoked at any time.

In fact, in most peasant societies outside Western Europe, several different categories of persons may hold rights in pieces of land. For this reason social anthropologists have found it unprofitable and even misleading to think of the simpler kinds of land tenure in terms of 'ownership'. To the question 'who owns this piece of land?' an enquirer may receive several different answers. This does not mean that his informants are inconsistent or mendacious, though of course they may be. It simply means that he is asking the wrong question: here as elsewhere in anthropology the investigator's categories of thought and those of the people whose ideas he is trying to under-stand may differ so radically as to make understanding in familiar Western categories impossible. The right question to ask in such contexts is rather: who are the people who have rights in this piece of land and what rights do they have?

In the kingdom of Bunyoro in East Africa, if this question were asked about a particular field, the answer to it would be somewhat as follows: 'The king has rights in it, for the country and everything in it belong to him and, in theory at least, he can do what he likes with any part of it. The local chief or headman also has rights in it, delegated from the king. For it was he or his predecessor who allotted it to the head of the family which at present cultivates it, and he has the power to dispossess him of it should he leave it for a long time, or should he be found guilty of a crime such as rebellion or sorcery. But the family or lineage head who occupies the land has rights in it too; he may cultivate any part of it if he wishes, and enjoy its fruits, and he may direct his grown-up sons to cultivate portions of it for their own and their families' use. And finally, the son who is actually digging the field in question has rights in it, even if they are limited and conditional ones; he may live there and cultivate undisturbed, so long as he remains on good terms with his father and with the local chief.'

I think it is plain that in situations of this kind (and often the system of rights involved may be very much more complex) a simple answer to the simple question 'who owns this piece of land' could only be partial and misleading.

Ideas about ownership and about property in general differ greatly from one culture to another, and the stress on private, individual ownership characteristic of Western society is absent in many other cultures. In most small-scale, pre-industrial societies there are few things in which particular individuals hold exclusive and uncon- ditional rights. There are always some such things, personal effects such as clothes and weapons are almost invariably such. But most property (and in many simpler societies there is not much material property anyway) is not. Like land, livestock is rarely owned by individuals, but is rather held by a group such as an extended family or lineage. Although the stock may be controlled by the senior member of the group, it is not his private property; he holds it on behalf of the group and as its representative. Even women, who in many patrilineal societies are regarded as a kind of property, are not always exclusively 'owned' by their individual spouses: we noted that sometimes wives are thought of as in some sense the wives or women (often the same term serves for both) of all of the members of their husband's agnatic group. Thus among many peoples (including the Nyoro) if a man cohabits with his brother's wife there is no adultery, and although the husband may object strongly there is not much that he can do about it.

I am not simply distinguishing here between individual and communal ownership. There is no evidence that any society ever practised a thorough-going primitive communism in which equal rights in everything were held by everybody. The important points are two. First, very usually rights in things are not held exclusively by indi- viduals, as they tend to be in Western societies, but rather by specified groups, often based on kinship. And second, these rights are usually limited and conditional, and not absolute. These considerations impose on the student who wishes to understand attitudes to property in other cultures the task of discovering what kinds of rights what kinds of people hold in what kinds of things, and on what conditions. These are issues in which Western stereotypes may be particularly pervasive and misleading.

(2)

So much for the production of goods, and attitudes to property, in small-scale societies. I now discuss in more detail how the goods that people produce are consumed and exchanged. First, many (though by no means all) of the societies which anthropologists have studied live at or near the subsistence level. This means that the people who produce the goods consume most of them themselves. This is so for almost all hunting and collecting peoples, also for most subsistence agriculturalists. But even among the poorest and technologically least developed peoples food is always something more than merely something to eat. Eating is a biological necessity, but feasting is not. Almost all peoples mark the importance of certain social occasions, like birth, initiation, marriage and death, by the commensal activity of eating and drinking together. They also do it just for the pleasure of having a party. An important effect of these activities, which essentially involve prestation, or gift giving, is to increase a community's sense of interdependence and mutual attachment. In other words, they are important socially, as well as biologically and economically.

There are few, if any societies, in which institutionalized exchange does not play some part. As Durkheim pointed out, exchange is especially characteristic of those societies in which there is some form of occupational specialization; when one section of the community produces one kind of commodity, another a different kind, then they can exchange their surpluses to their mutual benefit. Thus coastal Trobriand Islanders, who sometimes have a surplus of fish, exchange these for the yams of which the inland dwellers produce more than they need. This enables both groups to enjoy a mixed diet which neither could achieve alone. But here again the social relationships brought about by these exchanges may be just as important as the economic ones. In many parts of the world, even where trade is by barter only, market systems have developed; it is often convenient for the producers of different kinds of goods to meet at a pre-arranged time and place to make their exchanges. For example, markets in West Africa have considerable social importance; they provide a meeting place for many different kinds of people; they admit women, who are the principal primary producers, into a social world otherwise inaccessible to them; often they become centres of administration, since they are the most convenient places for the collection of taxes and other dues, and for the promulgation of orders and information by the rulers. Many of the great markets of the world, such as Delos in the ancient world and Timbuktu in medieval Africa, have become internationally famous, for in them men of many different nations and speaking many different tongues have met. Lord Bacon knew what he was doing when he called the kinds of illusions and misunderstandings which arise from the use of words 'the idols of the market-place'.

Where large-scale exchange systems have developed, price mechanisms with fixed (or relatively fixed) currencies have grown up, with all the complexities which money economies involve. A few of the simpler societies have developed a sort of monetary system, but for the most part the range of possible exchanges has not required the creation and use of some single value factor covering such transactions. The presence or absence of money is a matter of degree; where some single commodity becomes valuable not only in itself but also as a standardized medium of exchange for a number of other kinds of commodities (like blankets among some North American Indian peoples, gold weights among the Ashanti, and cowry shells throughout much of Africa), then we have the beginnings of such a system. Social anthropologists do not claim to understand the complexities of the wide-range price systems of the Western world; they are happy to leave this field to trained economists. But they can investigate the varieties of exchange and their significance in simpler, smaller-scale communities, and their findings may be more relevant than might appear to the understanding of some of the more sophisticated types of exchange found in Western societies.

Anthropological fieldwork has amply shown that economic value in the accepted sense of the term is not the only kind of value significant in exchange relationships. Even where economic advantage is sought, other social ends may also be served; often these other ends may be thought the more important. I noted in an earlier chapter that the bridewealth of cattle or other goods transferred at marriage by the bridegroom to the bride's family in many parts of Africa and elsewhere does have economic importance. In a patrilineal, virilocal society a woman and her labour are lost to her natal group when she marries, and the bridewealth paid for her may serve as an indemnity for this loss, since it provides that group with the means to replace her. But there is a great deal more to it than this. It is a mark of status, a means of validating a conjugal relationship, and a legitimization of the offspring of the union. Further, since the marriage payments are

196

rarely concluded in one transaction, but usually imply a series of exchanges of goods and services continued over a long time, it also provides a means of expressing and maintaining what are expected to be amicable social relations.

This is the crucial point. In very many kinds of exchanges, the maintenance of good relations is the prime consideration, rather than any economic advantage to either party. This may be so even where the parties to the exchange are well aware of this advantage. Sometimes institutionalized exchange provides a way of sustaining on a friendly basis a relationship in which there are possibilities of friction (and in what relationship are there not?). We noted earlier that in many cultures a man is not allowed to see or speak to his wife's mother. But he is none the less required to maintain good relations with her, for she has given him her daughter, and he does this by sending presents to her, through a third party, from time to time. The continuing aspect of such transactions is especially important, for what is at issue is a relationship between people. In the West of Ireland, a small farmer never quite pays off his account with the country shopkeeper on whom he depends for his supplies, even though he may be financially able to do so. If he did, it would imply that he wished to end his relationship with that shop. For him it is a friendly relationship between real people, not an impersonal relationship between a man and a firm or an institution, and he wants to keep it that way. And he does this by maintaining, as one does in gift exchange, a state of mutual indebtedness.[1]

The classical examples of the extra-economic significance of what at first sight appear to be economic activities are the *kula* of the Western Pacific, described by Malinowski in his monograph *The Argonauts of the Western Pacific*, and the *potlatch* of the American Indians of the North-West coast. The kula is a ceremonial exchange of certain valuables, participated in by the inhabitants of a closed circle of islands (including the Trobriands, where Malinowski carried out his fieldwork). The objects concerned in this cycle of exchange are of no practical or commercial value; they consist only of red shell necklaces and white shell bracelets. These two types of valuables circulate in opposite directions, as gifts exchanged between partners in the kula ring. Every participant has two kinds of partners, those from whom he receives arm-shells and to whom he gives necklaces, and those from whom he receives necklaces and to whom he gives arm-shells. Though these ornaments have no commercial value, they differ greatly in prestige value, and it is a matter of pride to have, or to dispose of, a good piece. There is no bargaining or haggling about

[1] Arensberg, C., *The Irish Countryman*, London, 1937.

kula gifts, and a return for a gift is not made at once, but after the lapse of a year or two. Not everybody may join in the kula exchange; it is necessary to be of a certain social status—women, for example, are excluded from it. Often it involves long canoe voyages from one island to another. This is why Malinowski called his book *The Argonauts*, for they also set out on a long sea voyage in pursuit of an economically useless object.

Now if this system of institutionalized exchange is not an economic one, what is the point of it? Social anthropologists answer this question by showing how the kula is bound up with a great many other social activities and values. First, like all ceremonial activity, it has an expressive aspect. Participation in the kula is an indication of social status, and to possess many partners and to handle exceptionally valuable pieces is to enhance one's social standing in the community. Secondly, the kula involves such other activities as canoe-making, and these in turn entail important cycles of economic and magical activity. Third, although kula valuables themselves are not traded, there is trading on kula expeditions, and Malinowski notes the contrast between the bargaining and haggling that takes place when ordinary goods are bartered and exchanged, and the formal ceremony of the kula exchanges. Fourth, the possession of a kula partner or partners in a foreign country provides protection from the dangers which are to be expected there from both the human and the spirit inhabitants. This leads to the final point, stressed by Marcel Mauss in his celebrated *Essai sur le don*, that the kula is a means to social integration; it brings people into institutionalized relationship with other people, and so, in some sense, makes them members of one society.

The potlatch of the American North-West is at first sight a very different kind of institution, but a closer look at it reveals some striking similarities. The Kwakiutl and some other tribes of this area live (I am using the ethnographic present tense) in a region of great natural wealth; there is often a surplus of fish and game, and also they possess certain 'treasure' items such as decorated slabs of copper. These people are organized in agnatic groups, and from time to time one such group gives a great feast, at which not only are huge quantities of food consumed, and generous gifts given to the representatives of other groups, but also large amounts of valuables, such as canoes, coppers and even (in former times) slaves are destroyed. Now by strictly economic standards these exchanges do not make any kind of sense; still less does the wholesale destruction often involved. Even though almost everybody has enough of everything already, to burn up valuable property is the reverse of sensible. The explanation lies elsewhere. These peoples are much concerned with prestige, and to give a potlatch more splendid than that of a rival is to lay claim to a higher social status than his. But—and it is this that constitutes the potlatch a system rather than merely a megalomaniac aberration—the giving of a grand potlatch is only a *claim* to status; not until further potlatches are given can it be known whether the claim has been acknowledged. For at subsequent potlatches the original giver will be a receiver, and the level at which his status is assessed will be shown by the amount of the gifts made to him; not in absolute terms, but relatively to the gifts made to others who are present as guests at the feasts. So every potlatch is at the same time both a claim to status and its public acknowledgment. In a society where social worth is implicitly equated with institutionalized liberality, it is in this, and not in economic considerations, that the function and significance of the institution lie. So it is quite beside the point to argue, as the early Europeans in the North-West did, that economically the potlatch was a ruinous waste of resources. The Kwakiutl knew this perfectly well but they didn't care; their interest in it was of quite a different kind.[1]

Many other examples could be quoted, and not only from the 'simpler' societies, to support Malinowski's point that 'economic man' is an absurdity. Nobody is activated only by motives of enlightened economic self interest; there are always other, often more highly regarded, values involved. Veblen and later sociologists have made this amply clear for Western society, and Vance Packard's *The Hidden Persuaders* has recently highlighted some of the considerations other than economic ones which motivate the purchaser of economic goods. 'Keeping up with the Jones's' is important in Melanesia as well as in Middletown; for the modern European or American a motor car is no less a prestige symbol than it is a means of transport. In all the cases we have considered the motive of profit or material advantage is replaced or at least supplemented by what Firth has called the 'status-increment motive'.

Always some valuable is being exchanged for another one, but the goods involved are not necessarily material ones. It is useful to distinguish between utilitarian or material value, based on usage, and ritual or 'status-increment' value, based on the particular kind of regard in which certain things and conditions are held, regardless of the use to which they are put. Even though in actual human affairs these values are not mutually exclusive (since the same objects may have both kinds of value), the distinction provides a useful fourfold

[1] A good account of the potlatch is Barnett, H. G., 'The Nature of the Potlatch' in *American Anthropologist*, Vol. 40, 1938.

classification of types of institutionalized exchange, as Steiner has pointed out.[1] A utilitarian value may be exchanged for another utilitarian value, as the Trobriand Islander exchanges fish for yams, or the modern housewife does her week's shopping for cash. But utilitarian values may also be exchanged for ritual ones, as when the Kwakiutl Indians trade goods for status, or the Yap Islanders of the Carolines exchange goods which they have taken years to accumulate for huge stone discs which they then bury under their huts and put to no economic use whatever. Conversely, a ritual value may be exchanged for an economic value, as when a University confers the degree of M.A. on its graduates on payment merely of certain dues, or when honours are conferred by a Government upon persons who have contributed substantially to party funds. And finally, a ritual value may be exchanged for another ritual value, as in the kula, or in the annual mass exchange of Christmas cards in the Western world.

In all this the key concept is exchange. I noted earlier that Durkheim was the first to give explicit sociological recognition to the importance of exchange, in his distinction between mechanical and organic solidarity, and the notion was further developed by Mauss, who makes three especially important points. First, he emphasizes that (as we have seen) a great many other things besides economic goods may be exchanged. Second, he stresses that exchanges are in a sense obligatory; there is always a social obligation to return, or at least to make a return for, a gift, even where the existence of such an obligation is conventionally denied. Mauss argues that this is because to give something to somebody else is in a sense to give him a part of oneself; the gift is not, in his phrase, 'inert'. Many peoples believe, he claims, that so to possess a part of another's personality is in some sense dangerous until a return gift has been made. Thus the Maori apparently have an explicit concept, *hau*, part of the meaning of which is the reciprocating 'spirit' or essence of a gift, which must sometime and somehow be returned to the original donor. Few people go so far in reifying the sense of obligation involved in gift giving as the Maori are said to do, but there is no doubt that the sense of indebtedness involved is ubiquitous in all cultures. Mauss's third important point is the essential one, already touched upon, that gift exchanges of various kinds are a means to the establishing and maintaining of social relations. Ethnography published since Mauss's book appeared in 1927 has fully documented this claim.

Broadened in the ways I have indicated, the concept of exchange assumes fundamental sociological importance. To exchange things,

[1] Steiner, F., 'Notes on Comparative Economics', in *British Journal of Sociology*, Vol. 5, No. 2, 1954.

and especially the kind of exchange between persons which Mauss included under the general concept of gift giving, is an essential element in every interpersonal social relationship. Exchange is not just a matter of economics, although of course it may and commonly does serve economic ends. Nor is it only a matter of status increment, though much gift giving implies a claim to prestige, like the Kwakiutl potlatch. Sociologically, the important thing is that by habitually exchanging goods and services with one another individuals constantly put themselves, as it were, in the hands of others. To give and receive gifts is to involve oneself in a network of mutual indebtedness, and so to increase mutual social cohesion and solidarity.

This is most particularly the case where the exchange relationships are between people who know one another personally. It is very much less true (though it is still so in a sense) in the case of the large scale economic exchanges of the modern world. It is a paradox of modern life that although nowadays it is technically possible for us to communicate with our fellow men over a vastly wider range than ever before, we are much less closely bound up with a group of other people in daily face to face relations of mutual interdependence and support than the members of simpler, smaller scale societies are. This is one of the reasons why gift exchange, which is essentially a relationship between persons, plays a much less important role in modern, Western societies than it does in 'simpler', preliterate ones.

SHORT READING LIST

FIRTH, RAYMOND, *Economics of the New Zealand Maori* (second edition), Wellington, 1959.

Primitive Polynesian Economy, London, 1939.

FORDE, D., *Habitat, Economy and Society*, London, 1934.

HERSKOVITS, M., *Economic Anthropology*, New York, 1952.

LEACH, E. R., *Pul Eliya, a Village in Ceylon*, Cambridge, 1961.

MALINOWSKI, B., *Argonauts of the Western Pacific*, London, 1922.

Coral Gardens and their Magic, London, 1935.

MAUSS, M., *The Gift* (English translation), London, 1954.

RICHARDS, A. I., *Land, Labour and Diet in Northern Rhodesia*, London, 1939.

TAX, SOL, *Penny Capitalism, a Guatemalan Indian Economy*, Washington, 1953.

12

The Field of Ritual: Magic

SOCIAL ANTHROPOLOGISTS have a special interest in symbols and symbolism. All symbolism can be regarded as a kind of language, a way of saying something, and the kinds of symbolic behaviour in which anthropologists are most interested usually assert the importance of some social value. But as well as expressing something, symbolic activity often (though not always) has an instrumental aspect. People who carry out institutionalized symbolic procedures or rites usually believe that by doing so they are either producing some desired state of affairs or preventing some undesired one.

Now the chief difference between what we call practical, common-sense techniques for doing things, and ritual or 'magico-religious' ways of doing them lies basically in the presence or absence of an institutionalized symbolic element in what is done. An example will make this clear. Every agricultural community knows which of the crops available to it should be planted at what season, and in which of the available soil types, if the best results are to be achieved: it has its own agricultural knowledge and skills, learned from and tested by experience. The readiness with which agricultural communities in the interior of Africa took over new food plants deriving from other continents (such as maize and manioc from America, bananas from the Far East) long before the European penetration of the continent shows that these communities have always had a practical, common-sense attitude to farming, and have been ready to try out new crops and to accept or reject them on the basis of trial and error. Every society, whatever its stage of technological development, must have a body of practical, common-sense knowledge, founded in and tested by experience: if it did not it could not survive.

But even in 'advanced' societies not all human activity is practical and 'scientific', although modern dependence on a complex technology means that in the everyday life of Western countries the major emphasis is on such activity. This emphasis has often led Western observers to misinterpret ritual behaviour in cultures other than their own. Nobody has ever had any difficulty in understanding, for example, the behaviour of a man who is hoeing a field and planting millet in it. This is a perfectly straightforward, practical thing to do; nothing is standing for anything else and there is nothing ritual or symbolic about it. But when, after he has planted his millet, the man goes off to a rain-maker, a ritual expert who, for payment, manipulates some special magical equipment and makes the appropriate incantations so that rain may fall, the Westerner is inclined to be puzzled. He sees that this is somehow a different kind of activity from the more 'practical' operations of digging, planting and weeding. But he finds it hard to see the point of it, to understand how anybody could possibly suppose that such childish 'magic' could possibly work. He tends to explain such behaviour (and as we shall see he is not altogether wrong) by reference to a belief in some kind of supernatural forces, and often he imputes to the culture concerned a clearly-marked distinction between the 'natural' and the 'supernatural'. This is the distinction which Durkheim expressed as that between the sacred and the profane.

But the trouble with such distinctions is that very often they commit the cardinal sin of social anthropology, by imputing to another culture a kind of category-making which is characteristic of our own practically oriented, 'scientistic' society. To an African or Melanesian peasant it is just as 'natural' for a rain-maker to make rain, or for a witch to bewitch his enemy, as it is for a woman to bear children, or for a man to harvest the crop he plants. Most peoples do not dichotomize the universe into two distinct and mutually exclusive spheres labelled 'natural' and 'supernatural', as Westerners do, although they often dichotomize it in other ways, and they can distinguish different kinds of causal agents in the world they live in.

There is, none the less, a distinction between these two kinds of activities, even though both may be regarded as equally 'natural', and although the distinction cannot always be clearly formulated by the members of the cultures concerned. It rests simply on the presence or absence in what is done of a symbolic element, in which something is standing for something else. This means that the whole procedure, or rite, has an essentially expressive aspect, whether or not it is thought to be effective instrumentally as well. In every rite something is being said as well as done. The man who consults a rain-maker, and the rain-maker who carries out a rain-making ceremony, are stating something; they are asserting symbolically the importance they attach to rain and their earnest desire that it shall fall when it is required.

This is why so many rites enact the state of affairs which it is hoped to bring about. It is not simply that some causal connection is believed to exist between things that resemble one another; it is rather that the use of like objects or situations is an appropriate way of saying what has to be said. Thus rain-making ritual often involves the simulation of rain or cloud, as by pouring water, or burning green herbs to make heavy smoke. And a sorcerer who wishes to kill someone may dramatically express and 'act out' his wish by making a wax model of his enemy and melting it in the fire or impaling it with pins.

Once the essentially expressive, symbolic character of ritual, and therefore of magic, has been understood, it becomes easier to answer the question, often asked: how is it that so many people continue to believe in and practise magic, without either noticing its ineffectiveness or attempting to test it empirically as they test their practical techniques? It is simply that there would be no point in doing so, for if and in so far as the central significance of a rite is expressive, it is thus far an end in itself. There are other reasons why people continue to believe in and practise magic; I note some of them later. But where what is basically important is to say something publicly and ceremonially, the consequences, if any, of saying it are rather less to the point than they are in more exclusively technical activities.

I am not saying that ritual and magical activities are not commonly thought to be causally effective; they certainly are. But they are expressive *as well as* being instrumental, and it is this that distinguishes them from strictly empirical, instrumental activity. Indeed often they are believed to be instrumental just because they are expressive; many people think that the word, the *logos*, has its own special power. Often it is believed that to say or even to think something solemnly and emphatically enough is somehow to make it more likely to happen. Even members of modern societies may be frightened and ashamed when they become conscious of hidden wishes for the death or injury of someone they dislike, and may feel guilt when the object of their antipathy is run over by a bus. Belief in the power of words, thoughts and symbols is by no means a monopoly of simpler peoples. Most members of 'advanced' societies have at least some non-scientific, non-empirical beliefs and practices, which may (or may not) be embodied in formal religious—or perhaps political— rituals. Since these beliefs are essentially expressive it would be inappropriate, even meaningless, to put them to the kinds of tests which might disprove them.

For Westerners, the distinction between these two kinds of activities and interests is perhaps clearest in the context of art. Like ritual, art is a way of saying something, and its worth as art lies in the effective-ness with which it says it, rather than in any end (the promotion of particular moral or social attitudes, the sale of a commodity, or whatever it may be) which it may be sought to bring about. This is not the place for a discussion of primitive art, which has been much misunderstood by Western critics. But it is worth stressing that most such art is a way of expressing, in sensory form and usually in an idiom comprehensible to the people for whom it is made, concepts, attitudes and values which are held in particular regard in a given culture. The 'primitive' artist is not, or not usually, pursuing 'significant form', or art for its own sake; he is trying to say some-thing important to his fellows (often about the spirit world), in language that they will understand.

It is understandable that expressive, ritual, patterns of behaviour should be much more prevalent in simpler, technologically primitive cultures. Of course there is always a body of empirical knowledge in such societies, but inevitably there is a very much wider field of daily experience in which scientific knowledge which might provide a recipe for effective action is lacking. Illness and death from disease, starvation or accident are not only commoner in such communities, they are also much more public. They form an inescapable part of everybody's daily experience. The urban citizen of a modern state may (with luck) grow to adulthood without any real, first-hand experience of these unpleasant facts; an African tribesman or an Asian peasant cannot. And in these less protected communities there is no adequate scientific understanding of these distressing and socially disruptive events, so for the most part there are no practical, empirically tested ways of dealing with them. But this does not mean that they cannot be dealt with at all: that would be intolerable. There is much that a member of such a community not only can but ought to do; his culture prescribes definite institutionalized ways of dealing with illness, death and other misfortunes, and with the fear of them. What these ways have in common is that they are symbolic and expressive, rather than scientific and experimental. Even though to deal with illness, for example, by magical means or by reference to the postulated activities of ghosts or spirits is not (or not usually) clinically effective—or at least not in quite the way in which it is thought to be by its practitioners—it may none the less have impor-tant psychological and social consequences.

Broadly, these consequences are of three kinds, and most explana-tions of magical and religious phenomena which are concerned with cause and effect rather than with meaning refer to one or other of them. First there is the cognitive level. Rituals almost always embody beliefs, and these beliefs may provide acceptable explanations for events which would otherwise be inexplicable. In this way they provide an antidote to ignorance and doubt. For most people, in all times and cultures, it is a necessity to know, even to know wrongly, rather than not to know at all. We noted in an earlier chapter that it was at this cognitive level that the great Victorians Tylor and Frazer tried to explain magic and religion. Tylor thought that primitive man resolved the intellectual puzzles of sleeping, dreaming and dying (where am I when I am asleep, dreaming or dead?) by supposing that there must be things called spirits, having some kind of existence separately from bodies. And Frazer, correctly observing that much magical activity involves the use of things that are like one another (as gold was supposed to be a magical cure for jaundice) or of things that have once been in intimate contact with one another (as a sorcerer is thought to be able to injure another if he can obtain a bit of his hair, a nail-clipping, a shred of his clothes, even the dust he has trodden on), was led to formulate his celebrated distinction between homeopathic magic, based on likeness, and contagious magic, based on physical contiguity. But Frazer erred in supposing that magic was simply a mistaken theory of causation. Nobody in their senses could possibly believe that all things that share some common quality, and all things that have once been in contact, are continually affecting one another; in a world so conceived almost everything would all the time be affecting almost everything else, and all would be chaos. Magicians and their clients know quite well that for most of the time like is *not* affecting like.

Magic is not thought to take place by itself, as Frazer's theory implies. It is only when men make magic, that is, when they perform rites, that results are to be expected. Magic is the acting out of a situation, the expression of a desire in symbolic terms; it is not the application of empirically acquired knowledge about the properties of natural substances. For the intelligent magician and his subjects it is the whole procedure, the rite, that is thought to be effective, not just the substances by themselves. And this is so even though, as we shall see more fully later, the nature of symbolic thinking is such that often a special kind of potency comes to be imputed to the substances used in or associated with ritual. I have already quoted Whitehead's dictum about symbolism's tendency to run wild, and in most cultures the potency implicit in symbolic activity tends to flow over into the symbols themselves.

Frazer failed to see that magic was not just a mistaken theory about natural causation because he was concerned with what people thought about things, rather than with what they did about them. He reached his theories about what 'primitives' thought by imaginatively putting himself, complete with his scientifically oriented, Victorian intellectual background, in their place, and then conjecturing what kind of theory about nature could possibly account for their behaviour. This is why Evans-Pritchard refers to his and Tylor's theories as the English 'intellectualist' interpretation of magic. The truth is that magic is a symbolic activity, not a scientific one, and the elements used in it are selected because they are symbolically appropriate, not because they have been found by careful experiment to possess certain kinds of causal effectiveness. Frazer was right in identifying two of the basic principles implicit in magical symbolism, but he was mistaken in basing on this symbolism a presumed primitive theory of causation.

So magic is not only a way of thinking about things; it is also a way of doing things. And people usually resort to it in situations of actual or potential danger or misfortune: if everything were for the best in the best of all possible worlds, there would be little need of either magic or religion. This brings us to the second important kind of consequence which ritual, 'magico-religious' behaviour may have. This is that it may provide a way of coping with situations of misfortune or danger with which there are no other means of dealing. It is a commonplace that in the face of actual or threatened disaster to do something is psychologically satisfying and a way of relieving anxiety; anything is better than just remaining passive and waiting for it to happen. Where there is no body of empirical knowledge to turn to for help, or where such knowledge is plainly inadequate, then ritual procedures, whose validity does not rest on experience, may provide an acceptable alternative. Malinowski's Trobriand Islanders carry out a number of magical rites before they set out on long and hazardous kula voyages, but they do not bother with magic when they are simply going for a day's fishing on the lagoon. This is just what we should expect. There are grave dangers to be faced on ocean voyages in fragile canoes; the sheltered lagoon is free from hazard. And where there are good grounds for anxiety, to relieve it may be an important function of magical activity.

In many parts of Africa—and elsewhere—illness, which naturally may be a source of grave anxiety to the patient and his kin, is believed to be due to the anger of a spirit or ghost, perhaps of a living witch or sorcerer. Any of these alternatives, one or other of which is likely to be diagnosed by divination, not only adequately explains the illness, it also provides a recipe for action. The victim or his relatives may attempt to conciliate the ghost or spirit by invocation and sacrifice; or they may seek out the witch or sorcerer and either request him to withdraw his evil influence or try to have him brought to justice. Or, like the Azande of the Southern Sudan, they may themselves make vengeance magic against the suspected witch. In all of these cases and in many others like them magical beliefs and techniques imply not just a theory of causality but also a way of acting. It is believed that by taking the proper action threatened misfortune can be averted and actual misfortune alleviated.

It has been pointed out with some justice that this is all very well, but that ritual beliefs and procedures do not always relieve anxiety. Sometimes they have quite the opposite effect. Victorian children were terrified by horrific accounts of hell fire, and Ganda peasants in traditional times were presumably disquieted by the possibility of arbitrary arrest and execution so that their shed blood might ritually 'strengthen the king'. But even if ritual beliefs and practices sometimes create anxiety, more basically they are designed to relieve it. The exceptions may be explained by ritual's proliferating character. One symbol leads to another, and the implications for human behaviour of some of these proliferations are often far from consistent with what may be presumed to have been the ritual's original intention. With regard to the two cases mentioned above, most people would agree that the core of the Christian teaching, to which belief in hell fire and damnation was peripheral, was a message of comfort and reassurance. And it may even be supposed that the Ganda monarchy, the importance of which was stressed symbolically by the ritual killings which were believed to sustain it, served for many people as a factor of social stability and cohesion.

The third important kind of consequences which magical and religious institutions may have are their implications not just for their performers' states of mind, but for other social institutions which co-exist with them in the same society. This is the functionalist question: how do the institutionalized beliefs and practices which we call magical or religious fit into their social context? We are concerned here mainly with what R. K. Merton called 'latent function' rather than 'manifest function'. That is, we are dealing with consequences of human behaviour of which most of the actors are or may be quite ignorant. But it is likely that in most societies at least some of the actors will be more or less aware of some of the social implications of their ritual institutions.

What then are the social implications of ritual, of magico-religious behaviour? Some have been indicated already. To take the matter further the best course will be to take an actual case, and the best, indeed the classic example is still Evans-Pritchard's account of *Witchcraft, Oracles and Magic among the Azande*. Among this people of the Southern Sudan, witches are persons who are believed to be able to make others ill or even kill them through the possession of a special kind of power. Most misfortunes are attributed to witchcraft: a victim knows that the witch is likely to be someone who is acquainted with him and has a grudge against him, for witches attack those whom they hate. A man who thinks he has been bewitched first of all consults an oracle. By means of an oracular technique, such as the manipulation of a special rubbing-board (when it sticks it confirms the suggestion put to it) or the administration of a strychnine poison to fowls, the victim determines or confirms the identity of the attacker. If the witch's activities have not yet resulted in death, the victim or his relatives may approach him and politely ask him to withdraw his witchcraft. To save trouble, the suspected witch usually agrees. If the victim died, in pre-European times his relatives might have avenged his death by killing the witch, provided that the chief agreed and that his oracles confirmed the original diagnosis. But more often the survivors would make magic against the witch responsible, even though they did not know who he was: after oracular confirmation, some subsequent death in the community was taken to be evidence of guilt and of the efficacy of the vengeance magic.

Thus Zande beliefs about witches and the behaviour associated with these beliefs form a closed system. They not only provide an acceptable way of thinking about the socially disruptive experiences of illness and death, but they also prescribe a socially approved way of doing something about them. They canalize and give institutionalized recognition to the hostile emotions which are inevitable in a small community, and they provide a means of expressing and dealing with these emotions. Also, in Azande as in many other societies where sorcery and witchcraft are still prevalent, they are important social sanctions against anti-social behaviour. For a man who is surly or unneighbourly not only risks antagonizing others and so incurring the danger of being bewitched by someone he has offended, but also he may himself be thought to be a witch (since witches are known to be bad-tempered and unsociable), and so may invite accusation by somebody, with possibly very painful consequences for himself. Finally, Zande oracles, like the political system itself, are hierarchically organized; the most powerful oracles are those operated by the chiefs and by the king himself, and a commoner must take matter of special importance to them. So the system of oracles is consistent with and may even be said to support the political system with which it is associated. In all these ways Zande witchcraft, oracles and magic form a coherent system on the levels of both thought and action, and as social institutions they have important implications for the life of the community.

Other forms of ritual or magical activity have important social consequences. First, they may provide a means of ordering and co-ordinating every-day, practical activities. Malinowski pointed out that among the Trobrianders practical activities like canoe-building are more efficiently carried out because the different stages of the work are associated with particular rituals, and joint participation in these is mandatory. Again, the duties implied in particular kinds of social obligation may be more willingly performed if their importance is emphasized and driven home by ritual. An example is the rite of the blood pact, common in many societies, whereby through the performance of a special rite two men enter into a relationship of mutual help and support. As we noted in Chapter 8, the ritual avoidance often prescribed between certain affines may be an important means of maintaining good social relations and avoiding conflict.

In all these cases it is a function of ritual to enhance the social importance of something which is held to be of value in the society which has the ritual. If ritual is a kind of language, a way of saying things, then Trobriand canoe magic stresses the importance of canoe building for the Trobrianders; blood pact ritual emphasizes the need for mutual support between the parties to it; and avoidance ritual asserts the need to maintain good relations between affinally linked groups. Since people's behaviour is largely determined by what they think to be important, the performance of ritual may have important social consequences. This was the central theme of Radcliffe-Brown's theory of ritual, which he derived from Durkheim. In *The Andaman Islanders* and elsewhere he argued that ritual's main social function is to express certain important social sentiments (or as we should nowadays call them values), such as the need for mutual support and solidarity between the members of a community. Unless enough people held and acted on these values the society could not survive, and through the performance of ritual they are kept constantly in the minds of the performers, and so the maintenance of the social system is secured. I return below to Radcliffe-Brown's theory of ritual; here I note only his argument that ritual is a kind of language, that what it says is often socially very important, and that the statements it makes have significant implications for action.

Here are two further examples of this general theme. In every society as people get older they move through different statuses. Sometimes these statuses are strongly institutionalized in systems of age grades and age sets, as among the Nilo-Hamites of East Africa. Where this is so, initiation into an age set, and the transition from one grade to another, are usually accompanied by extensive ritual. Often the rite of circumcision is practised, as a way of marking the transition from childhood to adulthood. Very commonly there is a period of separation from the normal life of the community, and certain ritual prohibitions have to be observed. Rites of these kinds have been called *rites de passage*, or transition rituals. The French ethnologist van Gennep has distinguished them as rites of separation, rites of segregation, and rites of integration. Rites of separation express the initiate's relinquishment of his former status. Rites of segregation express the fact that he is now cut off from normal community life; he now occupies no recognized status in society but is, as it were, betwixt and between. Rites of integration express the initiate's acceptance in his new status—adulthood, warriorhood, or whatever it may be—and his reintegration in the community. Transition ritual expresses the great social importance which a society attaches to changes of status among its members: the smooth working of any social system depends on everyone knowing and accepting his proper role in it, and this is so especially where (as among the Nilo-Hamites) the maintenance of a fighting force in a state of constant preparedness is essential. Often transition ritual involves the infliction of pain, and so of some fear and anxiety, on the subject of it. This not only serves to impress upon the candidates and all others concerned the social importance of the occasion, but it may also, through the bond of shared suffering, strengthen the tie between those who are initiated together.

Here is a second example. Numerous ritual and magical beliefs and procedures are often associated with kingship, and hereditary political authority generally. In this context myth, which often embodies a claim to divine or miraculous origin or imputes superhuman attributes to a ruler's ancestors, may be regarded as a kind of ritual, rather than as a kind of history. Like all ritual (and unlike history), it is not trying to prove something or to convey practical, verifiable information about some state of affairs. Rather it is saying something, and what it is saying is that the ruler is a very superior sort of being, quite different from ordinary people; therefore he should be respected and obeyed. The social significance of this assertion is, of course, that to accept the myth is also to accept the ruler and the system of authority which the myth validates. In this way social distinctions of power and status which are given in a society may be sustained.

Kingly ritual takes many other forms besides myth. Frazer's 'divine kingship' involves magical beliefs about the king's mystical identification with the country he rules (that is, he is himself a symbol), with their corollary beliefs that he should never become ill, deformed or feeble, lest the whole country suffer. Hence the widespread idea that the king should be ritually killed before his powers wane, and replaced by a stronger and younger successor. Though real evidence that this often or indeed ever happened is inconclusive, the belief that it does so is socially important. It stresses the king's uniqueness and power, and so helps to sustain the system of authority of which he is the head. Other royal rituals point the same moral, for example the food restrictions associated with some African (and other) kingships, which require the king to eat only high-status foods and not those consumed by ordinary people; the special court vocabularies associated with some kingships; and regalia of crowns, sceptres and other symbolic objects. All these ritual usages and things are essentially expressive, and they also have important social implications.

So far, I have intentionally not distinguished between magic and religion; both imply ritual, symbolic ideas and activities rather than practical, 'scientific' ones, and in some simpler cultures they are not clearly distinguished, if they are distinguished at all. I have throughout stressed the danger of attempting arbitrarily to impose our own category distinctions on those of other cultures. In fact, however we formulate the distinction, beliefs and practices which are usually called religious often contain a magical element, even in Western cultures. And much so-called magical activity (for example, sorcery, or the rain-making ritual referred to earlier) may involve reference to gods or spirits, and may even entail invocation and sacrifice, phenomena which are usually regarded as religious. What is common to all these kinds of activities is the ritual, symbolic element they contain. With this is combined the idea, implicit or explicit, that there is a certain kind of efficacy in the performance of the rites themselves. But so long as we bear in mind the complexity of the social and cultural situations involved, a broad distinction is possible. We may, with Tylor, distinguish between those kinds of beliefs and practices which involve reference to more or less 'personalized' spiritual beings, such as gods, ghosts and spirits, and those which do not, implying instead the notion of an impersonal, unindividualized power.[1] Even though there are numerous borderline cases in which it is difficult to say whether what is involved is a 'personalized' spirit or a diffuse, unindividuated power, the distinction has much practical convenience, and I adopt it here. In the rest of this chapter I deal more particularly with magic, in the sense just indicated, leaving those ritual activities which are concerned with gods, ghosts and spirits for Chapter 13.

Although magic *is* magic because it is essentially expressive and symbolic, the people who use it think of it as instrumental. They

[1] Tylor, E. B., *Primitive Culture*, London, 1871.

perform it to bring about ends which they desire. The ends which they wish to bring about may be socially regarded as good ones, such as rain in time of drought, a good harvest, plenty of children. Or they may be regarded as bad, like the death or illness of another person. In all societies black magic or sorcery is regarded as a bad thing, and in many when sorcerers are detected they are killed or banished. But here as so often in social anthropology, a clear-cut dichotomy misrepresents the facts. Sorcery is not always evil, for it may be employed against bad people, as the bereaved Azande practise it against the anonymous murderers of their kinsmen. The power which Nyakyusa witches possess to injure others is shared also by the village headmen, who may use it against unpopular or deviant members of the community. Malinowski tells us that Trobriand chiefs are expected to use 'black magic' to maintain their position.[1] But generally sorcery and witchcraft are bad.

What exactly does magical activity involve? Malinowski said that there are three elements in any magical act: the spell or the actual words used; the rite, what is actually done; and the moral or ritual condition of the performer. The latter, as Radcliffe-Brown also stressed, may be especially important. For example, much royal ritual must be carried out by virgins, male or female, or by persons who have been continent for a specified period. Often participants in communal ritual are required to be well disposed towards one another and free of mutual enmity. But the importance attached to those various elements differs greatly from one culture to another, and also the emphasis varies in different kinds of magical activity. A Zande witch is believed to injure his victim without the use of instruments or medicines; he does so, perhaps unknowingly, because he has a special power to bewitch. This power is supposed to be associated with a particular physical condition of the intestines, detectable by autopsy. But in most parts of Africa sorcerers use the most varied kinds of medicines to perform their evil magic: hair, blood or nail parings of their intended victim; human and animal bones; various plant species; 'eye of newt and tongue of frog'—the catalogue of sorcery medicines is almost endless. And almost all of them are selected because of some symbolic appropriateness to the end sought.

It is said (though it is very difficult to prove) that sometimes they include 'real' poisons, and in many cultures the clear-cut distinction drawn by Westerners between poisoning and 'black magic' is not made. This is yet another case where Western and 'native' categories may not coincide. Anthropologists have found it useful to distinguish

[1] Wilson, M., *Good Company*, London, 1951; Malinowski, B., *Crime and Custom in Savage Society*, London, 1962.

between witchcraft and sorcery on the grounds just considered; a witch brings about his evil effects simply because he is a witch and wants to; he has no need of medicines or techniques: a sorcerer deliberately uses magical techniques and substances to work evil on somebody or something. Here again there are borderline cases where the distinction is difficult to apply. But in many cultures in Africa and elsewhere these two kinds of magical evil-doing are recognized and have different names, so we shall do well to mark the distinction too.

A further variation in emphasis broadly distinguishes magical practice in Africa and Melanesia. In Melanesia the spell is essential; the right form of words for the performance of particular kinds of magic is handed down from generation to generation. It is disastrous to forget the right words, for a mistake will invalidate the magic. So in many Melanesian societies magical spells are an important kind of property. But in Africa the stress is rather on the power of the rite itself, and of the materials used in it; the actual form of the words used is relatively unimportant, although some sort of more or less formal invocation is almost always required.

I stressed earlier that magic does not make itself; usually it is the whole act or rite, not just the medicines or words by themselves, that is thought to be effective. Nevertheless in many cultures the potency believed to be involved in these activities is often thought of as somehow flowing over into and attaching itself to many of the objects, events and even words which are associated with the ritual. Since Western Europeans have no monopoly of Whitehead's 'fallacy of misplaced concreteness', this potency comes to be thought of as a kind of existent in its own right, capable of being transmitted from one person or object to another.

Polynesian peoples have a notion of a kind of impersonal power, associated especially with chiefs, but also with other creatures and objects which are in some way strange and out of the ordinary, and so in some degree awesome. This power is called *mana*, and it is believed that it may be dangerous to people who are not equipped either by birth or training to come into contact with it. It is thought that the mana of a chief can kill or injure ordinary people, and a Tikopian (for example) who accidentally touched his chief's head would think himself in grave danger. Readers of the Old Testament will remember that contact with the Ark of the Tabernacle could kill the impious. The Nyoro of East Africa have a concept which they call *mahano* (it may be assumed that the slight resemblance to the word mana is fortuitous!). This is a kind of magical power which is associated with a wide range of objects and events. What is common to these is simply that they are strange, apart from ordinary life; and therefore fearful. The king and his senior chiefs have much mahano; birth and death bring it about, and unusual events like the birth of twins, or the entry of a wild animal into a dwelling-house, involve it. Nyoro speak of mahano as a real quality or force, almost as a substance, inhering in certain persons, things and events. Like a physical contagion there are recognized means of acquiring and disposing of it, which entail the performance of special rites. But we need not range so far afield to find examples of the universal tendency to attribute power to symbols. In Tudor England to touch the king or even his garment was believed to be a specific for scrofula, and even today in many quite 'advanced' cultures many people impute special magical power to symbols in the form of mascots and charms.

Common to all these ideas and practices, then, is the notion that a special kind of potency attaches to symbols, and to symbolic, that is, to ritual, procedures. These are fundamentally expressive, but just because they are this they are often taken to be instrumentally effective as well. It is because, whatever else they are, they are essentially expressive that they are not usually thought of as experimentally testable, in the same way as practical techniques for doing things. It would be quite inappropriate so to regard them. No Nyoro, for example, thinks of mahano as something that can be measured and weighed; the idea of doing so would be as absurd to him as it is to us. This is why magic is totally misunderstood if it is thought of, as Frazer thought of it, as 'bastard science', and this is why in no culture do people try out the efficacy of different spells or magical substances in the same way as they test the efficacy of different kinds of clay for pot-making, or of bait for fishing. We have here two quite different kinds of human activity: each may be thought to be causally effective but in all cultures the causal efficacy of magical and religious activity is thought (where it is thought about at all) to be of a different kind from the causal efficacy of practical, everyday techniques. Naturally the degree of articulateness with which this difference is expressed varies from culture to culture. But the distinction, whether explicit or inchoate, derives from the fundamental fact that in one case we are dealing with the imagined potency of symbols and symbolism, and in the other with the directly experienced power of ourselves, of other people and of things.

Consideration of the notion of mana, and of the power believed to reside in symbolically significant objects and situations, leads to the concept of *tabu*, or taboo. Like mana, the word comes from Polynesia; there it means what is forbidden on pain of some ritual sanction.

that is, of some penalty which is believed to be brought about by the mere fact of performing the forbidden act. In many Polynesian societies it is taboo for a commoner to touch a chief's head. People who possess the necessary magical knowledge can make things taboo; for example a Polynesian who wishes to protect his standing crop from thieves may taboo it by performing the necessary magical rite, and then putting a recognized sign where all can see it. It is believed that the breach of a taboo places the offender in a condition of ritual danger, and in many cultures this can only be relieved, where it can be relieved at all, by the performance of specific cleansing ritual. Thus in Bunyoro the mahano which is brought about by twin birth can only be relieved by the performance of a long and nowadays expensive series of rites. In European society to spill salt at table is thought of by some as a kind of taboo, and the undesirable ritual condition which this entails (usually called 'bad luck') can only be relieved if the offender carries out a rite of throwing a pinch of salt over his left shoulder.

The concept of ritual prohibition or taboo is just as widespread as the idea of ritual force or power; indeed it is an aspect of it. Like it, it rests not on experience and experiment, but on a belief in the efficacy of symbols. We do not say that it is taboo to drive through a red traffic light, or to look for a gas leak with a lighted match; these prohibitions are sanctioned by bitter experience, either our own or other people's. This is not so, or at least it need not be so, in the case of taboos. There is (at least nowadays) no 'common sense' reason why, for instance, it is considered unlucky to spill the salt, or why a member of a totemic group among the Australian aborigines should not kill and eat his totemic animal, provided that it is plentiful and good to eat. These prohibitions are sanctioned not by practical experience, but by ritual. And this is so even though sometimes practical sanctions may be added to ritual ones, as when a breach of taboo is made punishable by law, or the whole community takes action against an offender. The force of these interdictions does not lie in remembered or learned experience of the actual consequences of their breach; it lies rather in their symbolic significance for the people who acknowledge them.

This is not to say that taboos do not have important social consequences: they do. A taboo on a field of ripe yams may be a powerful disincentive to theft; a taboo on (say) using the name of one's wife's mother may reinforce socially prescribed respect between affines; the taboo on touching or approaching too close to a chief may powerfully sanction a system of political authority. But, as in the case of other magical beliefs and practices, these consequences may not always be known to the members of the culture which has the taboos.

I have already referred to Radcliffe-Brown's theory of ritual. His argument was that one of its functions is to express and so to reinforce certain sentiments or values upon adherence to which the smooth running of the society that has the ritual depends. The important truth which this view contains is now plain. In this chapter I have argued that ritual, magic and taboo, are essentially symbolic and so expressive, although they are often thought to be instrumental as well. Certainly they may have important social consequences for the people who have them, and I have discussed some of these. But the difficulty with Radcliffe-Brown's account of ritual, as with some of his other theories, is that as he states it it is too general to be of very much practical use in investigating real human cultures. To say, as he does, that the communal performance of ritual may express, and so sustain, values which contribute to the maintenance of social solidarity may, sometimes, be true. But it is not always so. Communal ritual may be divisive as well as cohesive, and other notions besides social solidarity may be symbolically expressed by means of it. Some of the rites involved in sorcery, for example, can hardly be said to sustain patterns of behaviour which are conducive to social cohesion. Further, Radcliffe-Brown's hypothesis, as he tends to state it, can afford no hypotheses for testing. For social cohesion itself is taken to be exhibited by the very communal performances which are supposed to sustain it. There is circularity in an argument which reduces itself to the assertion that dancing together contributes to the kind of situation in which people like to dance together. The thesis could only be disproved by finding a society which failed to carry out the necessary ritual and therefore perished. But it was Radcliffe-Brown's great merit that, following Durkheim, he made the point that ritual is an essentially expressive activity, and that it can and does have important social implications.

SHORT READING LIST

EVANS-PRITCHARD, E. E., *Witchcraft, Oracles and Magic among the Azande*, Oxford, 1937.

KLUCKHOHN, C., *Navaho Witchcraft*, Harvard, 1944.

MALINOWSKI, B., *Magic, Science and Religion and other Essays*, Glencoe (Ill.), 1948.

MIDDLETON, J., and WINTER, E. H. (editors), *Witchcraft and Sorcery in East Africa*, London, 1963.

RADCLIFFE-BROWN, A. R., *The Andaman Islanders*, Cambridge, 1922.

STEINER, F., *Taboo*, London, 1956.

VAN GENNEP, A., *The Rites of Passage* (English translation), London, 1960.

WILSON, M., *Good Company*, London, 1951.

Rituals of Kinship among the Nyakyusa, London, 1957.

13

The Field of Ritual: Religion

I SAID EARLIER that any attempt to distinguish clearly between magic and religion is bound to be arbitrary, for the difference between the notion of a magical power in things and the idea of a more or less personalized spirit in things is very much one of degree. The beliefs and practices which we call totemism fall on the borderline. Sometimes, as among the Australian aborigines, the totem is thought of as a kind of spiritual agent for which special ceremonies are performed, so that it is the object of a totemic cult. More commonly, as among many Bantu peoples, it is little more than a clan symbol or emblem, though it may be the object of a ritual avoidance, and it is sometimes imbued with a magical power to injure members of the totemic group who abuse it. The chief difficulty in discussing totemism is that the term has been applied to many different social and cultural institutions. Indeed, as the American anthropologist Goldenweiser showed, there is no single criterion by which totemism might be defined which is not lacking in what is called totemism in some other society.[1]

The term *totem* comes from a North-American Indian language, but it has been widely used to refer to animal or plant species and occasionally other things which are held in special regard by particular groups (or, exceptionally, individuals) in a society. When social anthropologists speak of a totemic society, they usually refer to a society which is divided into a number of named groups, the members of which believe themselves to be descended unilineally from a common ancestor, and stand in a special relationship, usually involving respect and avoidance, to some object. So a number of features are generally associated with totemism besides the reference to some *thing*, the totem.

First, it is usually a group institution, though the group is not invariably one based on unilineal descent. But in some North-American

[1] Goldenweiser, A. A., *History, Psychology and Culture*, New York, 1932.

219

Indian tribes people may have individual totems. Whole communities are organized into distinct and mutually exclusive totemic groups in Australia, Bantu Africa, North America, and many other parts of the world. Second, these totemic groups are very often exogamous. But they are not always so; totemic clans among some African peoples are not. Third, the group may be named after the totemic species with which it is associated: thus in Buganda there is a leopard clan, a crocodile clan, a lungfish clan, and so on. But in the neighbouring Bantu kingdom of Bunyoro clans are not named after the species with which they are associated, although they are socially recognized units. Fourth, there may be a mythical belief that members of each totemic clan are descended from the totemic species associated with it: this is common in Australia and Melanesia, rare in Africa.

It is not even the case that there is always an attitude of reverence or respect towards the totem, although as befits a symbol, it is usually thought of as different from ordinary, everyday objects. Fortes reports that the West African Tallensi view their totems quite unemotionally, and the Indians of the American North-West hold theirs in no special regard. None the less a custom of ritual avoidance of the totem is widespread. In Africa members of totemic groups are generally prohibited from killing and eating their totem (if it is edible), though others may do so. A Nyoro believes that if he eats his totemic species he may become ill and perhaps die. He respects rather than fears it; certainly he does not worship it. He uses the same term, meaning 'respectful avoidance', for his relationship to his wife's mother as he does for his relationship to his totem.

Some Australian tribes, like the Arunta described by Spencer and Gillen, avoid their totems except on the occasion of special 'increase' ceremonies. It is said that these sometimes involve ceremonially eating the species concerned, and that the object of the ritual is to ensure its continued supply. Commonly the totem is an important article of diet, like a kangaroo or a witchetty grub. Thus the increase ritual of each totemic group is directed to ensuring the normal food supply of the rest of the community. This kind of totemism was at one time thought to be characteristic of totemism everywhere, but it is now recognized to be a peculiar type, probably limited to Australia.

How are we to understand this curiously widespread institution, or category of institutions? Durkheim, who based his analysis mainly on the Arunta data, was the first to offer a sociological explanation. He saw that totems were symbols, standing for something other than themselves, and he argued that what they stood for was the social group itself. In the rigorous conditions of Australian tribal life group membership, with its implied rights and obligations, is an indispensable condition of survival. But group solidarity and the maintenance of the social system on which it depends are concepts too abstract for Arunta tribesmen to represent to themselves in logical terms. Nevertheless the essential sentiments of attachment to these values can be given collective expression, and so reinforced, through the performance of joint ritual. Some concrete object which stands for these values is needed to serve as the object of this ritual, and this object is the totem. In Durkheim's metaphor, it is the flag of the clan, and the reason why real natural objects are chosen is that unlike the concepts and values they stand for, they can be easily apprehended and represented. Durkheim thought that all religion originated in totemism, for like most of his contemporaries he believed that the Australian aborigines represented a stage of social evolution through which all more advanced societies must have passed. Thus he was led to the view that all the gods that men worship are but man-made symbols of society itself. Society is the indispensable condition of human life as we know it, and in worshipping God man is really worshipping his own social system.

Durkheim's theory of religion has been subjected to a good deal of well-deserved criticism. But it is rather less naïve than it appears to be, when it is realized (and Durkheim sometimes failed to make this clear) that society is not a 'thing', but rather a system of relationships, in some sense a construct. Social relationships, involving as they do beliefs, expectations and values as well as human interactions in space and time, are not 'given' empirically, in the same sense that the data of the natural sciences are. It is one thing to say that totemism, or religion, means that a man worships the actual group of people, the social aggregate, of which he is a member. It is quite a different thing to say that what he is revering is a complex system of moral imperatives, of rights and obligations, the observance of which is a condition of ordered social life. It was the latter that Durkheim should be taken as having meant, not the former, though sometimes he was less than clear on this point. What he did was to raise to the level of a sociological principle the Christian maxim that all men are members one of another. Most modern students of religion would hold, as against Durkheim, that religious belief and practice are more than merely a system of social and moral symbolism. But such group symbolism can be very important, in secular as well as in religious contexts, and it was to Durkheim's great merit that he pointed this out.

But as a theory of totemism it is not quite adequate, although it makes the important point that totems, like flags and old school ties in Western societies, are symbols of group unity. It explains both too much and too little. It explains too much because, as we have noted, not all totemic groups worship or revere their totems. It explains too little because, as Radcliffe-Brown later pointed out, the preoccupation with the food supply implicit in Australian totemic ceremonies suggests that totems are chosen not *just* because they are easily represented, but for some other reason too. Radcliffe-Brown argues that they are selected because they are already objects of practical, and therefore ritual, interest to the community. Why, he asks, are food animals and plants so commonly chosen as totems, as they are in Australia? The answer, he suggests, is because man is dependent on natural products for his existence, and so, since ritual value tends to attach to objects of great importance, there already exists a ritual relationship between man and the natural world. This explains why people as remote from each other as the Eskimos of North America and the Andaman Islanders of the Indian Ocean, both of whom lack any form of totemism, have none the less a ritual regard for certain important features of their natural environment. So, Radcliffe-Brown argues, totems are not ritually important simply because they have been chosen as totems; they were chosen as totems in the first place because they were already symbolically important on other grounds. Totemism as it occurs in Australia (though hardly anywhere else) is really a kind of ritual division of labour. The society is segmented into a number of distinct totemic groups, and each group is responsible for the ritual needed to ensure the continued supply of a particular food.

This interpretation may somewhat advance our understanding of Australian totemism, and of ritual generally, but it is no advance on Durkheim's as a general theory of totemism. It is doubtful if the hypothesis that in general people have a ritual regard for objects and events which are of great practical importance to them can be sustained, at least without a good deal of qualification. Certainly many people do attach ritual significance to things that are important to them, but by no means all peoples do, and even when they do they do not so regard everything that is of practical importance. Many African peoples attach a very high value to cattle, but among none of them do cattle form the object of a cult, though they may be and are used in religious cults. And a theory which does not account for apparent exceptions to it is of little use.

Further, in many parts of the world where totemism is found, the totems are not natural objects of importance to the totemists, so the regard in which they are held cannot derive from any general ritual relationships between man and nature. Thus the totems of the Tallensi of Northern Ghana (for which in any case they have little regard) are

222

mostly animals of little or no practical importance to human beings. What they symbolize, Fortes tells us, is the power of the lineage ancestors, not any aspect of the natural environment. Since ancestors are often inimical, the fiercer animals are thought specially apt to symbolize them. In other totemic societies the choice of totemic objects is alleged to be due to some historic event linking the fore-bears of the totemic group with the totem. To quote an example already given, a Nyoro clan has as a totem a species of small bird, which, it is said, once warned an ancestor of the group that he was about to be attacked by a buffalo. In other cases the choice seems to have been based on whimsy or private predilection. It should be remembered, too, that in a simple, small-scale society where there are scores, perhaps hundreds, of named totemic groups, the environ-ment must be combed pretty thoroughly if the totemic emblems of the various groups are not to overlap confusingly. Radcliffe-Brown's emendation of Durkheim's theory tends to overlook the essential fact that totems are symbols, so that their significance for the people who have them must be looked for elsewhere than in themselves.

It is worth mentioning in passing, if only as light relief, the great psychologist Sigmund Freud's contribution to the study of totemism. Like Durkheim, he based his hypothesis on the Australian material. He surmised that the origin of the institution lay in the Oedipus complex, which he held to be universal. In the primeval family, he says, the sons covet their father's wives, and in order to acquire them they kill and eat their father. Afterwards they are smitten with remorse, and the totemic feast (which in fact may have occurred in Australia but is found nowhere else) is really a symbolic re-enacting of that first parricidal crime. Freud does not make clear at what point in human history he thinks that this happened, or whether it happened only once or on many occasions. His theory is not taken seriously by social anthropologists, who in any case are not greatly interested in the undiscoverable origins of human institutions. What Freud does is to translate what is undoubtedly a scientific insight of profound importance (at least in Western cultures) from psycho-logical into socio-historical terms. But this is to turn it into an un-demonstrable and therefore valueless hypothesis, significant only as itself a sort of mythical expression of psycho-analytic values.[1]

So the term totemism covers a multitude of phenomena. As it is generally used, however, it refers to situations where each one of a number of discrete social groups into which a society is divided maintains a particular regard—though not necessarily one of worship or reverence—for a particular object in the natural or cultural

[1] Freud, Sigmund, *Totem and Taboo*, London, 1950.

environment; or, more rarely, for some quality such as a particular colour. This object is not (or not only) regarded as valuable in its own right, but because it stands as a symbol for something else. This is why we reckon totemism to be a magico-religious institution. Usually, it seems, the totem symbolizes the unity and solidarity of the group which has it. But very often it symbolizes other things as well: sometimes, as in the case of the Australian aborigines, a particular kind of interdependency between man and the natural products upon which he depends; sometimes, as with the Tallensi, the power of the ancestral ghosts. Institutions which have been labelled totemism are so various that no single hypothesis is likely to be adequate to explain all of them. As with all symbols, we have to ask what it is that is symbolized and what the social consequences of symbolizing it are. There is no reason why all cultures should give identical answers to these questions.

I now consider those symbolic, non-empirical powers, equally creations of the human mind but believed also to be potent agents in human affairs, which are more or less individualized or 'personalized'. Individualization is evidently a matter of degree, and here as elsewhere no firm boundaries can be drawn. But gods, ghosts and spirits are thought of as different from the other impersonal magical forces discussed in the last chapter, however difficult it may be to draw a sharp line between them. First of all I discuss ghosts, then gods and then other kinds of non-human spirits. The important thing about all of them is that they are conceived to be non-human, even though they may have some human attributes. Even ghosts are not thought of as people, even dead ones; they are thought of as beings of quite another kind.

But the fact that they are endowed with some human attributes means that living people may enter into some sort of social relationship with them. Again, precise borderlines cannot be drawn. In some cultures a sort of social relationship can be entered into with forces which are usually thought of as impersonal, such as magical medicines of various kinds. This is why anything more than a rough-and-ready distinction between magic and religion is impracticable. In the ideologies of many simpler cultures nothing is quite inert; there is a force or power in everything which can be known, and 'personalization' is very much a matter of more or less. But nearly always there is a distinction between those powers with which a relationship of a more or less personal kind can be entered into, and those with which it cannot. It is upon this difference that we base a rough distinction between magic, concerned with impersonal magical forces, and religion, concerned with ghosts, gods and spirits.

224

I have said that in most cultures ghosts are not thought of as people; rather they are something that people may leave when they die. A Nyoro who wishes to threaten somebody with ghostly vengeance does not say, 'I shall haunt you after I'm dead!' He says, literally, 'I shall leave you a ghost!' But it is believed that ghosts, unlike other kinds of spirits, were once people, and this gives the world of ghosts a sort of continuity with the living. Something of what a person was when he was alive characterizes his ghost after he dies, but in most cultures it is thought that the softer, more 'human' qualities of his personality are lost. Generally, though not always, ghosts are inimical. This is what one would expect, since like other supernatural agencies, they are usually socially relevant only in situations of illness or other misfortune. What remains of a living person after death is usually thought to be the power which he wielded when alive, transmuted to another plane. Thus in many cultures the ghosts of the powerful, rich and important are the most feared; those of children or poor people are usually disregarded and quickly forgotten. Also, the ghost of a near relative, or of a person, like a blood partner, with whom one has had a particularly close association, is often thought to be especially powerful. In many cultures, if a man has offended someone standing in such a relationship to him, and if that person dies, it is very likely that any illness or other misfortune befalling the person who has offended will be attributed to the ghost of the man he has injured.

In many societies in Africa and elsewhere there is a cult of ancestor worship, or at least people have a special regard for the ghosts of their dead ancestors. Of course it is quite possible to have a lively belief in ghosts and their power over the living without actually worshipping them. The presence or absence of an ancestral cult is very much a matter of degree. Most people know that they had ancestors, and many believe that when their ancestors died they left ghosts behind them. The important questions are, first, what kind of importance, if any, are these ghosts believed to have for the living, and, second, what kind of attitudes do the living have towards them and what do they do about them? In some cultures the answer to these questions is 'none, and nothing, at all'; in others 'very little', and in others again 'a very great deal'. Ancestral cults are known to us from many parts of the world and from all periods of history. In the classical worlds of Greece and Rome an attitude of piety and respect was maintained towards the family ancestors: the Chinese had an elaborate ancestral cult; many simple, pre-literate communities in Africa and elsewhere have one today.

Societies which attach high value to unilineal descent, as the

Romans did, often have an ancestral cult. In such societies lineage forebears several generations back may be structurally important for the living, in defining the distinct lineage subdivisions in which the community is organized. Where this is so, an ancestral cult may stress importance of these key ancestors. But it is by no means the rule that lineage-based societies have ancestral cults: some do, but others do not. The Nuer of the Southern Sudan, whose social organization centres on patrilineal lineages, have no developed ancestral cult. But it is evidently a condition of such a cult that the people who practise it should at least know that they have ancestors, and should think it worth while to remember them, and this is often so where membership in a unilineal descent group is socially important. Sometimes, as among the Tallensi, the lineage is thought of as a single unit, including both the living and the ghosts of their dead ancestors. In such cases the ancestors are believed to be concerned above all with the unity and well-being of the lineages descended from them. They are thought to punish with illness or other misfortunes any behaviour by their living descendants which damages the solidarity and mutual cohesion of the lineage group. Quarrelling between lineage mates, failure to support a needy member of the group, or the territorial scattering of lineage members, may, it is believed, anger the ancestral ghosts and cause them to punish offenders. In these ways the cult may act as a social sanction for approved behaviour, and help to sustain the existing social system.

Obviously all of a man's ancestors cannot be individually remembered. Often they are lumped together as a collectivity, and in many societies as well as the named ghosts of remembered dead relatives, there is a residual category of unspecified forbears. So it is useful to distinguish between ghost cults, where for one reason or another individual ghosts have to be propitiated, and ancestral cults, where the ancestors as a whole are regarded as of vital importance to the living. For there are many societies in which there is a lively fear of and regard for ghosts, but in which ancestors as such are regarded as relatively unimportant, if they are thought of at all.

Ancestral cults may have important social implications. I have referred to their significance as a force for social cohesion, and as affording a social sanction for approved behaviour. But they can also have divisive implications. Middleton has shown how among the Lugbara of Uganda the struggle for authority among different lineage segments and their representatives is expressed through competition for the control of the more important of the ghost shrines. Only those men who can persuade others that they have successfully invoked the ancestral ghosts to punish the living can claim the status of elders, with the right to control shrines. Thus the struggle for political authority is conventionally expressed in, and validated by reference to, the supposedly ancestor-given power of invocation.

Later in this chapter I consider how the activity of ghosts may be diagnosed, and what is done when it is. But first something must be said of other kinds of spiritual powers. Almost every force which can affect human beings may be and has been spiritualized. The elemental powers of nature; sun and moon, rain, thunder and lightning, lakes and rivers, mountains, the forest and the desert; all these have been conceived of as spirits, and have become objects of worship and sacrifice. Individual places, trees, rocks and streams, are often endowed with a kind of personality in this way, especially if some striking and inexplicable event has been associated with them. Human and animal diseases are particularly liable to spiritualization. For people who lack the benefits of modern medical science, it is common for illnesses, especially those, like smallpox or plague, which strike suddenly and dramatically, to be thought of as due to the activity of witches, sorcerers or spirits, or as themselves manifestations of special spirits identified with them.

Why should human beings everywhere people their world with such multiplicities of non-natural agents, often fearsome and terrifying? The answer lies partly in the human condition, especially that of members of simpler, technologically undeveloped communities. Although life in the conditions of such societies may offer rewards unavailable to civilized man, everyday existence is surrounded by unpredictable and sometimes terrifying hazards, of which mortal illness is not the least. And there exists no adequate body of empirical knowledge which might enable men to cope with these hazards, or even to hope to cope with them, by means of practical, scientifically proven or provable techniques. So they must cope with them symbolically and expressively instead.

One answer is to spiritualize the universe. The members of a simple society may have no practical resources to bring to bear against a smallpox epidemic. But if they endow the force which is threatening them with quasi-human attributes, they can at least enter into some kind of social relationship with it. Then, by invocation and sacrifice, they may attempt to avert or ameliorate it. This way of regarding the world can survive long after Western knowledge and techniques have become known, if not always readily accessible. For it meets a universal need, which even in the modern world cannot be wholly satisfied in any other way.

In some, though not in all, societies there has developed the idea of a supreme spiritual being, a high god. Sometimes, as among the ancient Greeks, he is conceived as the oldest and most powerful of the gods, *primus inter pares*; sometimes, as among the Nuer (whose religious ideas have been brilliantly expounded by Evans-Pritchard), God, or the 'sky spirit', is thought of as a kind of universal and all-pervasive essence, of which lesser spirits are merely local aspects or 'refractions'. Where the high god expresses the generalized idea of spirit or 'power', the concept often tends to become depersonalized. So in many cultures the high god is thought to be very much less interested in the affairs of men than are lesser gods or spirits who may be thought to play a frequent part in everyday life. Many African peoples make sacrifices and utter invocations to the ghosts of the dead and to other spirits, but they do not attempt to enter into so personal a relationship with the high god. Often the idea of an otiose high god is expressed in mythical accounts of how after creating the universe he withdrew from it, being dissatisfied with his handiwork. Or, sometimes, human beings are represented as having severed their original relationship with divinity through pride or disobedience. The Christian doctrine of the Fall expresses this idea.

No more can be said here of the conceptual aspect of ghosts, gods and spirits, the ways in which they are thought about and their symbolic significance; these are topics which could (and do) fill many volumes. I now consider their significance in action: what do people do about them, and what is the social importance of what they do?

I have stressed that symbols and spirits tend to become relevant for human action when scientific knowledge is inadequate. Characteristically the spirit world becomes socially important in situations of actual or threatened misfortune. Nyoro culture provides a good example of the kinds of procedures that may be involved. In Bunyoro a man who becomes ill or suffers some other kind of misfortune is likely to consult a diviner to find out the cause of his trouble. The diviner uses one or other of a number of available techniques of divination. These include the use of various kinds of oracles, such as the throwing of cowry shells and the interpretation of the ensuing pattern; the rubbing oracle, in which the diviner rubs his fingers up and down a moistened stick, the point at which his fingers stick indicating the answer; and haruspication, in which the diviner examines the entrails of an animal or bird, nowadays usually a chicken. He then gives his answer. He may say that his client's trouble is due to the practice of sorcery or witchcraft by some living person; if he does he will be careful not to be too specific but will leave his client to draw his own conclusions, for to impute sorcery is a serious matter. He may say that it is due to the activity of a ghost, either of some recently dead person whom his client offended when he was alive, or of some remoter ancestor. Or he may say that it is caused by one or other of a number of powerful non-human spirits, many of which are associated with certain natural forces, and with various kinds of illness.[1]

Whatever the diagnosis, Nyoro culture, like other similar cultures, provides a specific response. If the activity of a ghost or spirit is diagnosed, the sufferer, or perhaps another person acting on his behalf, may have to undergo initiation into a spirit mediumship cult, so that he may be formally 'possessed' by the ghost or spirit responsible. This enables it to communicate, through its medium, with living people and so with the sufferer himself. It can then be interceded with; it can ask for what it wants—perhaps a sacrifice, or the erection of a shrine, or the discharge of a neglected obligation. When its demands have been met it may, Nyoro believe, withdraw its malign influence. In general, in Bunyoro and elsewhere, there are three ways in which the world of spirits can be dealt with; possession, invocation, and sacrifice: often all three are combined. It will be best to deal with them separately.

Given the belief that there are non-human spirits, and that these may affect living human beings, the idea that men may be possessed by them is an almost inevitable corollary. Spirit possession occurs in almost all cultures, though it may assume many different forms, and it is more strongly institutionalized in some cultures than in others. In dealing with it, we shall do well to adopt Firth's useful distinction between spirit possession, spirit mediumship and shamanism. We have spirit possession when a person assumes a state of apparent auto-hypnosis or dissociation, and his behaviour, which is not that of his ordinary self, is understood to be due to control by some spiritual agent normally outside him. Where the presumed spirit not only possesses someone but also communicates with other people through the possessed person, usually in a voice, accent and perhaps language not used by that person in ordinary life, but culturally accepted as appropriate to the spirit believed to be mediated, then we may speak of spirit mediumship. And when the medium is not only a vehicle for spirits, but is believed, like Prospero in *The Tempest*, to be able to command them, we have shamanism.

Possession by a spirit of some kind is often given as an explanation of illness or abnormality, especially in the case of states of mental derangement or dissociation, when the subject does seem to be, as we say, 'out of his mind'. The New Testament contains several references to spirit possession, and the social history of Western Europe provides numerous examples of possession by evil spirits, especially in connection with witchcraft. Since possession is usually (though not

[1] Beattie, John, *Bunyoro: an African Kingdom*, New York, 1960.

always) a bad thing the question then arises: what is to be done about it? Different cultures give different answers. Sometimes, as in the Christian tradition, a spiritual force conceived to be more powerful than the presumed spirit may compel it to leave its victim. In medieval Europe priests with bell, book and candle could exorcise evil spirits. Elsewhere, as in parts of Africa today, techniques of 'peaceful persuasion' may be used. A Nyoro shaman may, with soft words, cajole a minor spirit which is troubling a client to leave him and to enter an earthenware pot. The pot is then quickly sealed with clay, and is later destroyed or abandoned in the bush. In other cases, where the subject is not merely possessed but is also a medium, he may, as it were, come to terms with the spirit through the performance of appropriate ritual. Whether the spirit is the ghost of a deceased relative or some other kind of power, it may use its medium, while in a state of induced possession, to say what it requires if it is to leave its victim alone.

The ways in which spirits are believed to express themselves vary from one culture to another. Although mediums are often in a condition of dissociation, in most cultures the proper way for spirits to manifest themselves through mediums can be learnt, either through formal instruction by experts, or by experience and example. In all cultures with institutionalized spirit mediumship cults certain personality types seem to take more readily than others to cult participation. Sometimes types of deviant behaviour, such as homosexuality among some North American Indian tribes, and in many cultures a propensity to fits or other kinds of mental disturbance, are particularly associated with cult membership. But in many cultures anybody can become a spirit medium, provided that spirit activity is diagnosed, and provided—nowadays—that the candidate has the money to pay for the often quite costly course of initiation involved. When I was enquiring into the cult in Bunyoro one of my informants, formerly herself an accredited spirit medium, told me that even before she was initiated she knew that possession was simulated. 'But,' she said, 'I still thought that it would be good for me to do these things.'

I think that this provides a clue to the intriguing problem of whether or not spirit mediumship is just a fraud. Sometimes it may be, but since dissociation is largely a matter of degree, it is likely that in many societies in which spirit mediumship is institutionalized the practitioner really believes in what he is doing. Even where possession is consciously simulated the pretence may not be wholly fraudulent. For although the practitioner, and perhaps the more sophisticated among his audience, may know that spirits are not, or at least not always, really present in the mediums when they appear to be so, neither he nor they doubt that spirits exist. And it may be believed that a spirit is gratified by the performance of prescribed possession ritual, and so may be willing to withdraw the malign influence which it has been exercising. Here again what is fundamentally important is the symbolic, ritual quality of the performance. It is the whole act or rite that is believed to be effective, and its effectiveness derives in the last resort from what it says.

As well as providing a means of coping with inimical forces which, by being personalized, can be communicated with and so influenced, mediumship can also be turned to good effect as a technique of divination. We shall see in the next chapter how radically the advent of a cash economy has affected the institutions of most small-scale preliterate societies, and spirit mediumship cults are not exempt from this influence. In Bunyoro initiation into the cult of certain spirits may be a source of considerable profit to the experts who control the initiation ritual. Also, like the Greek oracles of classical times, certain spirits when they are 'in the head' of their mediums can, for a fee, answer their clients' questions and predict the future.

There is one other reason for the universality and persistence of spirit mediumship cults throughout the world, and this is their pronounced dramatic quality. Whatever else a rite of spirit possession is, it is a vivid dramatic performance. The medium assumes the role and character of a being other than himself, and often he plays the role with great histrionic effect. Special clothes, masks, ornaments and insignia may be worn, special gestures used, and often a special spirit language or vocabulary is employed. I can testify from my own experience in Bunyoro (where the cult, though rigorously proscribed by government and missions for many years, is still practised clandestinely) that for a peasantry whose lives are spent in the somewhat drab monotony of subsistence agriculture, and to whom the Western resources of theatre, cinema and television are not (yet) available, a spirit seance is an exciting, colourful and dramatic event. Jane Harrison has argued that the drama in ancient Greece began in possession by the spirit Dionysos, and in the contemporary spirit cults of Africa and elsewhere we may be witnessing a repetition of this ancient development. Anyway it is certain that a mediumistic seance, which is a public rather than a private affair and is usually accompanied by dancing, singing, drumming and the shaking of rattles, has usually a strikingly dramatic, cathartic quality. In many cultures the cult directs feelings of frustration and strain into socially acceptable channels. I return to this theme in the next chapter.

Shamanism, the presumed power to control and direct spirits by special ritual techniques, was first fully described for North Asian peoples, from one of whose languages the word comes. It is almost as widespread as spirit mediumship. I have referred to the power claimed by some African mediums to conjure a spirit to leave its human vehicle and so to encompass its own destruction. Often it is believed that shamanistic powers are used by sorcerers, who having once entered into a possession relationship with some harmful spirit—for example the smallpox spirit—can retain it as a kind of familiar and send it to afflict an enemy. Where spirit mediumship is highly institutionalized, as it is in some parts of East Africa, novices in the cult usually have to undergo a complex process of initiation. The ritual is controlled by experts, themselves often mediums for a number of spirits. These experts know all the techniques appropriate for raising spirits, and can teach these techniques to others.

It is often believed that some kinds of spirits can be exorcised and destroyed, but others are thought to be too powerful, and with them, as with God or the gods in non-mediumistic religions, some sort of more or less enduring relationship may have to be entered into. Prayers and invocations may be addressed to spirits, and sacrifices made to them, whether or not they are manifested through human mediums. As a rule, spirits are conceived as immaterial and, usually, as being diffused through space, or perhaps as not in space at all. But they are generally associated with specific places in the material world. If these places are made by men, usually at the behest of a god or spirit, they are called shrines. A huge cathedral is no less a shrine, dedicated to God, than a tiny pyramid of sticks and grass, dedicated by a pagan African peasant to his ancestral ghosts. Both Christian and pagan are concerned with the unseen spiritual world. And it is helpful to both to have a place where they can pray and sacrifice, and which stands as a sign and reminder of the spiritual power which both acknowledge.

So far I have discussed some of the ways in which the spirit world is conceived, and in which it is believed that ghosts and other spirits may affect the living. I have said something of one very general means of entering into a relationship with spirits, that is, through possession and mediumship. But what then? Having entered into such a relationship, what does the human party to it do? First, he usually speaks to it, rather as though it were a person. This is the point of having spirits. If the spirit, or God, is thought to be vastly greater and more powerful than men, as is the case in most of the advanced religions, then the address takes the form of humble entreaty. Man does not generally attempt to impose terms on God, still less does he threaten or abuse him; he approaches him submissively. But in many of the simpler religions the relationship between men and spirits is less one-sided. Peoples like the Nuer, who have a complex theology and a clear conception of a high god or sky spirit, are on the whole exceptional. Very often ghosts and spirits are thought of as being dependent on men, as men are on them; there are rights and obligations on both sides. In such cases the relationship, like so many social relationships, is thought of as involving reciprocity or exchange. Just as a man needs the good-will and protection of the spirits if he is to prosper, so a spirit is thought to need the attentions of men if it is to be remembered, and to be given the opportunity to manifest itself (as through spirit possession) in the human world. Here the underlying principle is *do ut des*, 'I give to you so that you may give to me'; and much intercourse between men and spirits is of this kind. In Bunyoro, a man may enter into a relationship with a particular spirit, which is then thought to guard and protect him so long as it is not neglected. If that man suddenly dies, his relatives may berate the spirit, telling it that if it wants to 'eat' (that is, to receive periodic sacrifices) it should go off and find someone else to possess: it has failed to take care of the person for whose well-being it was responsible, and the members of that household want no more to do with it.

Where the relationship between men and spirits is conceived in this way, as it is in many parts of Africa, its reciprocality is made quite explicit in the invocations used. If prayer is associated with sacrifice, as it usually is, the spirit's attention is drawn to the beast or other object which is being sacrificed to it; a hint that it should accept its reciprocal obligation to do what it is asked. I remarked earlier that in most so-called 'primitive' religions spirits tend to be regarded as potentially harmful unless they are propitiated. Even ancestral ghosts are potentially dangerous, although they are believed to help and protect their living descendants: illness is often attributed to their displeasure. The aim of much invocation, prayer and sacrifice is to turn away evil rather than to solicit positive good, though both ends may be and often are combined. It is consistent with this that the idea of assimilation or absorption into Spirit, characteristic of advanced religions, does not occur in most 'simpler' ones, except in the restricted context of spirit possession and mediumship, where the identification is a means and not an end. Much primitive religion is apotropaic; what is sought is the turning away of spirit, not its nearer approach.

Since there is usually an element of exchange in the relationship between men and spirits, it often involves the symbolic presenting or making over to them of some material—or sometimes non-material

—thing. Hence the almost world-wide institution of sacrifice. Some-times this involves the destruction of what is offered, frequently the immolation of some living creature. Sometimes, however, food or drink are left for the spirit, perhaps at a shrine, and sometimes living animals are dedicated to a ghost or spirit, and not actually killed. This last is a convenient arrangement from the donor's point of view, for although he may not sell or otherwise dispose of the dedicated beast (perhaps a cow or a goat), he can enjoy its produce and dispose of its progeny as he wishes. But usually ghosts and spirits are less easily satisfied, and what is sacrificed must be completely made over. The destruction of expensive livestock may be a real sacrifice for the donor, in all senses of the term. In some cultures, like that of the Aztec and some traditional African ones, even the sacrifice of a human being may be required, as Abraham was called upon to sacrifice his own son. Always there is the idea of some deprivation on the part of the sacrificer, and always something is made over, trans-mitted from man to god or spirit.

It is especially plain in the case of sacrifice that there can be no adequate comprehension of what is going on in other cultures unless the ideas in the minds of the actors are understood. An anthro-pologist who is watching a sacrifice must ask not only 'what are they doing?' but also 'what do they think they are doing?' And the mean-ing of sacrifice varies widely from culture to culture. Thus in Western Christian culture the notions of communion and assimilation are strongly stressed aspects of it, as they were in the Hebraic rites from which the Christian ideas of sacrifice derive. This led some Victorian anthropologists, like Robertson Smith, to suppose that communion was the essential element in all sacrifice. This view gained some support from the totemic practices of the Australian aborigines, whose religious behaviour was supposed, in accordance with the evolutionary theories of the time, to represent an early stage in all religious development. As we noted earlier, the Arunta are said to have eaten, in special rites, the totemic species which are the objects of their group cults. But far from being the universal type of primitive religion, the Australian cult is practically unique. The notion of eat-ing together with gods or spirits is found in many cultures; thus a Nyoro medium, while possessed by a spirit, may hand morsels of food to others who are present. But there is here no notion of god-eating, nor is there any idea that a mystical identification with the spirits is thereby achieved.

The idiom of commensality is one of mutual respect and good will; sharing food or drink with a ghost or spirit, like sharing it with any-body else, implies amity and especially reconciliation. I noted in

Chapter 10 that when two Nyoro have quarrelled, once the dispute is settled they eat a meal together, and after that the matter is supposed to be completely finished. In most simpler cultures men and spirits are thought of as essentially different; it is believed to be essential for men to secure and retain the good will of spiritual forces (or at least to avoid their ill will), but there is no idea that the difference between these two orders of being can be or should be transcended. Each category has its proper place in the scheme of things. Much primitive ritual expresses the necessity to keep separate things that ought to be kept separate; humans and spirits, male and female, senior and junior, left hand and right hand, inauspicious and auspicious. It is almost as though the category distinctions which every culture sustains were regarded as hard-won gains, which must be emphasized and reaffirmed in ritual lest they fall into disuse, and primal chaos return.

So not all sacrifices are communions, though some are. But the notion that something is yielded up, given over to god or spirit, is universal. Where ghosts and spirits are regarded as separate and individual powers, dependent on men as men are dependent on them, the rule of *do ut des* may prevail, and a sacrifice may be thought of as a kind of bargain. But it is never simply this. Ghosts and gods are not people, and the symbolic aspect of sacrifice is intrinsic. Sacrifice is a symbolic act; trading in the market is not. If we regard sacrifice as the making of a gift to a spirit, we must ask just what it is that is given and received. A Nyoro who puts a few grains of cooked millet at a shrine knows quite well that the grains may be eaten by birds and insects, and a Nuer who sacrifices an ox eats the meat himself, together with the others attending the sacrifice. Some Bantu peoples would say that it is the essence, the vital force, of the thing sacrificed that is taken by the spirit, so that only the appearance, the empty shell, remains. The Nuer, whose ideas about sacrifice have been analysed by Professor Evans-Pritchard, say (what is much the same thing) that it is the life that is taken, even though the flesh remains behind and is eaten by men. Here, as so often in the study of ritual, Western observers commonly make the mistake of regarding as exclusively instrumental an act whose significance is basically expressive, even though it may be regarded as instrumental too. Symbolic behaviour is not to be understood simply as a means of achieving something: I have stressed that it is also and essentially a way of saying something. It follows that its manifestations are not always to be taken absolutely literally, as though they were a kind of technology; though the very naïve may sometimes so regard them. The Western European who puts flowers on his mother's grave is not perturbed by the question whether he supposes that his dead parent can really smell them; he is performing a rite, and the gift of flowers is symbolic, not real.

Sacrifice, then, is symbolic gift-giving. Now in giving a gift a man gives, in a sense, part of himself. In sacrifice this identification is often made explicit. This is why the sacrifice of living things, in some cases even human beings themselves, is so often prescribed. For an ox or a goat or even a chicken shares the quality of life with the human who sacrifices it, and so may appropriately stand for him. Also, and more practically, when a man sacrifices a valuable beast like an ox he is giving up a most prized possession. Of an early Nyoro king we read that he loved cattle more than people, and Nilotes in the Southern Sudan develop deep attachments to individual oxen, and name themselves after them. For such peoples cattle, above all, are fitted to symbolize the living human beings who make the sacrifice. But always the giving of the gift is a symbolic act, a rite, and in the last resort it is the rite, and not the object sacrificed, that matters most. Ideally, when a sacrifice is required, a Nuer should sacrifice an ox to god. But if he has not got an ox or cannot spare one he may sacrifice a species of cucumber instead. When he does so, he does not ask God to accept a cucumber; he asks him to accept an ox. It is not that he thinks that God is stupid and can be more easily deceived than a man; it is rather that what he is performing is a rite and not an economic transaction. Whether he sacrifices an ox or a cucumber, a Nuer who makes a sacrifice is symbolically giving a part of himself.

The identification of the sacrificer with the object sacrificed is marked in other ways. Almost always there is an act of consecration, either by a laying on of hands or in some other way. By consecration the object sacrificed ceases to be just an ox or a chicken or a cucumber; it becomes something more—a man-made symbol. A Nuer who participates in a sacrifice places ashes on the back of the sacrificial beast; by doing this he believes himself to be conveying to the animal which is to be destroyed all the evil which was in his heart. Thus sacrifice is often a moral cleansing, a washing away of evil, a means of disposing of what Radcliffe-Brown called ritual impurity.

When the piacular, expiatory element is dominant, and the emphasis is rather on getting rid of evil and impurity than on making a gift to a specific spiritual power, we have, not sacrifice, but a rather different kind of institution, of which the most familiar example is the scapegoat. Where evil is conceived as a kind of real existent, like the other kinds of power discussed in the last chapter, it may be ritually transferred to a chosen animal, sometimes a human being, and that animal or person may then be either driven out of the community or destroyed. At times of grave crisis the ancient Athenians are said to have driven out and killed certain chosen individuals, called *pharmakoi*, who were believed to take with them all the evil of the city, which was thus purified. Here there is no idea of sacrifice to a spirit, but it is easy to see that the two ideas may readily combine, as they do in the Christian doctrine of the Atonement.

No more can be said about sacrifice here. It is plain that the concept is by no means a simple one. As so often in the comparative study of human institutions, what appears at first sight to be easily comprehensible turns out to be vastly complex: one simple-seeming term is found to denote a wide variety of different institutions. But what is common to all sacrificial rites, whether the emphasis is on gift exchange and propitiation, on communion with the spirit world, on purification, or on some other aspect of the relationship between man and spirit, is their symbolic character. Like all ritual, sacrifice is a way of saying something as well as a way of doing something. It is a drama, not a technique. So we can only understand it if we ask not only what the people who practise it are trying to do, but also what they are trying to say, and in what language they are trying to say it.

There is one further sphere of human behaviour which involves reference to spiritual beings or forces, that of blessing, cursing and oath-taking. In the first two a human agent gives verbal expression to his wish that something may happen to another person or persons, often through the instrumentality of some non-human power, which may or may not be specified. Thus the blessing or cursing which is generally believed to be most effective is that of a person to whose wishes the powers invoked are most likely to attend. That is why an elder's curse is particularly feared among many African peoples, for they are the closest of the living to the ancestral ghosts. And where there are religious specialists, such as shamans or priests, their blessing or curse is often thought to be the most potent of all.

In oaths the action of the non-human power referred to is invoked upon the swearer himself. And it is invoked conditionally: a man who swears an oath deliberately puts himself in a condition of ritual danger unless he does what he has sworn to do. It may be supposed that the power referred to may act directly upon the oath-taker, as a man who swears falsely on Bible or Koran may be thought to place himself in danger of divine punishment. Or the oath-taking may compel others to action. Thus in traditional Ashanti a man who wished to initiate legal proceedings against another was required to swear the chief's oath, usually a reference to some inauspicious day in the history of the chief's family. This compelled the chief to take action in the matter, for mention of the day in question was forbidden in all normal circumstances.

The expressive element in these forms of behaviour is evident. Often it is the mere saying of what is wished that is thought to be effective, and here as elsewhere its expression in symbol and rite is believed to enhance its effectiveness. The grotesque proliferation of symbolism in oath-taking among the Kikuyu at the time of the Mau Mau revolt in Kenya provides further dramatic confirmation of Whitehead's remark about the proliferating tendency of symbolism.

In this chapter it has hardly been possible to do more than to touch on some of the major issues discussed by social anthropologists in the comparative study of religious behaviour. I conclude it with a brief summary. I somewhat arbitrarily distinguished religious behaviour from other kinds of symbolic activity by defining it as ritual behaviour involving a belief in non-human spirits. Like all ritual, religious behaviour is essentially expressive, though it is generally thought of as instrumental as well. I said something of both of these aspects. Instrumentally regarded, religious and magical beliefs and practices form part of systems of action; they have consequences, even if they are not always those envisaged by the people who have them. On the cognitive level, they provide satisfactory answers to otherwise insoluble questions: they fill gaps in human knowledge and experience and so diminish areas of doubt and uncertainty. Thus religious belief and practice may give confidence in the face of dangers which would otherwise be overwhelming. They provide institutionalized means of coping with such dangers, and even if these means are generally scientifically ineffective, they are satisfying morally and emotionally. As Malinowski showed, ritual may serve to co-ordinate and regulate co-operative human behaviour in a variety of social situations. Religious and magical beliefs may serve as social sanctions, both through the fear of incurring supernatural punishment if approved norms are breached, and, in the more advanced religions, through the moral ideals which these faiths embody.

On the level of idea and meaning we find a similar variety. All the kinds of ritual forces and powers—mana, ghosts, spirits and gods—are highly important for the people who respect them. But none is given as an empirical datum, though their presumed effects are. Everywhere people are dependent, whether they like it or not, on extra-human forces lying outside their physical control, and much of the fascination of the anthropological study of religion lies in the vast range of forms in which man's fertile imagination has represented these powers. Ritual both enhances the importance of the things and events with which it is associated, and provides a means of dealing with them. I said that what was asserted in the various forms of symbolic behaviour that anthropologists study is always something of value for the people who have the ritual. And generally it is something more or less generalized and abstract, not concrete and individual; for there is no need to state symbolically what is already obvious.

This leads to a final point. What *is* symbolized in religious behaviour? Durkheim said that in totemism (for him the elementary form of religion) society is worshipping itself, or, to put it more sophisticatedly, men are asserting and so reinforcing the importance of the system of mutual interdependencies which constitute society. Radcliffe-Brown argued that ritual expresses symbolically certain sentiments or values, upon the acceptance of which the smooth running of society itself depends. This view is essentially a restatement of Durkheim's position, and, like it, it obscures the important fact that conflict and opposition may be important components of social systems as well as harmony, and may also become focuses of ritual. But Radcliffe-Brown argued also that ritual sometimes expresses more than man's need of society; basically it expresses his fundamental dependence on the natural world which he occupies and of which he is a part. We have seen that much ritual and religious behaviour translates uncontrollable natural forces into symbolic entities which, through the performance of ritual, can be manipulated and dealt with. Ritual is a language for saying things which are felt to be true and important but which are not susceptible of statement in scientific terms. Even if sophisticated modern man is less inclined to attach instrumental efficacy to the symbols which he has created to express his apprehension of the universe and of its ultimate meaning, he still feels the need to express this awareness. And in the areas beyond science there is no way of expressing it except symbolically. To say that religious symbols are man-made is not to decry the validity of religion, for ritual is a statement about something, not just about itself. But the comparative study of the religious beliefs and practices of other cultures may suggest that in religion, no less than in other forms of symbolic behaviour, reality is misrepresented if the symbol, and not the often indefinable thing that it symbolizes, is taken to be ultimate truth.

SHORT READING LIST

DURKHEIM, É., *The Elementary Forms of the Religious Life* (English translation), London, 1915.

EVANS-PRITCHARD, E. E., *Nuer Religion*, Oxford, 1956.

FORDE, D. (editor), *African Worlds*, London 1954.

FORTES, M., *Oedipus and Job in West African Religion*, Cambridge, 1959.

FORTUNE, R. F., *Manus Religion*, Philadelphia, 1935.

LESSA, W. A., and VOGT, E. Z. (editors), *Reader in Comparative Religion*, Evanston, 1958.

LIENHARDT, GODFREY, *Divinity and Experience, the Religion of the Dinka*, Oxford, 1961.

MARETT, R. R., *The Threshold of Religion*, London, 1909.

MIDDLETON, J., *Lugbara Religion*, London, 1960.

SMITH, W. ROBERTSON, *Lectures on the Religion of the Semites*, London, 1889.

14

Social Change

(1)

CHANGE IS TAKING PLACE in all human societies all the time. Sometimes it is sudden and catastrophic, as when a system of government is destroyed by revolution and replaced by a different one; sometimes it is gradual and hardly perceptible, so that even the members of the society themselves scarcely notice it. But it is always there, and social anthropologists who wish to understand the working of the societies they study must take account of it. Here, in particular, they must play the historian; changes take place in time, and they can only be understood as causal sequences of events leading up to new states of affairs. And it is these new states of affairs, 'the present', that the social anthropologist is trying to understand. He is a historian, but he is so only in a particular context and for a particular purpose.

Social change cannot be studied as though it were a separate social field, distinguishable from the other topics which have been discussed in the second half of this book. The student of change is concerned with all these fields of enquiry, regarded in their temporal, dynamic aspect. He can no more study 'social' change in general than he can study 'society' in general. His data are specific social and cultural institutions, and he has to study the modifications of these through time, in the context of other co-existing social, cultural and, sometimes, ecological factors. It may be doubted whether such a study will reveal any general laws of social change, though certain trends, characteristic of certain conditions, times and places, may be detected. One such is considered below. For it is now plainer than it used to be that changes in people's social and cultural institutions through time are not to be understood in terms of any single 'blanket' principle. A multiplicity of social processes is involved, and these often operate concurrently.

Earlier attempts by anthropologists to explain the origins of the customs they studied (some of which I discussed in Chapter 1) represented such simplistic attempts to understand change. But the evolutionary theories of Morgan and McLennan, which postulated that all societies everywhere, if not interfered with, develop through an ascending series of stages, became discredited when it was realized that almost all societies *were* being interfered with, and increasingly so. The opposite camp, the diffusionists, were on firmer ground in stressing that different cultures do borrow from one another, but some of them, too, went beyond the evidence when they claimed that most or all cultural and social phenomena had diffused from some common source.

Some anthropologists still write about social and cultural change as though it could be explained simply in terms of the diffusion of culture traits. This is understandable enough, for social change has become an important concern of anthropologists mainly in the context of what has been called culture contact. Usually this has meant the contact of advanced, complex and wide-scale Western or Western-type societies with technologically simple, often pre-literate or recently literate, small-scale ones. And this contact certainly has involved the transfer of ideas and artefacts from one group to the other. For British social anthropologists culture contact was represented mainly in the relations between European colonial powers and the various indigenous peoples whom they governed in Africa and elsewhere. Of course the alien *governments* were not the only agents of change: missionaries, settlers and traders often preceded them, and powerfully affected the indigenous cultures. And the changes brought about by impact with the Western world were not only political; radical alterations in the whole range of social and cultural institutions were brought about.

These contacts have obviously involved the transmission of new elements from one culture to another (however these elements be defined). In America the term 'acculturation' was first used to describe what happens when 'groups of individuals having different cultures come into continuous first-hand contact, with subsequent changes in the original cultural patterns of either or both groups'.[1] This formulation is useful, but it is a little too restricted. For instance it excludes as means of acculturation, television, radio and the printed word, which do not require continuous first-hand contact in order to effect quite important changes. But more importantly, it does not go far enough. Social change is not just a matter of two sets of social or cultural institutions being in contact—whatever this may

[1] Quoted and discussed in Herskovits, M. J., *Man and his Works*, New York, 1948.

242

precisely mean—so that either or both change by absorbing features of the other. Of course this does happen, and some work has been done, mostly in America, on the question why some small-scale societies in contact with Western culture adopt some institutions, while some adopt others, and yet others reject Western values altogether. This kind of enquiry raises interesting questions about cultural consistency. But it is inadequate as a complete account of social change, as Malinowski in particular stressed.

For social change cannot be adequately understood merely as a kind of borrowing or re-shuffling of culture traits: to use Fortes' metaphor, social institutions cannot be regarded as having been pitchforked, like bundles of hay, from one culture into another, What we are presented with in situations of social change is something new, 'a process of reorganization on entirely new and specific lines', in Malinowski's words. It cannot be comprehended simply as an assemblage of parts the whole of which can be understood by as it were invoicing each constituent part back to its place of origin. For in being adopted new usages and institutions are subtly (sometimes not so subtly) adapted. As the American anthropologist Keesing wrote, 'an element, in passing over from one context to another, tends to have its character made over to fit the new setting'.[1]

But this is not all. The innovations may also modify the pre-existing institutions and radically affect the complex network of relationships between them. The functional hypothesis that in any society the constituent institutions may be mutually interdependent, so that none can be fully understood without reference to the others, has obviated the error of too naïvely diffusionist a view of social change. Certainly the histories of particular institutions must be studied, but they must be studied in their whole social contexts: historical and functionalist methods must be combined.

To say that it is useful to regard societies, whether they are undergoing acute social change or not, as in some sense functional units, composed of interacting institutions, is not to say that every society is in a state of perfect equilibrium. Integrated does not mean well-integrated, as Gluckman has pointed out. When we discussed the functional analogy between societies and biological organisms we saw that this way of looking at societies tended all too readily to be taken as implying (not always explicitly) that societies were, or should be, like smoothly running machines, with all their parts in complete harmony. Gluckman legitimately criticized Malinowski for failing to see that far from being an abnormal state of society, conflict might

[1] Keesing, F. M., *Culture Change: an Analysis and Bibliography of Anthropological Sources to 1952*, Stanford, 1953.

rather be an essential aspect of it.[1] In our discussion of Nuer political organization we noted that the blood feud, which certainly involves conflict, is an essential component of the political system.

The idea that the 'natural' state of human society is somehow conflict-free has led to other misrepresentations of the nature of social change. Firth has made the point that social change (which almost always involves some degree of conflict) is not necessarily from better to worse, as some anthropologists have assumed, though it may fairly be argued that it very often is. This is a matter for investigation, not for dogmatism. The fact that change often has had evidently deleterious consequences (human nature being what it is concomitant beneficial ones often tend to be overlooked) has sometimes tended to create a presumption that it always does so. This presumption may induce in both students and victims of change a quite unjustified nostalgia for a golden age which in all probability never existed. But, more important, the notion that social change is necessarily degenerative tends to sustain the untenable hypothesis (which Firth calls 'the basic assumption of homeostasis') that societies are naturally species of equilibrium systems, whose social institutions may be regarded as feedback devices adapted to retain the *status quo*. If societies were really like this, any change in them would obviously be for the worse. But in fact, fruitful though the 'organismic' approach has been, it is only an analogy, and like most analogies it can be dangerously misleading if it is pressed too far. It is now more widely recognized that change and conflict are normal characteristics of social systems no less than equilibrium and harmony. What is perhaps a little less plain is that these changes and conflicts call for understanding in categories other than and additional to those of the functionalism of the twenties. Process must be considered as well as structure, and historical as well as sociological categories employed.

Though there is conflict in all societies, it may differ considerably in kind and degree: it is a sadly common observation of anthropologists (and others) that under the stress of culture contact many of the societies they study have ceased to function as they used, and in some cases have broken down altogether. Sometimes social systems, even peoples, have been totally or almost destroyed: the Tasmanian aborigines, the Tierra del Fuegians, and the North American Indians are examples. But often the damage has been more subtle, though hardly less radical. The functional, organic model seemed plausible enough when it was applied to those small-scale societies which were virtually unaffected by outside contact, and which had apparently

[1] Gluckman, Max, *Order and Rebellion in Tribal Africa*, London, 1963.

not changed significantly in generations. But when increasing contact with the West brought radical social change, and new and more disruptive social conflicts, and when the more intensive fieldwork of modern times disclosed these changes and conflicts, then this approach, by itself, became plainly inadequate. It was no use plastering up the cracks in institutional functionalism with concepts like dysfunction (a notion better expressed by Durkheim in his concept of *anomie* or 'lawlessness'; a state of affairs in which hitherto accepted and acceptable standards are no longer meaningful). For these still implied the untenable assumption that there was an ideally harmonious, 'functional' state of society, and that this had somehow been breached.

Social anthropologists, then, have increasingly concerned themselves with situations of conflict and social stress, and they have done so mostly in the context of culture contact. But 'conflict' is a vague term. Two problems, in particular, arise. We must ask, first, what are the things that are supposed to be in conflict, and second, what kind or degree of conflict is it that concerns us?

To begin with, we are primarily interested in conflicts between different kinds of social institutions, rather than in conflicts between individual people, or between groups or categories of people, although of course all of these may be involved. But, as I have stressed, social institutions are abstractions from what is observed. Here the distinction between the three aspects in which it is possible to regard systems of institutionalized social relationships becomes vital. I distinguished between the legal and moral values implicit in social relationships (what people think ought to be done), the modes in which people actually represent themselves and their social world (what they think is actually done), and, on the level of action rather than on the level of idea, the social situation as it presents itself to an outside observer in causal terms (what actually happens). In the real world of our experience, of course, these three levels interpenetrate and affect one another, but the distinction between them is analytically essential to the understanding of conflict and change. For a particular institutional complex may change in one or two of these aspects but not in all. For instance (I discuss this example further below) the institution of chiefship may change radically in fact (that is, chiefs may cease to be paternalistic, traditional figures, bound to their people by long-standing personal ties, and become instead salaried and sometimes transferable civil servants), while ideas about chiefship, both about what it is and what it ought to be, remain unaltered, or at least change at a slower rate. Where this happens, as it has in many parts of the world, various stresses ensue.

245

In the last resort, these stresses manifest themselves in and between individual people—where else could they manifest themselves? Here again our tripartite analysis of social institutions is indispensable. For we may speak of conflict on the level of action; thus a man cannot be in two places at the same time, or carry out two physically incompatible courses of action at once. And we may speak of conflict on the level of belief; a man cannot readily hold two contradictory opinions about a particular existing state of affairs at the same time (though Orwell and others have shown us how little perturbed men may be by breaches of the law of contradiction so long as they can manage to keep the contradictories more or less insulated from one another). And we may speak of a conflict of values; incompatible aims may be built into contemporaneous institutions, with consequent confusion and emotional disturbance. And as well as conflicts on each of these levels, there may be conflicts *between* them. Plainly it is important in any particular context to know which of these kinds of conflict is being considered. For the task of understanding them (and so also the task of solving them) may call for different approaches.

As a student of social change the social anthropologist is not interested in all kinds of social conflicts, though as a social anthropologist he is. The working of the Nuer blood feud is important to anyone who wishes to understand traditional Nuer polity. But unless the form of the institution itself is changing it is not of direct concern to the student of social change. It is obvious that some kinds of conflict are structurally more disruptive than others, for they bring about major changes in the form of social institutions. The difference is neatly illustrated by the distinction between rebellion and revolution. Where a traditional ruler is deposed by a rebellion and replaced by another man, the institution of kingship or chiefship itself may remain unchanged. Indeed periodic rebellion may be an essential feature of the political system, as it is among the Anuak of the southern Sudan. But if there is a revolution, and (say) a traditional kingship is entirely done away with and replaced by a popular dictatorship or by some form of republic, then the change is of a different order: the political system itself has been radically modified.[1]

Anthropologists have accordingly distinguished between two kinds of social conflict, and so between two kinds of social change. First there are those conflicts and changes which are provided for in the existing social structure. The Nuer blood feud, or the succession struggles which occur in many states when the king dies, are examples

[1] Gluckman, Max, *op. cit.*

246

of these. Obviously changes in personnel are a feature of every society, as people grow old and die, and are replaced by others. But so long as the roles themselves continue more or less unchanged, these conflicts and replacements do not affect the structure of the social system itself. They operate within its existing normative framework, are resoluble in terms of shared systems of values, and offer no challenge to the existing institutions.

The second kind of change is more radical. It is change in the character of the social system itself: some of its constituent institutions are altered, so that they no longer 'mesh' with other coexisting institutions as they used to do. This is structural or 'radical' change; and the conflicts to which it gives rise are not resoluble in terms of the existing values of the society. They are new kinds of conflicts, and tradition provides neither precedents nor cures for them. Hence they are specially disturbing, and involve confusion and strain. If the social system is to persist, sooner or later further radical modifications will have to be made in it, and so the society will become something other than and different from what it originally was. Here again, the ineptness of the organic analogy for the understanding of social change may be noted: organisms do not change from one species into completely different ones; under stress of social change societies often do.

To these two types of change Firth has added a third one, which he calls organizational change. Organizational changes are changes in ways of doing things, which themselves continue to be done, and in the extent and range of particular complexes of social relationships, which remain formally unaltered. This further distinction is useful, although in the last resort structure and organization are rather two aspects of the same reality than two different things. Organization is structure in action, its actual working out in practice, in space and time. There may be very great differences in the degree of structural change in any institution; and organizational change, as Firth conceives it, does seem to involve *some* change in the quality of the social relationships involved, and so in their structure. A decision as to the point at which organizational change, which may be gradual and cumulative, becomes important enough to qualify as structural change must be to some extent arbitrary. But sometimes distinctions in degree are as important as differences in kind, and even if Firth's distinction be regarded as marking two stages in the same process, it provides the student of social change with a useful half-way house between ordinary, 'built-in' change and conflict on the one hand, and that severer type of change which we call structural or radical, on the other.

Twenty years ago Godfrey and Monica Wilson made an original contribution to the subject by distinguishing these two major kinds of opposition, which they called 'radical' and 'ordinary' opposition. Further, they attempted to explain radical opposition (which was already a conspicuous feature of the African communities they had studied) by reference to what they called unevenness of scale. They pointed out that radical conflicts tend to arise when different but related spheres of social action vary widely in range and scope, the same individuals being involved at the same time in both. In many communities in Africa and elsewhere increase in the scale of some systems of social relationships, for example the economic ones involved in participation in world markets, is not balanced by corresponding increases in the scale of social relationships in other spheres, such as domestic life, race relations, or religious practice. It is certainly true that such differences of scale are a conspicuous feature of many changing societies, and conflict often does arise when wide-range systems impinge on narrow-range ones. But in the last resort relatively insoluble conflicts arise because the different institutions which social change brings into uneasy contact with one another involve radically different and incompatible ways of thinking and acting, rather than simply because there is a difference in scale. Thus we are brought back to the question raised earlier: what do we mean when we speak of conflict between social institutions?

Institutional conflict is not something than can be observed directly, any more than a social institution is; like all social facts, it must be inferred from what people say and do. This raises a further set of problems, which lie on the borderland between sociology and psychology. How is one to recognize radical or structural opposition when one sees it? It is not enough to say that a certain social institution conflicts with another when nobody seems to be at all bothered by the fact; it is because people *are* bothered and show signs of stress that these problems attract our attention. Nor is it just the fact that people are brought into conflict with one another, whether as members of social groups or as members of social categories, that indicates the presence of radical opposition and change: there is no society this side of Utopia which is free from all forms of inter-personal conflict. In the final analysis it is conflict *within* people rather than conflict between them that we have in mind when we speak of the dysnomic aspect of social change, although of course one may and often does involve the other.

More work has been done in this field by American than by British scholars. This is not surprising, in view of the American emphasis on man in society rather than on the society man is in. Social stresses and strains of the sort which we have been considering can only be inferred from the behaviour of individual people. But a case of crime or of mental breakdown, in itself, may give no indication whether the social stress which may underlie it is 'ordinary' or 'radical'. A significant increase in crime or in mental illness, whether in particular communities or among certain social classes or categories, may well suggest the presence of radical conflict. Later in this chapter we shall see how the imposition of incompatible social demands on the same individuals may, sometimes must, lead to the breach of *some* accepted norms, either old or new. American 'culture-stress' theory has highlighted such phenomena as increases in witchcraft and sorcery accusations, in suicide and homicide rates, and in other forms of anti-social behaviour, as indices of social strain. A difficulty is that statistical evidence adequate to provide a basis for estimates of increase or decrease is not always available, especially in many of the 'simpler' societies most recently affected by change. Also, cultural relativity may lead observers to stress unduly attitudes which are deviant by the standards of one culture but which are not so, or at least are less so, by those of another. These difficulties can be and are being dealt with. But it is plain that still more precise techniques of diagnosis are needed in the field of social change study, as well as clear formulations of the questions to which answers are being sought.

We have now a good deal of information about the dynamics of culture contact, what actually happens when cultures meet. Much of it has been contributed by social anthropologists who have studied societies which were undergoing rapid social change when they were studied. Since most of these changes derived directly or indirectly from the subjection of pre-literate or only recently literate peoples to Western influence, it was natural that the anthropologists who studied such peoples, mainly in the less developed areas of the British Commonwealth but also elsewhere, should have found themselves compelled to take an interest in processes of change.

It is too early yet to say whether such changes reveal any uniform pattern of development. Firth has suggested that the social changes consequent on the impact of a rich and powerful Western culture on a technologically less advanced and smaller-scale one are likely to move through four stages. First, on initial impact there is ready acceptance of such Western artefacts as guns and tools, but little modification of the traditional social structure. Then, as the process of interaction gathers momentum, there is a more radical absorption; the old group values give way to a growing individualism, and strains begin to appear between the old values and the new. This may lead to a third stage in which there is a reaction of hostility against the new order, a tendency to revert to traditional practices; sometimes a vain attempt to put the clock back. Finally, if the story ends happily, there emerges a more sophisticated synthesis of old and new: a novel social organization is achieved which is unique and viable in itself, but which owes something to both modern and traditional influences. Professor Firth's thesis is a historical one, and it accurately characterizes the history of change among the Polynesian peoples whom he has studied intensively. Whether it is equally applicable in all contexts of social change is more doubtful; and in any case its author does not claim universality for it. It would be over-sanguine to suppose that the happy ending it postulates will always be achieved. But the pattern which Firth describes, or some part or variety of it, undoubtedly occurs in certain conditions. His schema provides a useful paradigm for the historical analysis of change.

In any event recent ethnography has documented, with a wealth of detail, processes of change in particular societies in Africa and elsewhere. These studies have amply demonstrated that nothing approaching an adequate understanding of the complexities of the contact situation can be achieved simply in terms of a naïve (or indeed any other kind of) diffusionism, still less in terms of old-fashioned views of independent evolution. In this context historical enquiry must be combined with functional and structural analysis. In the rest of this chapter I discuss a few examples of actual processes of social change in some of the major dimensions of social and cultural life.

(2)

I give one or two examples of such changes in the contexts of political organization, domestic and family life, economic relations, and the field of religion and ritual. Most of my illustrations are from Africa, because this is the area which I know best, but nearly all of them could be duplicated from other parts of the world. We shall find that here, as elsewhere, the different dimensions of social life interpenetrate one another. Often, for example, the discussion of political organization involves the consideration of economic relations; that of ritual institutions the study of the kinship groupings with which they are sometimes associated. This is how social anthropology is: we must focus on one thing at a time, but this does not mean that we can consider it without reference to other things.

My first political example comes from the Newala district of southern Tanganyika. In this district live the Makonde, a matrilineal people who were traditionally organized in small kin groups. Although there were senior men who played an arbitrative and advisory role in group affairs, there were no specifically political authorities. In the late 1920's special emphasis was laid in British Africa on the principle of indirect rule; that is, government through the indigenous political authorities and not directly through European or European-appointed administrators. So the attempt was made to find the traditional Makonde chiefs, in order formally to invest them with administrative and judicial powers, under the new Native Authority Ordinance. This was easier said than done. But in the end something over seventy 'chiefs' were formally gazetted, provided with court warrants, and authorized to enforce government regulations. The result was chaotic. The so-called 'chiefs' had no idea what they were expected to do, for the notion of chiefly authority was completely foreign to them; and the ordinary people were not prepared to take orders in all sorts of matters from men whom they had known all their lives not as territorial authorities, but simply as the heads of small family groups. After a very few years this experiment in indirect rule was abandoned. The district was divided more or less arbitrarily into four sections, each of which was put under the authority of a trained African administrator from the Islamic coastal region. From this point onwards political progress was rapid. Soon the 'foreign' rulers were replaced by trained Makonde, and a new, more centralized form of administration, appropriate to the changed conditions of Makonde society, was successfully instituted.

In this case the strains consequent upon government-introduced change were quickly recognized, and the situation was remedied. Other problems introduced by political development and change are less tractable. Even where there were indigenous rulers, the expectations and values traditionally held by and about them were quite different from, often incompatible with, those appropriate to the impersonal and bureaucratic type of administration into which they were being assimilated, and to the standards of which they were now expected to conform. The old type of political bond was essentially personal, based on a sustained face-to-face relationship between chiefs (who usually held their positions on a hereditary basis) and their subjects. This bond was expressed through the provision of service and tribute by the people, and the giving of feasts, and of occasional gifts to the needy, by the ruler. It has not always been clear to either chiefs or subjects that this personal kind of government simply cannot be sustained if an effective administrative system adequate to modern conditions is to be achieved. Nowadays taxes have to be collected if central and local government services, schools, hospitals, roads, are to be maintained; impartial justice has to be administered; regulations covering a wide range of new economic and other activities have to be enforced. These tasks demand new kinds of officials, more like Western-type civil servants than the old 'feudal' or, better, 'patrimonial' kind of chiefs, characteristic of many traditional centralized states in Africa and elsewhere.

When I was in Bunyoro in the 50's, peasants often complained that modern chiefs are no longer, as they used to be, members of aristocratic families with a tradition of ruling: now they are merely paid employees, more interested in their salaries and personal advancement than in their people. One man told me: 'in the old days chiefs trusted and depended on their people, for their living [in the form of tribute] came from them. But now they do not care about their subjects, for their money comes not from them but from the government'. A very common complaint is that chiefs no longer provide feasts for their people as they used to do. In fact, of course, they cannot, since the peasants no longer bring them the food and beer to do it with, as they did in former times. Again, Nyoro complain that chiefs no longer know their people personally; instead of visiting them in their villages they spend most of their time working in their courts or offices. Also, they are liable to frequent transfer from one chiefdom to another.

The chiefs themselves are well aware that times have changed, but they do not always understand clearly how or why they have done so. They complain that people no longer respect them as they used to; they no longer bring them gifts of food or beer, but think that when they have paid their taxes they have discharged all their obligations to their rulers. It is not easy for either chief or subjects to understand fully what has happened and is happening to their traditional polity. They do not always see that a traditional political organization, in which political links were also personal ones expressed through the constant interchange of goods and services, is changing into a modern, civil service administration, in which bureaucratic norms are inevitably paramount, and chiefs and subjects can no longer know each other personally. In Professor Parsons' terms, political authority is ceasing to be diffuse (affecting all dimensions of the subjects' lives) and particularistic (conceived in terms of personal statuses and relationships), and is becoming increasingly specific (to particular spheres of the subjects' lives, such as their tax-paying capacity and their conformity to enacted laws) and universalistic (implying that the same rules apply to everybody regardless of particular relationships or statuses). But the important thing is that changes do not proceed evenly on all fronts: often values and expectations long outlive the institutions to which they were appropriate. When this happens, old ideas about government and administration co-exist, sometimes very uncomfortably, with modern and very different ones. It is easier to make formal alterations in social and political institutions than it is to change people's ideas and values. Very often the conflict between old and new, between 'feudal' and patrimonial ideas and modern, democratic ones, becomes most explicit in the context of territorial administration.

This has been well documented for the Soga of eastern Uganda by Lloyd Fallers.[1] Here local government has been carried out through traditional chiefs, who under a British administration have increasingly adapted themselves to Western norms. But the adaptation is still incomplete. Universalistic civil service norms of disinterested public service co-exist with particularistic values of kinship and personal dependence. This inevitably leads to conflict, both between individuals and within them. Chiefs frequently have to choose between applying one standard or the other, since they cannot apply both. Thus a chief may have to choose between favouring a kinsman or friend in a court case, an acceptable mode of behaviour in terms of traditional values, and applying the law absolutely impartially, as modern civil service norms require. Since he is constrained by both sets of norms, he is faced with an insoluble dilemma; either course of action will be wrong by one set of standards. In many parts of Africa this state of affairs has imposed considerable strain upon chiefs, and has involved a high casualty rate among them. As Fallers points out, many chiefs were dismissed by their European superiors during the colonial period because they failed to uphold civil service norms, yielding instead to traditional pressures which were still held valid by their subjects and to some extent by themselves. Even the opposite course may lead to dismissal. A subordinate chief who resists the traditional, particularistic demands of a superior may be 'framed', and find himself dismissed for the very offence which he refused to commit. At this stage of political evolution the lot of the African chief is often not a happy one. What is remarkable is that so many men have succeeded brilliantly in bridging the gap.

In the context of domestic and family life, too, there have emerged new kinds of conflict, not provided for by tradition. I consider these under two heads; first, the breakdown in attachment to and dependence upon traditional types of domestic grouping, and second, changes in the institution of marriage due to Western influence.

I spoke in an earlier chapter of the vital importance in simple societies of attachment to a group; in many such societies to be cut

[1] Fallers, L. A., *Bantu Bureaucracy*, Cambridge, 1956.

253

off from the group virtually amounted to a sentence of death. But Western influence, especially the advent of a cash economy and the suppression of inter-group hostility and tribal warfare, has for the first time made it possible for individuals to disregard traditional group ties with impunity. Sometimes, indeed, men can no longer sustain these ties, even though they may wish to do so, and may feel guilty if they do not. The African tribesman who moves to paid employment in an urban area cannot, as his country cousins still can, provide food and shelter for numerous relatives over long periods. Here again two sets of obligations, both more or less accepted, conflict. A town employee's obligation to sustain his needy relatives, and his obligation to meet the costs of rent, food and shelter for himself and his elementary family, cannot both be met. Even in rural areas the development of individualistic values, unthinkable in traditional times, has led to the break-up of the traditional large domestic units. Increasingly in Africa and elsewhere smaller groupings, centred on the elementary family, are becoming the basic domestic units. Correspondingly, there has been a breakdown in the old autocratic patriarchal family structure, common in many less developed societies. Older Nyoro complain that sons are no longer obedient as they used to be; they no longer build their homes in or near their fathers' compounds as they did in the past. Nowadays there is nothing to prevent them asserting their independence and going off on their own, and many of them do.

Women as well as men may take advantage of the new social and economic opportunities. I consider the economic aspect of this more fully below, but it is worth noting here that in many parts of Africa a woman who resents the restraints of the traditional way of life, perhaps as a junior wife to an old man who already has several other wives, can now, if she wishes, leave her family and go off to seek a more exciting life in the towns. There is evidence from South Africa and elsewhere to show that where the early missionaries have been successful in eliminating the payment of bridewealth at marriage, parties to unions contracted without bridewealth have hardly considered themselves to be married at all. Many women, no longer bound by the knowledge that if they leave their husbands a substantial bridewealth will have to be returned by their probably reluctant parents, have felt free to drift from man to man in a kind of promiscuity which was no doubt very far from the missionaries' intentions. Even where bridewealth (nowadays often commuted from stock to cash) has been paid, the new economic opportunities available to both sexes enable many women to repay it themselves and so to escape from unattractive spouses.

Here again people's attitudes are ambivalent. Men, especially younger men, value the new freedom, while at the same time they resent the fact that women can take advantage of it as well as they can. A Nyoro school teacher succinctly summed up the confusion that has resulted: 'Nowadays, Europeans have put the idea into girls' heads that they should find husbands for themselves; this has led many of them into unsuitable marriages or into informal liaisons, leading to promiscuity and disease. Some girls prefer not to get married at all; they like to live as prostitutes which means that young men who want to get married have to remain as bachelors. The result is that people play with one another in the fields and on the paths like animals.' Similar statements could be recorded in very many parts of Africa and in other recently developed areas.

The gradual decline in polygyny in many parts of Africa, largely a consequence of mission influence, has given rise to similar dilemmas. The Wilsons have documented for the Nyakyusa of southern Tanganyika the extent to which the fulfilment of traditional obligations of hospitality and generosity could only be met by polygynous households. Food production and beer-making were mainly women's tasks, and a man with only one wife could not compete with his polygynous neighbours. The traditional value of hospitality, and the new Christian value of monogamy, were mutually incompatible. Polygyny is still common in many parts of the world, but attitudes to it have become increasingly ambivalent. A young schoolteacher whom I knew well in Bunyoro had one wife, married in church, with whom he lived when he was resident at the school. At his home he had another wife and two children, who lived in a house he had built for them in his parents' compound. He had married this wife after his first marriage, with bridewealth and in full accordance with tradition. He asked me not to say anything about this second union if I should meet his superiors at the school. If they learned of it (the school was mission-run like most Uganda schools) he would have had to give up either job or wife. Like the traditional chiefs discussed above, this man— and there are many like him—had to subscribe at the same time to two quite incompatible standards of morality and family life. It is plain that such a situation must conduce to conflict and strain.

It is worth while interjecting here parenthetically that it is no part of the anthropologist's business to pass judgment on policies or events: his job is to observe and record the facts as carefully as he can, and to try to contribute towards a better understanding of them. He is not opposed to social change, or concerned to preserve some pre-existing *status quo*. He recognizes change's inevitability, and tries to understand it. He knows quite well, for example, that although

polygamous marriage is appropriate to certain kinds of social systems it is not so to others: the growth of education, increased economic opportunity for both sexes, the replacement of group values by
individual ones—all these and many other factors are incompatible
with it. Like all people of good will, anthropologists hope that successful adaptations will be reached in those societies which are now
undergoing radical changes of the kinds being considered here. But
since these changes are taking place, it is an important part of the
anthropologist's job to investigate them.

It has been possible here only to touch on a few of the major
dimensions of change in domestic and family organizations: I now
consider some aspects of economic change. Some of the consequences
of the provision of new incentives and of the advent of a cash economy
have already been mentioned; they have affected the working of
many traditional institutions. In Chapter 11 I discussed the social
importance of exchange in small-scale societies, in creating and
maintaining bonds of mutual solidarity and interdependence. This is
most noticeable when what is exchanged are real commodities like
food and drink. For gifts like cattle, grain and beer cannot readily be
concealed, as money can; in the absence of a cash economy they can
only be eaten or drunk, or given away again, or (in the case of livestock) retained against a rainy day. In most traditional political
systems the tribute of produce which people brought to their chiefs
was sooner or later returned to them in the form of feasts and gifts,
for the chiefs could not consume it all themselves. And joint participation in feasting renewed and reasserted the bonds of loyalty and
attachment which bound community and chiefs together. When
tribute in the form of goods is commuted to a cash payment, and
still more when tribute payment is done away with and an impersonal tax system introduced, the whole chief-subject relationship is
radically changed. Unlike foodstuffs, cash can be hidden and
hoarded, and nowadays it can be spent in a variety of ways unavailable in traditional times. Consumption has become a private,
not a public matter. The chief who formerly had to plough his
takings back into the community may now spend his salary, which in
any case no longer ostensibly comes from his subjects but from a
superimposed, sometimes alien, government, on permanent build-
ings, motor cars, foreign travel, higher education for his children,
and in a host of non-traditional ways. He no longer uses his revenues
in the performance of his traditional role as provider for and sus-
tainer of his people; instead he spends them in ways which tend to
separate him from and not to identify him with them.

In traditionally centralized societies, where chiefs were both the

richest and the most powerful men in the community, the introduction of a cash economy has significantly altered their relationship
with their subjects in another way. Wealth is now available to many
others besides chiefs. Trade, cash cropping and emigration may en-
rich industrious or fortunate commoners, while chiefs, often living
on tiny salaries, have no such opportunities. This has involved the
destruction of the traditional identification of wealth with high
status, and has sometimes led to jealousy and resentment. Chiefs are
looked down on because they are no longer wealthy, and in their turn
they resent the *nouveaux riches* who by traditional standards are
asserting a status to which they are not entitled. In some parts of
Africa this has led to the defection from the ranks of the chiefs of the
more intelligent and able, and so to a progressive deterioration in the
calibre of the chiefly class itself.[1]

The effect of the new economy on traditional attitudes to land has
also been radical. We noted that in most parts of the world land is
traditionally regarded as a resource available for all, rights in it being
vested not in private individuals as such but in specific social groups.
Modern land use is simply not compatible with this traditional
pattern. A man who, out of his own cash earnings, has built a
permanent house and has planted his land with a perennial cash crop
like coffee, cannot continue to be satisfied with traditional tenure.
Land has ceased to be a communal resource and has become a means
of private investment. In East Africa especially the demand for free-
hold rights has been emphatic. Whether such rights will continue to
proliferate, or whether in some areas forms of co-operative land
holding may be developed, it is certain that the old types of communal
tenure cannot survive.

In those societies in which a bridewealth of livestock is an essential part of traditional marriage, its commutation to cash has had
similar implications for the personal relationships involved. We saw
in Chapter 8 that in some societies in South Africa and elsewhere
a particular form of cross-cousin marriage involved the establishment of lasting relationships of friendship and co-operation between
separate social groups. Each group stood to any of a number of other
similar groups either as wife receiver and stock giver or as wife giver
and stock receiver. These relationships served to bind the whole
community together in a network of reciprocal exchanges. Even
where preferential or prescribed marriage rules are lacking, bridewealth serves to create and sustain such relationships.

But the content of these relationships is radically altered when cash

[1] For a discussion of the changing role of chiefs see Audrey Richards (editor),
East African Chiefs, London, 1960.

is substituted for cattle. The assembling of a cash bridewealth, unlike the amassing of a herd of cattle, does not demand group collaboration. Traditionally a man depended on his father and kin for contributions from their herds, which were owned not individually but collectively. But in these days he may collect a cash bridewealth (or the wherewithal to purchase stock for bridewealth) by assiduous cash cropping, or by emigrating to a mine, a town or a large estate in search of paid employment. Further, the incentives increasingly available in a cash economy make it unlikely that a man who has received a cash bridewealth for his daughter will keep it, as he might have kept a herd of cattle, against the time when he will have to provide bridewealth for his son's marriage. There are now too many other things to spend it on. I noted before that the missionaries were wrong in supposing that bridewealth was simply wife-purchase. But ironically, with the advent of the cash economy which followed Western impact, it has tended increasingly to become so. Sometimes young girls are forced to return to husbands they dislike because the bridewealth paid for them has been spent, and so cannot be returned to secure their divorce. In Bunyoro I recorded several suicides which arose from this cause, and the same thing occurs elsewhere. In this context again traditional standards are in conflict with modern ones; the old norms of filial obedience, wifely submission and family solidarity are at odds with the modern individualistic values implicit in commitment to a cash economy.

Everywhere traditional forms of economic activity are dying out and being replaced. These used to entail either close reciprocal relationships between producer and consumer (as in the case of potters, blacksmiths and a few other specialists), or co-operative activity by groups of neighbours or kin, as in agriculture, hunting, house-building and such activities. But now in technologically simple societies locally made artefacts such as pots and hoes, formerly obtained from craftsmen neighbours in exchange for stock or grain, are increasingly being replaced by machine-made kitchen and agricultural implements from Europe, America or China, and purchased in the shops for cash. A group of neighbours used to build a traditional-type African house in a day, and they were rewarded by a meal and beer, and by the knowledge that they could count on similar help when they needed it. Nowadays a man who wants a proper cement-floored, iron-roofed house with several rooms must pay cash to a contractor to have it built. In these and in many other ways individuals are gaining increasing economic independence of their neighbours and kin. 'I'm all right Jack' rather than 'do as you would be done by' is becoming the order of the day.

These new attitudes to the production and distribution of goods involve attitudes to labour and to 'hard work' very different from those which were traditional in most simple societies. The characteristically Western value of work for its own sake, classically analysed by Max Weber in his *The Protestant Ethic and the Spirit of Capitalism*, had no place in traditional economics. This is why wherever Europeans have been in contact with simpler cultures they have almost always referred to the 'natives' as lazy and inefficient. But the difference was really in values, not in capabilities. Traditionally members of simpler communities worked, and worked with amazing endurance, when work was socially prescribed, or was demanded by practical necessity. But in such communities labour was an intrinsic part of a primary subsistence cycle, or else it was bound up in a particular context of social relations. It was not, as it so often is now, a tedious and in itself unsatisfying obligation, to be undertaken only in order to earn money so that the demands of governments, schools and shopkeepers can be met. Here as elsewhere differences in behaviour are due to differences in people's notions about what is important, and not to differences in their innate capacity.

So economic change, and in particular the advent of a money economy and all that this implies, have radically altered traditional methods of production and exchange, and, with these, almost all other areas of social life. And here, too, the incompatibility of traditional norms and values with those implicit in the new economies has given rise to much confusion and stress.

In the field of ritual, of magical and religious behaviour, change has been no less radical. Since one important function of ritual is to relieve situations of strain and anxiety, and since change often gives rise to such situations, we should expect magical and religious behaviour to be both an index and a consequence of social change. While being careful not to adopt an over-simple 'atomistic' view of change, it may in this field usefully be regarded from two aspects. First, we may consider how traditional cults have become adapted (sometimes changed almost out of recognition) to the new strains and pressures to which they have been subjected. Second, we can investigate the ways in which new religious ideas, while partially accepted, have been greatly modified to accord with traditional values. Indeed most ritual phenomena of change may be regarded in both of these aspects, since they generally combine features of both old and new. But in any event what we are presented with is not just an amalgam of items from different contexts assembled in new patterns, but rather totally new situations, *sui generis* and to be studied as such.

It is a commonplace that people often react to unusual or particularly severe stress by falling back on the magico-religious resources of their culture. Not only does church-going increase in Western countries in time of war or crisis, but also recourse to fortune-tellers, spiritualists, and other purveyors of irrational consolations, mounts steeply. The stress of social change in simpler societies often produces similar effects. Observers in many parts of Africa have sometimes been puzzled by recent increases in recourse to divination, sorcery and witchcraft, despite two or three generations of devoted mission activity. The explanation is simple. The various changes in traditional institutions, some of which have been considered above, often lead to increased stress in inter-personal relations. An important function of sorcery and witchcraft beliefs is to express and canalize such strains. Where this happens, it is not so much that there is a total rejection of what is new, as that people are utilizing the traditional magico-religious resources of their own cultures in order to cope with it. And these resources may themselves be changing. New magical medicines and techniques, owing something to modern influences, may be absorbed into the traditional pharmacopoeia. Especially where mediumistic cults form a part of the traditional religion, new spirits expressive of the modern forces impinging on the traditional culture may find a place in it.

Reverting once more to the Nyoro of Western Uganda, recent modifications in their spirit mediumship cult provide a good example. Traditionally Nyoro had a cult of spirit mediumship centring primarily on a pantheon of quasi-historical hero-gods, who as well as representing a wonderful race of people believed to have lived in the country long ago, stood also for certain elemental natural forces, such as the sun, the moon, rain, thunder and the bush. This was essentially a group cult, associated with the traditional division of the people into separate unilineal descent groups. Other kinds of spirits, such as the ghosts of the dead and certain kinds of illness, could also be mediated through the spirit cult. Thus through ritual the community could come to terms with forces which could not be dealt with by means of practical techniques. Now instead of dying out with the spread of Christian teaching, this cult has proliferated in recent years. Instead of the spirits becoming fewer and fewer they have become more and more numerous, and they include many new ones which derive directly from the more alarming and disquieting aspects of the new world imposed upon them by European contact. These new spirits include the 'aeroplane' spirit, the spirit of military tanks (this is a very powerful one), the spirit of 'Europeanness'—not, be it noted, the spirit of any particular European—and a great many others. A striking one is the spirit known as *Mpolandi*. This derived from the presence in Bunyoro during World War II of a camp containing several hundred expatriate and displaced Poles. Such a large congregation of Europeans was an ominous and alarming phenomenon to Nyoro peasants, and before long it was adopted into the mediumistic cult. In this way, through the possession ritual, the situation became in some measure comprehensible and manageable. It is rarely possible to deal directly with the new and intimidating forces associated with social change, but through a possession cult people may translate these forces into the familiar idiom of their own culture, and so cope with them, at any rate for a while.

But sometimes the ritualization of social change has implied the rejection, or at least a very selective acceptance, of what the new Western world has offered or imposed. The Mau Mau revolt in Kenya was primarily a physical attempt by some Kikuyu, most of whom were crowded into inadequate reserves, to eliminate Europeans from the country so that they could regain the land for themselves. But it involved also a grotesque proliferation of ritual, chiefly in the context of oath-taking. Now oath-taking was traditionally institutionalized in Kikuyu culture. But the macabre lengths to which the symbolism was carried was something new and untraditional, hardly less obnoxious to old-fashioned Kikuyu than it was to Europeans. More usually, however, the negative reaction has not involved all-out physical attack on the European agents of change (after all they generally had the guns), though sometimes it has threatened to do so. Two different types of reaction are familiar to anthropologists. One implies the total rejection of the European and all his works, and is typified by the famous ghost dance of North America: the other, implying the acceptance of what is seen as good and the rejection of what is seen as bad in the new way of life, is exemplified in the so-called cargo cults of the Western Pacific.

Both of these kinds of movements have generally been initiated by particular individuals, who prophesy that if the people will act in a certain way, the desired state of affairs, usually involving a return to a happy and more stable existence, with or without certain of the more desirable amenities of the Western way of life, will somehow come about. For this reason the movements thus begun have been described as millenarian. Sometimes, when the prophet has emerged as an inspired leader, they have been messianic as well.

The ghost dance spread widely among the Plains Indians of North America in the second half of the last century.[1] These tribes were

[1] Mooney, J., *The Ghost-dance Religion and the Sioux Outbreak of 1890*, Washington, 1896.

losing their lands rapidly to the incoming Europeans, and the great herds of bison on which their economy traditionally depended were vanishing before the white man's guns. The prophets of the ghost dance preached that if the proper ritual, which included a special dance, were performed, then the Europeans would vanish, the ancestors would be resurrected, the buffalo would return, and all would be as it had been before. In North America, as elsewhere, the impact of social change on simple, non-literate peoples had been predominantly painful, and dissatisfaction with present conditions and a longing for happier times is an obvious precondition of the emergence of millenarian movements of these kinds. It is worth noting that one North American Indian tribe, the Navaho, whose traditional way of life was very much less disrupted than that of other Indian peoples by the European advance, and who managed to retain their flocks and herds, laughed at the prophets of the ghost dance and declined to take it up.

The conditions in Melanesia in which cargo cults arose and proliferated were comparable. There had been contact between the native Melanesian islanders and the white men, but in its early stages this had offered little advantage to the islanders (who were largely exploited as cheap labour), while the power and wealth of the Europeans were there for all to see. What was not evident was where the Europeans had obtained this wealth and power, and it was believed that this was due to some secret which they were keeping to themselves. In the first half of this century certain prophets began to emerge in various parts of the area, claiming that if the people would perform certain rites a special 'cargo' would arrive, generally by steamer but later, in some cases, by aeroplane. The rites often involved a symbolic repudiation of the people's own past, such as the formal abandonment of traditional attire and the adoption of European dress. The cargo was to consist of all the most desired European goods, destined this time not for the white men, who would soon disappear, but for the islanders themselves. In many manifestations of the cult, the ancestors would also return to the world of the living. Thus the people would have the best of both worlds; the familiar consolations of the traditional way of life, and at the same time all the desired new goods associated with the intrusive Europeans.[1]

Millenarian movements of this kind have often arisen in human history. When, in times of severe stress, men have felt themselves dissatisfied with the existing world and looked forward to a better one, they have usually found prophets to assure them of its imminent arrival. Christianity itself has of course a millenarian character, and

[1] A good account of such a cult is Burridge, K., *Mambu, a Melanesian Millennium*, London, 1960.

this was very much more marked in the Church's earlier days. But in recent years the circumstances in which most millenarian cults have arisen have been those of acute social change, where old ways of life have been disrupted, but full assimilation into the new culture has not been achieved.

As well as in North America and Melanesia, prophets have also emerged in Africa. Here, although in many contexts disruption was often severe, the populations themselves were for the most part too substantial to be threatened with physical extinction, as the North American Indians and some Pacific islanders were. One of the most striking movements in South Africa was among the Xhosa. These people had experienced with particular severity the impact of the white men from the south. Much of their land had been taken, and their stock had been decimated. In 1856 there developed a prophetic movement the leaders of which commanded, as an act of faith, the destruction of stock and food reserves: when this was done a new era would dawn, when cattle and food would be miraculously renewed, and the Europeans would have disappeared. When this failed to happen there was a disastrous famine.

In many parts of Africa, and especially in the south, ritual reaction to social change often involved the adaptation of the new Christian teaching to traditional African values, rather than (or sometimes in addition to) a reassertion of traditional values. No one knows better than the social anthropologist how great a contribution to African well-being has been made by many thousands of devoted missionaries of all denominations. But, as most of them themselves realize, their message has not always been understood, and often its effect has been—perhaps more often than it need have been—to disrupt traditional institutions, the morally innocuous as well as the (from the Christian standpoint) morally objectionable. It would of course be unjust to reproach the early missionaries, or even present-day ones, for lacking the kind of sympathetic understanding of the institutions of the societies in which they laboured which anthropologists have only recently, through intensive fieldwork, begun to achieve with any adequacy. In fact many of them possessed this understanding. Nevertheless misunderstanding has often been, and sometimes still is, total. In the 1950's many Nyoro peasants believed that the missionaries' strong condemnation of the traditional spirit mediumship cult merely reflected the Europeans' desire that the Nyoro people should die out, so that they (the Europeans) could take over the country. A central concern of the traditional possession cult was with fertility. Missionary objection to polygyny has also often been regarded as directed to the same end.

For such reasons as these there have sprung up in Africa, chiefly in South, Central and East Africa where contact with Europeans has been most intense, a number of separatist churches. Those in South Africa have been admirably described by Bengt Sundkler (a missionary) in his book *Bantu Prophets in South Africa*. They have sprung almost entirely from the various Protestant missions, with their sectarian tradition, and they have usually grown up around the person of a particular leader. While most of these sects have continued to regard themselves as Christian, they have usually incorporated a number of traditional features, of which, not surprisingly, polygamy is the commonest. Sometimes they have involved elements, such as possession, which are traditional in many indigenous African religions. And occasionally, as in some manifestations of the Watch Tower Movement, they have assumed an explicitly or implicitly anti-European quality.

So social change, deriving from the impact of technologically developed cultures on relatively simple and small-scale ones, has not, at any rate in its early stages, involved any decrease in people's recourse to ritual. Rather, in many cases, resort to religious and magical consolations has increased, the form of the rites involved sometimes being drastically modified to accord with changed conditions. If it is a main function of ritual to provide, on the level of action, a means of coping with problems which cannot otherwise be coped with, and, on the level of idea, an indispensable means of making important symbolic statements about the changing world, then this is not surprising. For ritual and symbolic activity may be both subject to change and a statement about change, and its full understanding requires that it be analysed from both of these points of view.

SHORT READING LIST

FIRTH, RAYMOND, *Social Change in Tikopia*, London, 1959.

MAIR, LUCY, *Studies in Applied Anthropology*, London, 1957.

MALINOWSKI, B. (editor), *Methods of Study of Culture Contact in Africa*, London, 1938.

MALINOWSKI, B., *The Dynamics of Culture Change* (ed. P. M. Kaberry), Yale, 1945.

REDFIELD, R., *A Village that Chose Progress*, Chicago, 1950.

SOUTHALL, A. (editor), *Social Change in Modern Africa*, London, 1961.

SUNDKLER, B., *Bantu Prophets in South Africa*, London, 1948.

WILSON, G. and M., *The Analysis of Social Change*, Cambridge, 1945.

WORSLEY, PETER, *The Trumpet shall Sound*, London, 1957.

15

Conclusion and Assessment

IN THIS BOOK I have tried to explain what social anthropology, as the subject is understood in Britain, is about, and I have described some of the work that social anthropologists have done in various fields. They study social and cultural institutions, primarily in the context of small-scale communities (though not necessarily 'primitive' ones), and they investigate these institutions through intensive observation and enquiry 'on the ground'. Then they attempt to make sense of the information thus gained, in the light of an existing and growing body of knowledge about human institutions. And finally, they try to communicate their findings to others. I have argued that the data which social anthropologists study require to be understood on two distinct but interrelated levels. On the one hand, they must be regarded as systems of action, having causal implications for other co-existing institutions in the society, and on the other hand they must be seen as systems of beliefs and values, which must be understood if we are to see other people's institutions as they themselves see them. Only when the dominant beliefs and values of a particular community have been adequately comprehended can an anthropologist fairly claim to have understood that community. For only then can he represent to himself and (what is even more difficult) to others what it would be like to be a member of it. Both functional analysis in terms of causal interrelatedness, and ideal analysis in terms of meanings, values and symbols, are essential in the study of human institutions. A social anthropologist must be equally at home in both.

In this chapter I consider what use social anthropology has been and can be, both to practical people who have direct dealings with simpler, small-scale communities, such as government officials, missionaries or businessmen, and, more generally, to all those who have any dealings with people of other cultures than themselves. Nowadays this latter category includes most of us; in a sense all of us.

265

First, what can social anthropology do for those, mostly administrators and missionaries, part of whose job it is to maintain, alter or adapt other peoples' social and cultural institutions? It would seem reasonable to assume that the more such people know about the institutions they are dealing with the better. More than sixty years ago the explorer Mary Kingsley wrote: 'in colonial rule goodwill is no substitute for knowledge which will act in the direction of preventing us from engineering our good intentions in such a manner as to make them appear tyrannies and hateful to those whom we wish to benefit by them.[1] This is as true today as it was then, and it applies no less to the African district commissioner administering a tribe other than his own, than it did to the old-fashioned European colonial official in charge of a 'native area'. It is better to act in knowledge than in ignorance, and if there are contexts in which an anthropologist is better qualified than anyone else to say what the effects of a particular course of action are likely to be, then anyone who contemplates such a course of action will do well to consult him.

But are social anthropologists' guesses any better than anyone else's? Administrators have sometimes argued that they can perfectly well be their own anthropologists. Often they live in the country longer than the anthropologist does; they know the people well, and they speak and write a language which other administrators can understand. This argument had a good deal of validity in the early days of anthropology, when fieldwork was simply a matter of asking selected groups of elders a number of leading questions on matters of interest, probably through an interpreter. Many very important contributions to ethnography have been made in this way by administrators and missionaries. But anthropology is no longer like this. The fact has to be faced that we live in an age of specialization. And the background knowledge which competent fieldwork demands, both in sociology and in comparative ethnography, is simply not attainable without at least some professional training. Also, modern fieldwork is a full-time occupation; unless an administrator or missionary is seconded for a long period, both to acquire the necessary training and to carry out intensive fieldwork (and so himself becomes a qualified social anthropologist), he cannot in the nature of things be expected to produce information of the same quality—and so in the last resort of the same usefulness—as a professional research worker.

There is a further qualification which administrators and missionaries lack. This is the quality of neutrality; however open-minded they may be they are already professionally committed, to

[1] Gwynn, S. *Life of Mary Kingsley*, 1933, quoted in Lord Hailey, *An African Survey* (revised edition), London, 1956.

Christian moral standards or to the norms of good government as they understand it; in some cases to both. It is difficult for them to attend beer-drinks or magical ceremonies on anything like an equal footing with the participants. Though a professional anthropologist cannot—and should not—cut himself off altogether from his own culture and values, if he is lucky and takes sufficient pains he can achieve a remarkably informal and egalitarian relationship with the people among whom he chooses to spend a year or two of his life. So, in the end, he can learn to understand them better than any other 'outsider' can. This is why he is better placed to make predictions about the society he has studied than anyone else can be. It is not that he is infallible; the springs of human behaviour are so complex that he may very well be wrong in any individual case. He can only say what is likely or unlikely to happen, not what is certain to happen. But if a social anthropologist has really understood a particular system of land tenure, a form of marriage, or the significance of a chief-subject relationship, then he is better placed than anyone else to assess the probable consequences of outside interference with any of these institutions.

His practical responsibility ends here. Social anthropologists cannot, or at least they should not, tell administrators or missionaries (or anyone else) what they should do. Like all scientists, their job is simply to ascertain the facts, and to assess the likely consequences of altering them. If administrators or missionaries wish to take the anthropologist's opinions into account they do so. But although, like all sensible decisions, their decisions should take account of the facts so far as these can be ascertained, they are inevitably influenced also by considerations of policy, by aims and considerations with which the anthropologist, *qua* anthropologist, has nothing to do. It is usually most difficult to separate fact from value judgment, and on the whole anthropologists are no less committed to certain moral standards than other people are. But objectivity and disinterestedness, however imperfectly they are achieved, are an essential part of the social anthropologist's stock in trade, and he must guard them jealously.

Practical people sometimes criticize social anthropologists on the ground that they are too much concerned with 'theory', with academic rather than practical issues, and that this vitiates the usefulness of much of their work for those who have to act and take decisions. But on the whole this objection is misconceived. Obviously the practical man is not concerned with theory for its own sake; there is no reason why he should be. But very often a framework of theoretical and comparative knowledge is an indispensable condition for the discovery of new facts, which may turn out to be highly important for administrator, missionary or trader. It is only because the social anthropologist has in mind a body of theory, a system of hypotheses based on comparative analysis, that he knows what to look for. An investigator who has no idea of what he is looking for is unlikely to find it. For example, it was not until the theoretical analysis of segmentary lineage systems (to some people one of the more arid branches of anthropological theory) had been fairly well advanced that it became possible to understand how societies lacking any form of specialized political authority could possibly work. But once this was known, it became easier to avoid the mistake of supposing that chiefs must exist in every pre-literate society, if only they could be discovered. An example of this mistake was given in the last chapter.

The development of a body of comparative knowledge and of general theory, though it may not always be of immediate practical use, very often proves to be so in the long run. The American anthropologist Sol Tax made this point neatly. Writing about the Indian administration in the United States, he said: 'If one wishes to apply anthropological knowledge to a given Indian tribe, science would hold that knowledge about that tribe is less important than knowledge about all Indians, or generalizations about human nature and society. To the administration, this may seem to be a reversal of common sense; but it should be apparent that just as a sheep breeder applies to his sheep knowledge of sheep genetics rather than knowledge of *his* sheep, so the administrator applies to the Indian tribe knowledge not about that tribe but knowledge about some aspects of human nature'.[1] Even from the most practical view, there is a strong case for allowing social anthropologists to be 'theoretical'.

In any case, the proof of the pudding is the eating, and in fact governments in the British Commonwealth, the United States and elsewhere have made much use of trained social anthropologists. They have done this in various ways. First, they have sometimes taken trained sociologists or social anthropologists on to their permanent establishments. Thus the anthropologist becomes a civil servant. As such, his primary business is with practical problems, upon which he brings to bear the techniques and special knowledge with which his professional training has equipped him. Government anthropologists have been asked to advise on such matters as labour migration, succession to political authority in particular tribes, and the likely social consequences of proposed land reforms. An anthropologist who takes such a post becomes a sort of anthropological general practitioner. If he stays permanently in government service he

[1] Tax, Sol, 'Anthropology and Administration', in *América Indígena*, V, 1, 1945.

is unlikely to become a specialist, or to make any major theoretical contribution to anthropology. We should not expect him to. We do not expect our family doctor to be a specialist, but we do expect him to tell us what is the matter if we feel unwell, and to call in a specialist if need be. But governments which take on permanent anthropologists in this way, if they are wise, leave them as much freedom as possible in framing their approaches to the problems to which solutions are sought. The anthropologist and not his employer must be allowed to be the best judge of the relevance of any particular line of enquiry to the problem in hand.

For social anthropologists of markedly practical bent there is much to be said for such a career, and if a government gets the right man it is well served. In the past some East African governments have very successfully made use of professional social anthropologists in this way. But such employers, whether they are governments, missionaries or businessmen, should allow their anthropologists sufficient leisure to enable them to keep reasonably abreast of current theoretical developments in their subject, as well as permitting them wide latitude in their approaches to the problems set for them.

A second way in which a government can make practical use of social anthropology is to employ a professional on contract for a period of a year or two, to carry out a specific piece of research. This method can work well when a particular problem is considered sufficiently important to justify the expense of full scale, professional study. An anthropologist who has made a special study of religious institutions might be taken on to investigate the emergence in a particular area of a separatist movement; or an expert on political organization might be engaged to make a study in a community for which major administrative changes were proposed. The Sudan Government employed the anthropologists Evans-Pritchard and Nadel in this way before World War II. For such specialized tasks governments do best to take on experienced and established scholars, rather than young anthropologists without previous field experience. First field studies are best controlled and financed through universities or other research bodies and institutes, for a social anthropologist on his first tour of fieldwork is still very much a student, and if he is to become a fully-fledged professional his supervision should be academic rather than administrative.

A third method by which governments have availed themselves of information provided by anthropological investigations is by supporting, encouraging or merely tolerating research by workers academically attached to universities or other research-sponsoring bodies. In recent years many anthropological studies in the British

Commonwealth have been financed by grants made by the home Government, and much research has been carried out by scholars attached for varying periods to overseas institutes subsidized wholly or partly by local governments. Such institutes are the East African Institute of Social Research at Makerere in Uganda, the Rhodes-Livingstone Institute in Northern Rhodesia, and the Nigerian Institute of Social and Economic Research at Ibadan, to speak only of Africa; other research institutes exist or have existed in Malaya, the West Indies and in other parts of the Commonwealth. Most of the field research of the past half century or so has been carried out under the auspices of such organizations, or with help from other grant-giving bodies like the Ford and Wenner-Gren foundations in America, and the Horniman Fund (through the Royal Anthropological Institute) and the Goldsmiths' Company in England. And much—though not all—of this research has been of acknowledged interest and use to governments.

So although administrators have sometimes criticized social anthropology, and although some of their criticisms have been merited (for example the charges that some anthropologists delay inordinately in publishing their material, and that when they do it is often written in a barely intelligible jargon), on balance social anthropologists have served governments well, and this service has been acknowledged. The case is rather different in regard to missions, for they are ordinarily in no position financially to subsidize professional research by scholars outside their own denominations. But perhaps more than administrators, they have been able to do their own anthropology. Though in a way even more *parti pris* than civil servants, they have the advantages of long residence in a single community and, usually, of knowing the native language well. Some of the most profound studies of native institutions and ways of thought have been made by missionaries; Roscoe's work among the Baganda, Smith's among the Ila, and Tempels' among the Luba, are among the best known,[1] but there are many others. If some of this work lacks the scientific rigour which only a professional training can provide, it should be noted that at the present time missions are increasingly making use of the training facilities available in universities in Britain and abroad. This is already showing fruit in important work.

But it is not only for those who are professionally concerned with cultures different from their own that social anthropology can be of practical use. What are loosely called race relations are of concern to

[1] Roscoe, J., *The Baganda*, London, 1911; Smith, E. W., and Dale, A. M., *The Ila-Speaking Peoples of Northern Rhodesia*, London, 1920; Tempels, P., *Bantu Philosophy* (English translation), Paris, 1959.

very many people both at home and abroad, and social anthropology can contribute significantly to their understanding. The physical anthropologists have cleared the ground by showing that there is no biological evidence which could provide a ground for race prejudice. Although members of the different main biological stocks of mankind obviously look different, they are all of the same species. No satisfactory evidence has ever been produced that there are any inherent differences in mental capacity or personality which are associated with physical 'race' differences. A statement on race relations published in 1950 under the auspices of UNESCO said categorically that 'according to present knowledge there is no proof that the groups of mankind differ in their innate mental characteristics, whether in respect of intelligence or temperament'. No form of intelligence testing yet devised has produced any findings to refute this: such slight differences as have been recorded are always attributable to cultural and other environmental differences in the upbringing and conditioning of the subjects tested. As Confucius said two thousand years ago, 'men's natures are alike; it is their habits that carry them far apart'.

But although there are no physical grounds for treating members of different physical stocks (so far as these can be clearly distinguished) differently, unfortunately there have, in the context of history, been other grounds of discrimination. These may be based on economic considerations, as when it is supposed that immigrant West Indians, or Irish, are taking jobs from Englishmen. They may be based on religious factors; history provides all too many examples of religious discrimination. They may derive from educational differences, and from a variety of other grounds. Even the mere fact of being an outsider, not one of 'us', may be a sufficient ground for discrimination. I began this book by noting how widespread in human societies is the fear and distrust of strangers, just because they are strangers. Whatever the underlying social or cultural differences upon which discrimination is ultimately based, it sometimes happens that these coincide with clearly visible differences in physical appearance; for example, in skin colour, hair shape, and cast of features. Where this is so, these physical differences provide a convenient and easily recognized symbol for the social and cultural differences which, though implicit, are really crucial. In this way 'race', and not culture, belief or economic interest, comes to be regarded as the essential factor. Here again, a symbol becomes imbued with an importance which really belongs to the thing it symbolizes. Thus the real problems which are involved in the coming together of people of different cultures often become obscured.

271

CONCLUSION AND ASSESSMENT

The fact is that where there *are* important differences between people of different races, these are social and cultural, not physical: they are learned, not inborn. This does not mean that they do not exist; they do, and evidently they may be of great moment. This is where social anthropology comes in. When it is understood that human beings, endowed everywhere (so far as we can tell) with pretty much the same constitutions and capacities, have evolved for themselves a huge variety of different cultures, just as they have evolved for themselves a great number of different languages; and when it is recognized that translation from one culture to another, though sometimes difficult, is always possible; then it becomes easier to recognize the common humanity which underlies them all. Whether one culture can be regarded as 'superioɪ' to another depends on the kinds of standards that are applied. Owing to the development of writing and a complex technology some are vastly richer than others, at least quantitatively. But every human culture, however 'simple', represents a more or less successful adaptation to its environment, and if nowadays the wiser of us are less ready than we used to be to apply wholesale the terms 'better' and 'worse' to cultures other than their own, this may be in some part due to our recognition of the intricacy and subtlety of many so-called 'primitive' cultures.

I am not saying that evaluational comparison of different cultures is impossible; social anthropologists are not committed to the view that every culture is 'just as good' as every other culture. But more, perhaps, than most people, anthropologists are aware of the dangers of 'holistic' cultural comparisons; different aspects of cultures, different institutions, may usefully be compared, but not whole cultures. Belief in sorcery and witchcraft, with the cruelties it involves, is no doubt a bad thing, but so is the Cold War with its threat of atomic holocaust; we are right to disapprove of domestic slavery and the subjection of women, but an increase in juvenile delinquency and a rising crime rate afford no grounds for complacency. At least sometimes, *tout comprendre, c'est tout pardonner,* and the better people can understand unfamiliar cultures and societies, the more tolerant of people of different cultural backgrounds from their own they are likely to be.

Today different cultures are coming into contact everywhere and all the time on an increasing scale. This is an important reason why an understanding of cultures other than our own has become essential. Some day, perhaps, a single, 'admass' culture will be universal, but happily that time is not yet. And this understanding is required on both sides. In the last chapter I spoke of the belief held by some simpler peoples that Europeans wished to destroy them and take

272

their land. Unfortunately they were sometimes right, but even where they were not the belief still existed. When I was an administrator in Tanganyika, it was widely held that Europeans were cannibals, who kidnapped African children and others and processed them for sale as tinned meat. Some European stereotypes about Africans were no less absurd. I have heard Europeans who had lived for many years in Africa (but who had never bothered to learn an African language properly, or to get to know any African outside the master-servant relationship) assert that Africans are lacking in natural family affections, that they do not know the meaning of gratitude, and that their languages lack a word for 'thank you'. These stereotypes are due to ignorance, and sometimes ignorance affords political or moral advantage. It does so where it provides a ground for maintaining an élite, or justifies a system of economic exploitation. Respect can come only from understanding, and only from respect can come any genuine sense of equality. Men are still a long way from achieving this, but a deeper understanding of other peoples' ways of life, and of their beliefs and values, may contribute a little towards it.

It is entirely natural that so-called 'native' peoples should, in achieving respect from others, have gained a newfound respect for themselves. Many Africans now feel it right to emphasize what is distinctively and uniquely 'African' about their history and culture. Certainly the depth and poetry of African thought, and the importance of African achievements in the arts, government and trade, have until recently lacked adequate recognition. And it may be, as Léopold Senghor and the *Présence Africaine* group claim, that there is a special 'African personality', based on what is distinctive in the various African cultures; a personality which is different from that of inhabitants of other continents. But if this be taken (as it sometimes has been) to imply that there is a specific African way of thinking, an innate African metaphysic, so that the products of the African intellect are to be measured not by the universal standards of human reason, but by standards proper and peculiar to African culture, then cultural separatism is being carried too far. Relative and contextual standards are appropriate and necessary where social and cultural values are being considered; this is one of the most important lessons which social anthropology has to teach. But they are very much less so when the nature of man's universe, shared by Africans with all other human beings, is in issue. Beliefs about the power of ancestral ghosts, for example, are highly important as cultural facts, and it is the social anthropologist's job to investigate them systematically and sympathetically. But it is another matter when what is in question is not the existence and significance of such beliefs, but their validity.

The criteria by which their correctness as beliefs is to be assessed are not a monopoly of African, Western, or any other culture. They are imposed by the nature of human reason. It would be a pity if the mystical and pre-logical quality supposedly imputed to 'primitive' thought by Lévy-Bruhl, and shown by later anthropologists to afford no ground for any clear-cut distinction between peoples, were to be reinstated by Africans themselves. There is indeed an African culture; or rather there are many African cultures, and these shape the personalities, the beliefs and the values of their members. But the mentality which these influences shape is something that is shared by everybody, and its laws are universal. If social anthropology shows how human cultures differ, it also shows that the people who have these cultures are fundamentally alike.

So the study of social anthropology is worth while both because of other cultures' uniqueness, and because of their basic similarities. Every human society has somehow developed its own distinctive culture and social system; its own way of life. As members of the same human family, we are bound to be interested in the different ways in which different peoples have solved for themselves the problems of living together. An edge is given to our interest in those small-scale societies whose members still live on a subsistence level, who are still pre-literate or only recently literate, and who are still little affected by culture contact, by the fact that few of them can long survive in their present form. They are rapidly and radically changing, so unless they are studied now they will never be studied at all. Societies are not organisms: they are not animals on the verge of extinction, and no one would wish to preserve traditional cultures in reserves, like nearly extinct animal species, regardless of the wishes of their members. What really matters are people, not societies. None the less, many kinds of social system which still exist will soon disappear, as many have disappeared in the past. So there is every reason to preserve some record of those that are left.

Basically, the fundamental similarity of all human cultures everywhere justifies the study of all their varieties. In understanding other cultures, we may come to understand ourselves better. It is not only that by entering into the beliefs and values of other peoples we may learn, to some extent, to see ourselves as others see us, though this is always salutary. Every human culture is unique, but the institutions it comprises are variations on themes that are shared by all. By learning something of these varieties we may learn to see ourselves in ethnographic context; we may come to see that our solutions to the common problems of living in a community are not the only possible ones. So in learning about the practical importance of witchcraft beliefs for the Azande, the Westerner may come to understand something of his own past; it is not so long since Western Europeans also firmly believed in witches and destroyed them when they were detected. Attitudes towards Jews or communists still held by some people today reflect many of the same irrational fears and anxieties. The search for prestige which we can so readily identify in the Trobriander's earnest participation in the kula exchange, or the North-West Coast Indian's addiction to the potlatch, may be discerned no less clearly, if we are willing to look, in many of the economic and social preoccupations of more developed nations. What is the Space Race but a kind of potlatch on a cosmic scale? The stresses of radical social change are as present a feature of Western societies as they are of those simpler societies which are now for the first time undergoing culture contact on a massive scale. The mote in another's eye is always more visible than the beam in one's own, and to recognize and understand these various social and cultural phenomena in other cultures may help us to recognize and understand them in our own.

If the researches of social anthropologists can help us to understand our own present, they may contribute too to the understanding of our past. The study of contemporary small-scale states in Africa may throw light on the working of similar polities in medieval Europe. In Western history they can only be studied through documents; in Africa some of them can still be investigated as working systems. The importance of oracles and the role of spirit mediumship in ancient Greece may become more intelligible when their significance in many contemporary cultures is fully understood. Jane Harrison made fruitful use of Frazerian anthropology in her investigation of ancient Greek religion, and the field is still hardly explored. The application of the findings of contemporary social anthropology to historical material is an enterprise to be pursued with caution, but it may well provide some new and interesting hypotheses.

These are some of the reasons, both practical and theoretical, for studying social anthropology. But the most important reason of all is simply that human societies and cultures, though less tangible than the material entities which for many centuries have formed the subject of the empirical sciences, are no less real and certainly no less interesting than they are. In the last resort social anthropologists study human communities and cultures because they are there.

Index

ability, and task differentiation, 190
abstraction(s), 38, 41
  and symbols, 70
acculturation, 242
administration, and social anthropology, 266 ff
adoption, 94, 107
affines, relations between, 135 ff
affinity, 93
age, and task differentiation, 189
age-grades, 146
age-set systems, 145 ff, 210 f
  functions of, 147
aggregate, social, 35, 36, 140
agriculture, 185 f
  and land rights, 192 ff
Alur, 159
amateur, place in social anthropology, 42, 79
Amba, 123
ambivalence, in affinal relations, 136 f
American Indians, *see* Indians
ancestors,
  and land rights, 192
  and totems, 223
  cult of, 225 f
Andaman Islanders, 10, 58, 72, 222
animals,
  domestication of, 185
  social behaviour of, 18
Ankole, 190
Année sociologique, 66
anomie, 245
anthropologists, social, how used by governments, 268 f
anthropology,
  American, 21
  cultural, 20 f, 31
  divisions of, 16 ff
  physical, 17 f, 31
  social: development of, 5 ff; subject of, 12 ff, 35; use of, 4, 265 ff
Anuak, 246
anxiety, and magic, 207 f
archaeology, 8
  prehistoric, 18, 31
Arensberg, C., 30 n, 197 n
aristocracy, emergence of, 186
art, 204 f
Arunta, 220, 221, 234
Ashanti, 113, 129, 154, 196
  advice to chief, 162
  chief's oath, 237

cross-cousin marriage, 129
ntoro, 97
political organization, 160
assistants, in fieldwork, 86
Athenians, 237
Australian aborigines, 3, 142, 145, 180, 184
  expiatory encounter, 176
  marriage systems, 127
  totemism among, 70 f, 219 ff
authority
  and force, 142 f, 155 f
  defined, 141
  specific and diffused, 156
  see also political authority
avoidance, 210; *see also* mother-in-law; totemism
Azande,
  beliefs, 67
  oracles, 87
  witchcraft, 74, 181, 208 f, 213, 275
Aztecs, 234

Bachofen, J. J., 6
Bacon, Francis [Lord], 196
Baganda, *see* Buganda
Bahima, 190
Bairu, 190
Baluhya, 148
Bantu,
  clan systems, 121
  sacrifice among, 235
  totemism, 219
  see also Baluhya; Interlacustrine Bantu; Kamba; Kikuyu; Luba; Nyakyusa; Nyamwezi; Ruanda; Southern Bantu; Yao
barter, 195
Beattie, John, 164, 229 n
Bedouin, 119, 121, 176
behaviour, expressive and instrumental, 71, 203 ff, 238
beliefs,
  and ritual, 206
  and sanctions, 173
  study of, 29, 36, 40, 65 ff
Benedict, Ruth, 27, 33
Berbers, 175
birds, and twins, 68
blessing, 237
blood feud, 142, 148, 167, 171, 177, 181, 244, 246

INDEX

Malaya, 270
Malinowski, B., 10, 49, 56, 57, 64, 93, 108, 131, 138, 154, 168, 169, 170, 176, 177, 182, 186, 188, 197 f, 199, 201, 210, 213, 217, 238, 243, 264
mana, 214 f
Maori, 200
Maquet, J. J., 134
Marett, R. R., 240
markets, 195 f
marriage, 6, 117 ff
  and bridewealth, 123 ff
  and residence, 130 f
  and social change, 254 f
  as exchange, 122 f
  as involving groups, 119 f
  ceremonial, 124
  Christian, and bridewealth, 125
  cross-cousin, 127 ff, 257
  'ghost', 120, 129
  leviratic, 107, 108, 110, 119, 129
  matrilocal, 130 f
  patrilocal, 130
  polygamous, 112, 118, 255 f; *see also* polyandry; polygyny
  preferential, 128
  preliminary definition of, 117
  prescriptive, 127 f
  prohibited, 125 ff
  stability of, 131
  uxorilocal, 130 f
  virilocal, 130
Masai, 73, 126, 145, 185
'matriarchy, primitive', 123
matrilineality, 6
  and cross-cousin marriage, 129
  and father-son relationship, 107 f
  and inheritance, 97
  and marriage, 129 ff
Mau Mau, 238, 261
Mauss, Marcel, 66, 67 n, 77, 198, 200, 201
Mead, Margaret, 27
'mechanical model', 39
'mechanical solidarity', 186, 200
medicines, magic, 213, 224
mediums, spirit, 229 ff
  Nyoro, and social change, 260 f
Melanesia, 10, 44, 214, 220, 262
  see also Trobriand Islands; Dobuans
Merton, R. K., 46, 48, 54, 181, 208
Middleton, John, 74, 164, 218, 226, 240
millenarianism, 261 ff
missionaries, 263
  and social anthropology, 270
model(s)
  mechanical and statistical, 39, 62
  structural-functional, 63
money, 196
Montesquieu, 5
Mooney, J., 261 n
morality, incompatible standards of, 255
Morgan, Lewis H., 6, 7, 10, 103, 242
mother-in-law avoidance, 12, 46, 135 f
myth
  and authority, 160 f
  and history, 24
  and royal ritual, 154

Nadel, S. F., 43, 48, 79, 269
Nagel, Ernest, 64
Nandi, 145
Navaho, 262
Needham, Rodney, 138
'needs'
  biological, 57
  'derived' and 'integrative', 57
  social, 56 f
Newala, 250
Nigeria, 159
  see also Ibo; Nupe, Yakö
Nilo-Hamites, 147, 189, 210, 211, 236
  see also Masai; Nandi
norms, and sanctions, 165 f
Notes and Queries in Anthropology, 90, 117
ntoro, 97
Nuer, 40, 142, 143, 167, 226
  and cattle, 75
  and twins, 68
  blood feud, 149 f, 171, 175 f, 181, 244, 246
  concept of spirit, 228, 233
  lineages, 100, 149 ff
  marriage, 119 f
  sacrifice, 235
Nupe, 159
Nyakyusa, 125, 173, 213, 255
Nyamwezi, 152
Nyoro, *see* Bunyoro

oath-taking, 237 f, 261
obloquy, public, 176
Omaha system of cross-cousin terminology, 114
opposition,
  balanced, 148
  radical and ordinary, 248
oracles, 87, 209, 228
organic solidarity, 187, 200
organismic approach, 11 f, 50, 56 ff
organization, and structure, 247
Orwell, George, 246
ostracism, 172
ownership, notions of, 193, 194

Packard, Vance, 199
paintings, paleolithic, 18
parents-in-law, *see* mother-in-law avoidance; relationships
Parsons, Talcott, 36, 48, 187
pastoralists, 185, 191
  and age-set systems, 147
pater and *genitor*, 107, 120
patria potestas, 108
Perry, R. B., 73, 77
Perry, W. J., 8
personality, 'African', 273 f
pharmakoi, 237
photography, aerial, 18, 89
Pilling, A. R., 138
Pitt-Rivers, J., 30 n
Plains Indians, 261 f
Pocock, D. F., 48

INDEX

political authority,
  and age-sets, 145 ff
  and myth, 24
  checks on abuse of, 161 ff
  delegation of, 157 f
  difficulty of defining, 141 f
  grounds of, 158 ff
  interpersonal relations and, 156 f
  patrimonial, 156
  ritual and, 153 f
  scope of, 155
  succession to, 161 f
  territorial range of, 154
  types of (charismatic, traditional, rational-legal), 160
political organization, 139 ff
  centralized, 151 ff
  segmentary, 143, 148 ff
  types of, 143 ff
political science, 32
pollution, ideas of, 121, 179 f
polyandry, 6, 118
polygyny, 112, 118, 129, 134
  and social change, 255
  missionaries and, 263
Polynesia, 214, 215 f, 250
  see also Maori; Tikopians
Popper, K., 64
popular representation, 160
possession, by spirits, 229 f
  and social change, 260 f, 264
potlatch, 44, 198 f, 275
Pound, Roscoe, 167
power, 140 f
  'absolute', 161
prehistory, 18, 31
prestation, *see* exchange
'primitive', meaning of term, 4 f
progress, idea of, 6
promiscuity, 'primitive', 6, 125
property, ideas about, 194
Prospero, 229
psycho-analysis, and totemism, 223
psychology, 25 ff, 31
punishment, 178 f
  as inducing conformity, 186
  by state, 180
  in Western society, 180
pygmies, 145, 184

qualitative and quantitative analysis, 39, 85
questionnaires, 85

race relations, 270 ff
Radcliffe-Brown, A. R., 10, 23, 29, 33, 34, 45, 47, 49, 56 ff, 60, 69, 72, 103, 104, 107, 111, 116, 142, 167, 168, 170 ff, 177, 178, 179, 182, 210, 213, 217, 218, 222, 239
rain-making, 203 f
rebellion, 158
  and revolution, 163, 246
reciprocity, 168, 181
  economic, 176 f, 187, 195 ff
  see also exchange

Redfield, Robert, 38, 39, 264
relationship(s)
  as subject-matter of social anthropology, 14, 29, 35
  brother-sister, 113, 126
  'cousins', 113 ff
  father-daughter, 108 f
  father-son, 106 f
  grandchildren-grandparents, 111
  husband-wife, 132 ff
  joking, 110
  kinship, 96, 105 ff
  kinship, reciprocating and non-reciprocating terms for, 106
  mother-son, 109
  parent-child, 106 ff
  sibling, 112 f
  social, meaning of, 35 ff
  with parents-in-law, 135 f
  with siblings-in-law, 136 f
religion, 219 ff
  and magic, 212, 224
  and social change, 259 ff
representations, collective, 27, 66
responsibility, individual, 180
Reth, 153
Rhodes-Livingstone Institute, 270
Richards, Audrey, 90, 164, 201, 257
rights,
  in land, 191 ff
  in personam and *in rem*, 134
  of ownership, 194 f
rites de passage, 211
ritual, 202 ff
  and magic, 206 f
  and social change, 259 f
  royal, 154
  sanctions, 173
  social implications, 58, 208 ff, 239
  study of, 71 f
Rivers, W. H. R., 116
role and status, 36
Romans, 98, 108, 225 f
Roscoe, J., 270
Ruanda, 134
rulers,
  admonition on appointment, 162
  grounds of authority, 160 f
  range of authority, 154 f
  sanctions relating to, 162 f
  scope of authority, 155 f
  see also chief; king; political authority

sacred and profane, 203
sacrifice, 53, 173, 180, 232 ff
  as communion, 235
  as exchange, 233 f
  as expiation, 236
  human, 234
  identified with sacrificer, 236
Saint-Simon, 11
sanctions, 165 ff
  and norms, 162, 165
  and political authority, 161 f
  defined, 165
  organized and diffuse, 171 f
  positive and negative, 170 f